JEWISH LAW AND MODERN IDEOLOGY

A Confrontation Based on Source Materials

ELLIOT N. DORFF

Published by
THE UNITED SYNAGOGUE COMMISSION
ON JEWISH EDUCATION

COPYRIGHT 1970 BY
THE UNITED SYNAGOGUE OF AMERICA

All rights reserved. No part of this book may be reproduced in any form without permission in writing from the publisher except by a reviewer who may quote brief passages in a review to be printed in a magazine or newspaper.

PRINTED IN THE UNITED STATES OF AMERICA

In memory of

Rabbi Isaac Leon Bonder, ז"ל

Known to us all as "Zicky"

David said: "O Lord, many groups of Zaddikim shall be admitted into Thy presence. Which one of them is most beloved before Thee?"

God answereth: "The teachers of the youth, who perform their work in sincerity and with joy, shall sit at My right hand."

                                    Pesikta Buber, p. 180a
                                    Pesikta Mandelbaum, p. 406

Table of Contents

Page

Page	
1	**UNIT I: THE NATURE AND FUNCTIONS OF RELIGION**
3	Chapter 1: Defining Religion 　　Wm. Alston, "Religion"
12	Chapter 2: Attack on the Nature of Religion 　　Karl Marx, "Contributions to the Critique of Hegel's _Philosophy of Right_ (Introduction)"
16	Chapter 3: Response on the Nature of Religion
16	a) John Macmurray, _The Structure of Religious Experience_
33	b) Martin Buber, _I and Thou_
41	Chapter 4: Attack on the Functions of Religion 　　Friedrich Nietzsche, _Beyond Good and Evil_ and _The Genealogy of Morals_
48	Chapter 5: Response on the Functions of Religion: I 　　Robert Gordis, _A Faith for Moderns_
55	Chapter 6: Response on the Functions of Religion: II
55	a) Abraham J. Heschel, _Between God and Man_
57	b) Mordecai M. Kaplan, _The Future of the American Jew_
62	c) Carmichael and Hamilton, _Black Power_
66	**UNIT II: THE SPECIAL FUNCTIONS OF JUDAISM**
67	Chapter 7: Jewish Values Distinctive in Degree 　　Abraham J. Heschel, _The Sabbath_
73	Chapter 8: Jewish Values Distinctive in Kind 　　Mordecai M. Kaplan, _The Meaning of God in Modern Jewish Religion_
82	Chapter 9: Jewish Values Distinctive in Degree and Kind 　　Eric Fromm, _The Forgotten Language_

Page		
88	**UNIT III: THE NEED FOR LAW**	
90	Chapter 10: Attack on Law	
90		a) The New Testament, The Letter of Paul to the Romans
92		b) The New Testament, The Letter of Paul to the Galatians
94	Chapter 11: The Need for Law: I	
94		a) Emile Durkheim, Sociology and Philosophy
98		b) Emile Durkheim, The Division of Labor in Society
101		c) Morris Adler, The World of the Talmud
105	Chapter 12: The Need for Law: II	
105		a) Abraham J. Heschel, Between God and Man
112		b) Franz Rosenzweig, On Jewish Learning
121	**UNIT IV: THE PROCESS OF AMERICAN LAW**	
121	Chapter 13: Early Sources on Segregation	
121		a) The Fourteenth Amendment
122		b) Plessy v. Fergusen
128		c) Brown v. Board of Education
135	Chapter 14: Subsequent Developments on Segregation	
135		a) The Congressional Record
145		b) The Civil Rights Act of 1964
148	**UNIT V: THE PROCESS OF JEWISH LAW**	
148	Chapter 15: Historical Survey	
148		a) Morris Adler, The World of the Talmud
164		b) Herman Wouk, This Is My God
171	Chapter 16: Illustrations of the Major Stages of Development in Jewish Law	

(cont.)

Page		
171-4-5	a)	The Bible, Exodus
172-4-5	b)	Mekhilta: Bo, Mishpatim, Ki Tissa
176	c)	The Talmud: Shabbat 17b-18a, 18b-19a, 121a, 122a-b
183	d)	Moses Maimonides, *The Mishna Torah*, Hilchot Shabbat
188	e)	Joseph Karo, *The Shulkhan Arukh*, Hilchot Shabbat

192	UNIT VI: MODERN APPROACHES TO JEWISH LAW

192	Chapter 17: The Orthodox Response to Jewish Law
192	a) Samson Raphael Hirsch, *Judaism Eternal*
203	b) Emanuel Rackman, "Can We Moderns Keep the Sabbath?" in *Commentary*

208	Chapter 18: The Reform Approach to Jewish Law
208	a) W. Gunther Plaut, *The Rise of Reform Judaism*
208	1) J. W. Schorr
209	2) Michael Creizenach
213	b) Solomon Freehof, *Reform Responsa*
218	c) Jakob Petuchowski, *Ever Since Sinai*
224	d) W. Gunther Plaut, *The Rise of Reform Judaism*, Bernhard Wechsler

231	Chapter 19: The Conservative Approach to Jewish Law
231	Mordecai Waxman, ed., *Tradition and Change*
231	1) Mordecai Waxman, "The Ideology of the Conservative Movement"
247	2) Robert Gordis, "A Modern Approach to a Living Halachah"
257	3) Arthur H. Neulander, "The Use of Electricity on the Sabbath"

PREFACE

I will admit it from the very beginning: this book is outrageously pretentious. It presumes to investigate a number of very complex problems -- far too many for its size -- and it totally neglects a variety of viewpoints on almost every issue it touches. Even those positions which appear are treated with a brevity and a simplicity unbecoming to any mind trained in philosophy and/or religion.

But that is precisely the point: it is not meant for those preciously few people in the world today who have investigated any of these issues in depth. It is rather intended for the many Jews of today with no motivation to concern themselves with Judaism because of the encouragement of parents or friends (indeed, there is usually <u>discouragement</u> from those quarters), but who are willing -- often eager -- to confront the Tradition and engage in a dialogue with it -- to give it a chance, as it were. For such people, and especially for those in their teens and twenties who are in the midst of making many decisions about the pattern of their lives, the dialogue must be frank, uncondescending, and intellectually sophisticated, because it is undertaken with utmost intelligence and seriousness. But it cannot assume much familiarity with the Tradition, and it cannot get bogged down in scholarly details because their level of interest in this whole area will not sustain a prolix discussion of any one topic, at least at the outset. So the pace of this book is very brisk and its approach is rather cavalier; but, if it engages such Jews and communicates the notion that Judaism need not be abandoned as childish, once one has gone beyond fifth grade, but, as a matter of fact, is intellectually quite respectable and mature and even wise, and if this serves as an entree to further Jewish study and commitment, then it will have achieved its highest aims. My task, then, has been to bring together sources which will present a few intelligent approaches to the issues, and which are sufficiently different in viewpoint, and wide in scope, to motivate discussion. Of course, in the process I have tried to be as faithful and sympathetic to each of the source readings as I could be, but my purpose was, frankly, not a scholarly and thorough exposition of texts.

This has immediate consequences for the way in which this material should be used. Whether you are reading this book on your own or in conjunction with others, I would strongly recommend -- indeed, plead -- that you approach each of the readings with as much openness of mind and sympathy that you can muster, making your dialogue with this material (and, if it happens, with the other members of your discussion group) as open and frank as possible. I would also recommend that you not spend too much time over the details of any one reading. Try to arrive at a general notion of what the position is and the major reasons advanced for holding it, and then try to evaluate it in terms of its strong points and weak points. The questions and introductions will attempt to guide you in this process.

It is fitting that the core of this book was formulated for discussions at Camp Ramah in Wisconsin, where I first began my intellectual testing of Judaism. Rabbi Burton Cohen and Mr. Leon Waldman were largely responsible for getting me involved in this project, and have continued to contribute to it throughout. For their stimulus and continuing inspiration and ideas I am sincerely thankful. The late Rabbi Isaac Bonder, Mr. Alan Cohen, Rabbi Michael Menitoff, Mr. Barry Mesch, Rabbi Bezalel Porten, Mr. Joel Riemer, and Mr. Melvin Sirner have all taught significant parts of this material to a variety of groups, and the comments and criticisms which they were good enough to share with me so tactfully are deeply appreciated. Under the good advice and kind encouragement of Rabbis Efraim Warshaw and Neal Kaunfer, the original material was changed in format so that it could be used in a long-range series of discussions in the Hebrew High School of Temple Israel of Great Neck, New York. I taught it there as a "Seminar in the Philosophy and Process of Jewish Law," and, as one might expect, the comments of my students there, as at Ramah, were most valuable.

The enthusiasm and efforts of Dr. Morton Siegel, Director of the Department of Education of the United Synagogue of America, have been almost totally responsible for making the publication of this material possible, and, needless to say, I am sincerely grateful. The Textbook Materials Committee of the United Synagogue Commission on Jewish Education, chaired by Dr. William B. Lakritz, was most helpful. I would like to thank the Committee and the readers designated for this book, namely, Rabbi Reuven Kimelman, Mr. Gabriel Schonfeld, Dr. Saul I. Teplitz, and especially Rabbi David Wolf Silverman, whose comments were particularly helpful. I would also like to thank Mr. George Levine, who has taken care of the many tasks involved in producing the book, and Henrietta Cohn, who patiently readied it for publication through painstaking and meticulous text editing. And, throughout, my wife Marlynn has shared in the development of this book and has undertaken more thankless jobs in its preparation than a husband has a right to request.

Elliot N. Dorff
New York, New York
Fall 1970

Sources

A book of this nature draws upon many different sources and could not exist without them. As a result, I am sincerely grateful to the authors and publishers of the readings for permission to reprint the material under their respective copyrights. I shall list them by chapter so that this list can serve as a ready reference for those readers who wish to do further reading in these books.

Chapter 1

William Alston, "Religion," in *The Encyclopedia of Philosophy*, Paul Edwards, ed., The Macmillan Company and The Free Press, ©Crowell, Collier and Macmillan, New York, N. Y., 1967; volume 7, pp. 140-42.

Chapter 2

Karl Marx, "Contributions to the Critique of Hegel's *Philosophy of Right* (Introduction)"; numerous editions.

Chapter 3

a) John Macmurray, *The Structure of Religious Experience*, Yale University Press, New Haven, Connecticut, 1936; selections from pp. 4, 5-10, 13-26, and 37-38.

b) Martin Buber, *I and Thou*, Charles Scribner's Sons, New York, N. Y., 1958; pp. 3-6, 11-12, 33-34, 75, 77, 78-9, 80-81.

(cont.)

Chapter 4

a) Friedrich Nietzsche, <u>Beyond Good and Evil</u>, Helen Zimmern, trans., The Macmillan Company, New York, N. Y., 1914; sections 259-260.

b) Friedrich Nietzsche, <u>The Genealogy of Morals</u>, Francis Golffing, trans., Doubleday and Company, Inc. (Anchor Books), Garden City, New York, 1956; pp. 166-168.

Chapter 5

Robert Gordis, <u>A Faith for Moderns</u>, Bloch Publishing Company, New York, N. Y., 1960; pp. 15-16, 18-21, 23-24.

Chapter 6

a) Abraham J. Heschel, <u>Between God and Man</u>, Fritz Rothschild, ed., The Free Press, New York, N. Y. (Now published by Harper and Row), 1959; pp. 251-2.

b) Mordecai M. Kaplan, <u>The Future of the American Jew</u>, The Jewish Reconstructionist Press, New York, N. Y., 1967; (first edition: Macmillan, 1948); pp. 82-3, 94-5, 96, 100, 102.

c) Stokeley Carmichael and Charles V. Hamilton, <u>Black Power: The Politics of Liberation in America</u>, Random House (Vintage Books), New York, N. Y., 1967; pp. 37-39.

Chapter 7

Abraham J. Heschel, <u>The Sabbath</u>, Farrar, Strauss and Giroux, New York, N. Y. (now published by Harper and Row), 1951; pp. 3, 5-6, 8-10, 14, 16, 17, 18-19.

(cont.)

Chapter 8

Mordecai M. Kaplan, *The Meaning of God in Modern Jewish Religion*, The Jewish Reconstructionist Press, New York, N.Y. (originally published by Behrman House, 1937); pp. 59, 60-61, 62-63, 81-83, 90-91, 96, 102, 103.

Chapter 9

Eric Fromm, *The Forgotten Language*, Holt, Rinehart, and Winston, Inc., New York, N. Y., 1951 (now published by Grove Press, Inc., New York); pp. 243-248 (in Grove Press edition).

Chapter 10

The New Testament, The Letters of Paul to the Romans and to the Galatians; numerous editions.

Chapter 11

a) Emile Durkheim, *Sociology and Philosophy*, D. F. Pocock, trans., The Free Press, New York, N. Y., 1953; pp. 54-55, 59, 73.

b) Emile Durkheim, *The Division of Labor in Society*, George Simpson, trans., The Free Press, New York, N. Y., 1947; pp. 105-106, 106-107.

c) Morris Adler, *The World of the Talmud*, B'nai B'rith Hillel Foundation, Washington, D. C. (now published by Schocken Books, Inc., New York), 1958; pp. 61-65, 66-67 (in Schocken edition).

Chapter 12

a) Abraham Joshua Heschel, *Between God and Man*, Fritz Rothschild, ed., The Free Press, New York, N. Y. (now published by Harper and Row), 1959; pp. 155-158, 161, 162.

b) Franz Rosenzweig, <u>On Jewish Learning</u>, Nahum Glatzer, ed., Schocken Books, Inc., New York, N. Y., 1955; pp. 75, 76, 77, 78, 79, 80, 81, 82-4, 85-6, 87, 88, 90, 91.

Chapter 13

a) The Fourteenth Amendment of the Constitution.

b) Plessy v. Fergusen (1896) and Brown v. Board of Education
c) (1954) in <u>United States Reports</u>, Volumes 163, 347.

Chapter 14

a) <u>The Congressional Record</u>, Volume 110, part 12 (July 2, 1964).

b) The Civil Rights Act of 1964 in the <u>United States Code</u>, Public Law 88-352, July 2, 1964, 78 Stat. 241.

Chapter 15

a) Morris Adler, <u>The World of the Talmud</u>, B'nai B'rith Hillel Foundation, Washington, D. C. (now published by Schocken Books, Inc.), 1958, 1963; pp. 19-20, 21-25, 28-29, 30-31, 35-36, 37-39, 39-40, 41, 43, 44-47, 48-50, 52-55, 57-58 (in Schocken edition).

b) Herman Wouk, <u>This Is My God</u>, Doubleday and Company, Inc., Garden City, New York, 1959; pp. 212-13, 213-14, 214-15, 216, 216-17, 219-20, 220-21, 221-22, 224-25.

Chapter 16

a) Exodus from <u>The Torah</u>, The Jewish Publication Society of America, Philadelphia, Pa., 1962; pp. 118, 134, 140, 156-7.

b) Jacob Z. Lauterbach, *The Mekhilta de Rabbi Ishmael*, The Jewish Publication Society of America, Philadelphia, Pa., 1933; Vol. I, pp. 70-71; Vol. III, pp. 178, 199, 204.

c) *The Babylonian Talmud*, The Soncino Press, London, 1938; *Shabbath*, H. Freedman, trans., pp. 73, 77-8, 599-600, 604-5.

d) Moses Maimonides, *The Code of Maimonides*, Book Three, *The Book of Seasons*, Solomon Gandz and Hyman Klein, trans., Yale University Press, New Haven, Conn., 1961; pp. 32-33, 34-35, 38-39.

e) Joseph Karo, *The Shulkhan Arukh*, my translation.

Chapter 17

a) Samson Raphael Hirsch, *Judaism Eternal*, **Isidor** Grunfeld, trans., The Soncino Press, London, 1956; Vol. II, pp. 213-14, 215, 216, 217, 229-30, 231-2, 233, 234-36, 220, 221, 223, 245-47, 248-50, 250-51.

b) Emanuel Rackman, "Can We Moderns Keep the Sabbath?" in *Commentary*, Vol. 18, No. 3, September, 1954.

Chapter 18

a) W. Gunther Plaut, *The Rise of Reform Judaism*, The World
d) Union for Progressive Judaism, New York, N. Y., 1963; pp. 113-14, 117-19, 185-88.

b) Solomon Freehof, *Reform Responsa*, Hebrew Union College Press, Cincinnati, Ohio, 1960; pp. 3-4, 15-18, 21-23.

c) Jakob Petuchowski, *Ever Since Sinai*, Scribe Publications, Inc., New York, N. Y., 1961; pp. 108-114.

Chapter 19

Mordecai Waxman, ed., <u>Tradition and Change</u>, The Rabbinical
   Assembly of America, New York, N. Y., 1958; pp. 12-23,
   377-80, 383-86, 390-91, 401-407.

Dedication: Louis I. Newman, ed., <u>The Talmudic Anthology</u>,
   Behrman House, Inc., New York, N. Y., 1945; p. 478.

UNIT I

THE NATURE AND FUNCTIONS OF RELIGION

To be an observant Jew is a very difficult thing indeed. Consequently, it is a very natural reaction for the modern Jew to ask whether Judaism is worth the bother. Or, in other words, we ask, quite legitimately, whether religion serves the individual and/or society in any vital way so that it should merit our concern.

As you might have expected, there are many people who answer this question in the affirmative, and many in the negative. Often, the reasons given on each side concern the failure or success of a religious institution to function effectively. Some like (or dislike) religion because of the personality of a particular religious functionary. Some like (or dislike) it because of their friends' attitudes toward it. And indeed, there are many, many justifications which people offer as reasons for being concerned, or unconcerned, with religion, some good, and some bad.

We, however, will deal with two very broad attacks against religion, attacks which ask, in effect, whether the whole enterprise is not misconceived. Briefly, we shall discuss the claims that (1) religion does not deal with the real world, as does science, but rather, with some sort of illusion, i.e., religion is _false_ (Marx); and (2) religion functions in perverse ways, i.e., religion is _bad_ (Nietzsche). But, before we examine each of these arguments in detail, we shall briefly describe what it is that we mean by the term "religion."

Two final words before we begin. First, you ought to know that the Nietzsche selection (chapter 4), and especially the Marx material (chapter 2) are by far the hardest readings in this book, so do not be discouraged by them. Things will get considerably easier later, and your exposure to these great giants of thought will be well worth your while.

And, secondly, please remember to be completely frank in your discussion of these issues. You are _not_ supposed to take the opinion of anyone in these readings or in your group (including your discussion leader or teacher) as dogma to be memorized and spouted back on cue; you _are_ supposed to confront the issues raised, evaluate some of the approaches to the issues, and eventually try to work out your own position. So go to it!

PREVIEW QUESTIONS to Unit I, Chapters 1-6

1. What is "religion"?

2. What faults does religion have? Be frank.

3. What good points does it have?

4. Summing up your answers, do you think that religion is a good thing to have around or something that we should get rid of as soon as possible?

Chapter 1

Defining Religion

When we seek to define something (say, what a "table" is), we want our definition to state the <u>necessary</u> and <u>sufficient</u> conditions for anything to be a table. We have stated the <u>sufficient</u> conditions when anything which fits our definition is, in fact, a table; and we have stated the <u>necessary</u> conditions when everything in our definition is required in order for an object to be a table (i.e., when our definition does not demand anything extra). So, for example, if I defined a "table" as "a flat surface," I would not have given a <u>sufficient</u> definition because there are many flat surfaces which are not tables, such as walls or floors. And if I said that a "table" is "a flat surface with legs and painted blue," I would not have given a <u>necessary</u> definition because there are many tables which are not blue. An example of a necessary and sufficient definition (and therefore a totally adequate one) is this: "A bachelor is an unmarried man"; for all unmarried men are, in fact, bachelors (therefore the definition is sufficient), and there are no bachelors who are not unmarried men (and therefore the definition states only the necessary conditions for bachelorhood).

Generally, however, there are too many variables and we cannot arrive at a completely adequate definition, as you might have guessed from our attempts to define "table." For example, how many legs (if any) does a table have to have? How high does it have to be? What is it made of? What is it used for? How can you distinguish real tables from other things (e.g., floors) which are only sometimes used as makeshift tables? Or are all these questions irrelevant because a table can vary in all of those aspects so long as it has one or two characteristics? But, then, what are those characteristics?

These difficulties led a twentieth century philosopher by the name of Ludwig Wittgenstein to the notion that when we "define" something, we often only state the "family characteristics," as it were, either because we cannot do any more than that, or because that is all we want or need to know in the first place. That is, we state a few of the characteristics which most commonly appear in the thing we are trying to define (e.g., a "table" is "a flat surface with legs"), and we understand that, because of the very nature of the process of defining something, there will be certain "tables" which are not quite flat, and certain "tables" which have no legs, and all the rest will differ greatly in shape, design, materials, use, and so forth, but the classical examples of tables will be flat with legs.

Now that you know something about what is involved in defining something, we are ready to come to some notion of what our subject matter is, i.e., of what we mean by "religion."

Question:

1. Try to define "religion." Jot down your definition so that you can check it later.

    Reading: "Religion" by Wm. P. Alston, in The Encyclopedia of Philosophy.

    Religion. This article is not a survey of the various forms that religion has taken in human history; rather, it treats the nature of religion as a problem in the philosophy of religion. It will be concerned with attempts to develop an adequate definition of religion, that is, to make explicit the basic features of the concept of religion.

    General Definition and Characteristics. Examination of definitions. A survey of existing definitions reveals many different interpretations.

    "Religion is the belief in an ever living God, that is, in a Divine Mind and Will ruling the universe and holding moral relations with mankind." -- James Martineau

    "Religion is the recognition that all things are manifestations of a Power which transcends our knowledge." -- Herbert Spencer

    "By religion, then, I understand a propitiation or conciliation of powers superior to man which are believed to direct and control the course of Nature and of human life." -- J. G. Frazer

"Religion is rather the attempt to express the complete reality of goodness through every aspect of our being." -- F. H. Bradley

"Religion is ethics heightened, enkindled, lit up by feeling." -- Matthew Arnold

"It seems to me that it (religion) may best be described as an emotion resting on a conviction of a harmony between ourselves and the universe at large." -- J. M. E. McTaggart

"Religion is, in truth, that pure and reverential disposition or frame of mind which we call piety." -- C. P. Tiele

"A man's religion is the expression of his ultimate attitude to the universe, the summed-up meaning and purport of his whole consciousness of things." -- Edward Caird

"To be religious is to effect in some way, and in some measure, a vital adjustment (however tentative and incomplete) to whatever is reacted to or regarded implicitly or explicitly as worthy of serious and ulterior concern." -- Vergilius Ferm

If we take these definitions as attempts to state necessary and sufficient conditions for something to be a religion, it is not difficult to show that none of them is adequate. With respect to necessary conditions, consider Martineau's definition. It is clear that such a belief does not have to be present in a religion. No polytheistic religion recognizes a single divine ruler of the universe; and there are religions, such as Hinayana Buddhism, in which beliefs in personal deities play no role at all. Bradley and Arnold identify religion with morality, but there are primitive societies in which there is no real connection between the ritual system, with its associated beliefs in supernatural beings, and the moral code. The latter is based solely on tribal precedent and is not thought of as either originating with, or sanctioned by, the gods. If, as would commonly be done, we call the former the religion of the culture, we have a religion without morality. As for McTaggart and Tiele, it seems likely that if we specify "piety" or "feeling of harmony" sufficiently to give them a clear and unambiguous meaning, we will be able to find acknowledged religions in which they do not play an important role. It would seem that we could avoid this only by construing "piety," for example, to cover any state of feeling that arises in connection with religious activities. It does seem plausible to regard some of the definitions as stating necessary conditions, as in Caird and Ferm. However, it is doubtful that these are sufficient conditions. Does any "ultimate attitude" or any "vital adjustment" constitute a religion? As William James points out (<u>The Varieties of Religious Experience</u>, Ch. 2), it seems doubtful that a frivolous attitude toward life constitutes a religion, even if it is the fundamental attitude of a given person. And Ferm's overcarefully worded statement would seem to admit any attitude with respect to anything considered important to the ranks of the religious. This would presumably include one's attitude toward one's wife, toward one's vocation, and, in many cases, toward one's athletic activities. At this point one wonders what has happened to the concept of religion. Many of the definitions are deficient on grounds of both necessity and sufficiency. To return to Martineau, it is quite conceivable that such a belief might be held purely as a speculative hypothesis, without affecting the believer's feelings and attitudes in the way that would be requisite for religious belief. And as for McTaggart, it seems clear that one could, from time to time, have such a sense of harmony without this being integrated into anything that we would call a religion.

It is noteworthy that most of these definitions stress one aspect or another of religion to the exclusion of others. Thus, Martineau and Spencer represent religion as some sort of belief or other cognitive state; Frazer, as ritual (conceived in a utilitarian fashion); Bradley and Arnold, as a kind of moral attitude and activity; and McTaggart and Tiele as a certain kind of feeling. One might attribute the failings of these definitions to their one-sidedness. One could hardly expect to get an adequate statement of the nature of so complex a phenomenon as religion, essentially involving, as it does, all these forms of human activity, by restricting one's self to belief, feeling, ritual, or moral attitude alone. Caird and Ferm escape this particular failing by concentrating on a comprehensive term like "attitude" or "adjustment," which itself embraces belief, feeling, and moral attitude. But, as we have seen, these formulations do not come measurably closer to providing a set of necessary and sufficient conditions.

Question:

2. Was your definition both necessary and sufficient? Was it neither? Was it one but not the other? What facts about religion, or what types of religion, did your definition fail to account for?

Reading:

There are other ways of construing definitions of religion. Instead of taking the above statements as attempts to specify features that are common and peculiar to cases of religion, we might take each of them as an attempt to state the *essence* of religion, that central feature in terms of which all religious phenomena are to be understood. This approach to the matter is explicit in the following statements:

> "The essence of religion is a belief in the persistency of value in the world." -- Harald Høffding

> "The heart of religion, the quest of the ages, is the outreach of man, the social animal, for the values of the satisfying life." -- A. E. Haydon

> "The essence of religion consists in the feeling of an absolute dependence." -- Friedrich Schleiermacher

There are two distinguishable interpretations of claims of this type. They might be interpreted genetically, as accounts of the origin of religion. The claim would then be that what is specified as the essence of religion is the original root from which all phenomena of religion have sprung. Thus, Julian Huxley, like Schleiermacher working with a conception of the essence of religion as a kind of feeling, says, "...the essence of religion springs from man's capacity for awe and reverence, that the objects of religion...are in origin and essence those things, events, and ideas which arouse the feeling of sacredness" (*Religion Without Revelation*, p. 111). Similarly starting with Høffding's formulation, we might try to show how typical religious doctrines, rites, and sentiments grew out of an original belief in the persistency of value. However, since we know virtually nothing about the prehistoric origins of religion, speculation in this area is almost completely unchecked by data, and it seems impossible to find any rational basis for choosing between alternative genetic accounts.

However, we might also give a nongenetic interpretation. Saying that the essence of religion is a feeling of absolute dependence, for example, might mean that the full interrelatedness of the various features of religion can be understood only if we view them all in relation to a feeling of absolute dependence. This claim would be independent of any view of the origin of religion. The difficulty with this is that there would seem to be several different features of religion that could be taken as central -- such as ritual, a need for reassurance against the terrors of life, or a need to get a satisfactory explanation of the cosmos -- and it is illuminating to view the rest of religion as related to each of these. How is one to settle on a unique essence?

Question:

3. Why can't we define religion in terms of its origins, either in society or in the psyche of men? Make up some examples of "alternative genetic accounts." (Try this one as a starter: "Religion springs from man's need to eat. Therefore it has food prohibitions, sacrifices, feasts, and fasts, and from the feasts and fasts prayer arises.")

Question:

4. What is wrong with defining religion in terms of some central feature of it (e.g., ethics), and viewing all the other aspects of it in terms of that feature?

Reading:

Characteristic features of religion. Despite the fact that none of the definitions specifies a set of characteristics which is present when, and only when, we have a religion, or gives us a unique essence, it does seem that they contribute to our understanding of the nature of religion. It appears that the presence of any of the features stressed by these definitions will help to make something a religion. We might call such features, listed below, religion-making characteristics.

1. Belief in supernatural beings (gods).

2. A distinction between sacred and profane objects.

3. Ritual acts focused on sacred objects.

4. A moral code believed to be sanctioned by the gods.

5. Characteristically religious feelings (awe, sense of mystery, sense of guilt, adoration) which tend to be aroused in the presence of sacred objects and during the practice of ritual, and which are connected in idea with the gods.

6. Prayer and other forms of communication with gods.

7. A world view, or a general picture of the world as a whole and the place of the individual therein. This picture contains some specification of an over-all purpose or point of the world and an indication of how the individual fits into it.

8. A more or less total organization of one's life based on the world view.

9. A social group bound together by the above...

Definition in terms of characteristics. If it is true that the religion-making characteristics, neither singly nor in combination, constitute tight necessary and sufficient conditions for something being a religion, and yet that each of them contributes to making something a religion, then it must be that they are related in some looser way to the application of the term. Perhaps the best way to put it is this. When enough of these characteristics are present to a sufficient degree, we have a religion. It seems that, given the actual use of the term "religion," this is as precise as we can be. If we tried to say something like "for a religion to exist there must be the first two plus any three others," or, "for a religion to exist, any four

of these characteristics must be present," we would be
introducing a degree of precision not to be found in the
concept of religion actually in use.

Another way of putting the matter is this. There are cultural phenomena that embody all of these characteristics to a marked degree. They are the ideally clear paradigm cases of religion, such as Roman Catholicism, Orthodox Judaism, and Orphism. These are the cases to which the term "religion" applies most certainly and unmistakably. However, there can be a variety of cases that differ from the paradigm in different ways and to different degrees, by one or another of the religion-making characteristics dropping out more or less. For example, ritual can be sharply de-emphasized, and with it the demarcation of certain objects as sacred, as in Protestantism; it can even disappear altogether, as with the Quakers. Beliefs in supernatural beings can be whittled away to nothing, as in certain forms of Unitarianism, or may never be present, as in certain forms of Buddhism. And, as mentioned earlier, in certain primitive societies morality has no close connection with the cultic system. As more of the religion-making characteristics drop out, either partially or completely, we feel less secure about applying the term "religion," and there will be less unanimity in the language community with respect to the application of the term. However, there do not seem to be points along these various dimensions of deviations that serve as a sharp demarcation of religion from nonreligion. It is simply that we encounter less and less obvious cases of religion as we move from, for example, Roman Catholicism through Unitarianism, humanism, and Hinayana Buddhism to communism. Thus, the best way to explain the concept of religion is to elaborate in detail the relevant features of an ideally clear case of religion, and then indicate the respects in which less clear cases can differ from this, without hoping to find any sharp line dividing religion from nonreligion. (Cf. Ludwig Wittgenstein's notion of "family-resemblances" among the things to which a term applies.)

Question:

5. Explain what Alston means when he says that there is no "sharp demarcation of religion from nonreligion." Why not?

Does this mean that we do not know what we are talking about at all when we use the term "religion"? Show how the same thing is true about "government" (are your parents a "government"? your friends?); "athletics" (is ping-pong a form of athletics? is walking? is lifting your finger?); or any other complex phenomenon.

Question:

6. Would you make any changes in Alston's nine characteristics? Would you add to them? Delete from them? Why, or why not?

Chapter 2

Attack on the Nature of Religion

Reading: Contributions to the Critique of Hegel's Philosophy of Right (Introduction) by Karl Marx

The abolition of religion as the illusory happiness of the people is required for their <u>real</u> happiness. The demand to give up the illusions about their condition is the <u>demand to give up a condition</u> which needs <u>illusions</u>. The criticism of religion is therefore in <u>embryo the criticism of the vale of woe</u>, the <u>halo</u> of which is religion.

Question:

1. What does "illusory" mean? What is the opposite of "illusory"?

Question:

2. The phrase that Marx uses to describe religion is "the illusory happiness of the people." If you were Marx, what features of <u>Judaism</u> would you say lead only to such an illusory happiness? <u>Why</u> is this happiness only illusory? What do you think <u>real</u> happiness would be, according to Marx? (Marx will answer this later on, but try to guess intelligently at the answer now.)

Question:

3. The "condition which needs illusions" is another term which Marx uses for "religion." But even if we agree with Marx for a moment in saying that religion does need illusions, why is that so bad? That is, why does he "demand" to give up religion just because it has illusions?

Points to be watched for as we continue reading:

   A. <u>Why</u> does religion need illusions? (So far, Marx has only told us that it <u>does</u> need them; we still do not know why.)

B. What is real (or true) as opposed to the illusion which Marx says that religion is?

Reading:

Criticism has plucked the imaginary flowers from the chain, not so that man will wear the chain without any fantasy or consolation, but so that he will shake off the chain and cull the living flower. The criticism of religions disillusions man to make him think and act and shape his reality like a man who has become disillusioned and has come to reason, so that he will revolve round himself and therefore round his true sun. Religion is only the illusory sun which revolves round man as long as he does not revolve round himself....

Question:

4. What is the "chain" to which Marx is referring? What are the "imaginary flowers"?

Question:

5. "Marx wants us to <u>realize</u> that religions are full of illusions so that we will then obey religious teachings, but without putting any faith in the illusions." True or false? Why?

Reading:

The basis of irreligious criticism is: <u>Man makes religion</u>, religion does not make man. In other words, religion is the self-consciousness and self-feeling of man who has either not yet found himself or has already lost himself again. But <u>man</u> is no abstract being squatting outside the world. Man is <u>the world of man</u>, the state, society. <u>This</u> state, <u>this</u> society, produce religion, a <u>reversed world-consciousness</u>, because they are a <u>reversed world</u>. Religion is the general theory of that world, its encyclopeadic compendium, its logic in a popular form, its spiritualistic <u>point d'honnour</u>, its enthusiasm, its moral sanction, its solemn completion, its universal ground for consolation and justification. It is the <u>fantastic realization</u> of the human essence because the <u>human essence</u> has no true reality. The struggle against religion is therefore mediately the fight against <u>the other world</u>, of which religion is the <u>spiritual aroma</u>.

Question:

6. "Man makes religion, religion does not make man"; and this world (that is, the world around us, including men and the opinions that they commonly hold) is a "reversed" world because men commonly believe that religion makes man, which is the reverse of what really is true -- i.e., that man makes religion. When Marx says these things, what part of Judaism is he denying? (Consider Genesis I:1)

Question:

7. What, then, is religion? (Note that your answer is -- hopefully -- the "true" position which religion conceals, according to Marx.)

Question:

8. Now that we know what religion is for Marx, we must decide why such a thing ever came into existence. To do that, consider the following:

> Religion consists of the tentative beliefs that we have in the areas where we as yet have no knowledge. As soon as science is able to give a definite description of a phenomenon, however, continuing to adhere to the religious description of that phenomenon is sheer stupidity. For instance, the Genesis Creation story was fine until we gained scientific knowledge about evolution; now that we have that knowledge, however, if anybody still believes Genesis, he is simply a fool. Eventually science will probably answer almost all our questions, and religion will no longer serve any purpose.
>
> This is the "residue" theory of religion. Would Marx agree with it? (Hint: consider the second and the last two sentences of the paragraph, and make sure you know what "essence" means.) If yes, point out other examples of such residue in Judaism which he would give. If not, why not?

Reading:

Religious distress is at the same time the _expression_ of real distress and the _protest_ against real distress.

Religion is the sigh of the oppressed creature, the heart of a heartless world, just as it is the spirit of a spiritless situation. It is the <u>opiate</u> of the people.

Question:

9. Given the analysis that Marx has given of religion, explain why he believes that it leads to "distress." In other words, explain why religion is detrimental to society.

Question:

10. What does opium do? How is religion, as Marx sees it, like opium?

SUMMARY QUESTIONS ON MARX:

Question:

11. What is the false premise on which religion is based?

Question:

12. What bad effect does religion have on society as a result of this false premise?

Question:

13. What is the true position, as opposed to the false one of religion? How would the life of a person who lives according to this true premise differ from the life of a religious man?

Chapter 3

Response on the Nature of Religion

Reading: John Macmurray, The Structure of Religious Experience

What are the normal and universal facts of human experience out of which religion, as a special kind of human behavior, arises? This is the question to which we have to find an answer....

The first difficulty which meets us when we try to answer our question is that it seems impossible to distinguish any special set of facts which form the field of religion. All the facts of experience seem to be data for the religious consciousness. We shall see this clearly if we try to distinguish the field of religion from the field of science. There is no fact of experience which the scientist will not claim as part of his data. Science takes the whole world of experience and leaves nothing over for religion. But equally, religion claims the whole world of experience for itself. The artist does likewise. We are driven, therefore, to suppose that the difference between them must lie, not in their fields, but in the attitudes of mind in which they deal with the same field. The facts are there. But the religious man brings a different attitude of mind to bear upon them from the scientist or the artist. Starting from the same facts, religion and art and science move in different directions because they deal with the facts differently. The religious man comes to worship, the artist to admire, the scientist to observe. But they all come to the same world of common fact. Before accepting the truth that lies in this remark, there are two qualifications which we must make. In the first place, science, art, and religion are not three sets of people. The same person may be at once religious, artistic, and scientific. The three attitudes of mind which we have distinguished can be combined in one and the same mind. We ought to restate the distinction by saying that if we approach the facts in an attitude of worship, we shall find that we are in the field of religion, whereas if we approach the same facts in the attitude of mere observers, we shall find ourselves in the field of science. The second qualification is this. The scientist, though he claims all the facts as his field, finds that certain groups or aspects of the facts lend themselves much more readily to his manner of approach than others. The artist and the religious man find themselves at home with quite another group of facts or another aspect of the field. Certain things are easier to observe and analyze than others. Certain things are easier to admire and contemplate with satisfaction than others, and certain facts are much more easily reverenced. Thus, though when we generalize we have to say that the field is one and the same for science, art, and religion, when we come down to earth and begin to grapple with the field in all its complexity, we find that in practice there are three fields which overlap to a considerable extent but which have distinct centers. It is as if the same field of general experience became organized in three different ways round three different centers of interest. The velocity with which a body falls to the earth lies very near the center of interest for science. But for religion, it lies somewhere near the circumference. In practice, therefore, the scientist will find himself continually preoccupied with one set of facts and the religious man with another, because it is in terms of the selection defined by his attitude of mind that he must deal with all the facts. In this sense, science, art, and religion, though they are concerned in an abstract sense with the whole of experience, will actually start from different fields, and seek from their different centers to bring an ever enlarging range of experience into relation with their own starting-point. When we remember this, our question about the field of religion becomes manageable. It means, "What are the facts and aspects of common human experience to which we turn, and in which our interest centers, when we approach the world in a religious frame of mind?"

Question:

1. At this point, Macmurray assumes that science, art, and religion each deal with the whole of reality. Nevertheless, they are to be distinguished in terms of (a) the attitude

which we have toward reality in each of the three fields, and (b) the section of reality with which we are most concerned in each of the three.

>   a. What attitude do we have in science? art? religion? Given those attitudes, give examples of bad practice in each of the three. For example, can a scientist, in his scientific work, express his political opinions? Can an artist, in his art work? A religious person, in his religious activity? Give other examples of modes of conduct which are acceptable in one or two of the fields, but not in the other(s) (or less so in the others) because of the initial attitude (state of mind) that underlies and directs the activity. What types of conduct are frowned upon in all three settings?
>
>   b. Give examples of the common topics of discussion in scientific, artistic, and then religious circles. Do they interrelate? Why? (Hint: see question #2.)

Question:

2. Why is it that nobody is just a scientist or an artist or a man of religion? That is, why is it that "science, art, and religion are not three sets of people"? What, then, do we mean when we call a man, say, a "scientist"? When a man devotes himself almost totally to science (or athletics or politics or religion, or anything else), what do we think of him as a scientist (etc.)? As a human being?

Reading:

These considerations reveal a factor of real importance for our inquiry. The three attitudes of mind in which we approach the world of common experience have the effect of selecting parts of it for special attention. Now, selection is valuation, and we cannot select one thing from among a number of others without assigning it a higher value than the others, at least in respect of our immediate purpose. If an attitude of mind toward the whole field of experience selects a particular part of the field as central, it organizes experience thereby in terms of a scale of relative values. What it makes central becomes, for that very reason, the most important fact, and the one in terms of which all the others gain or lose importance. The scientific attitude selects as central those facts of experience which are most clearly and accurately observable, that is to say, what can be measured and counted. These become for it the most important facts in the world, while the others become less important and lie further from the center. This enables us to understand the tendency of a scientific age to think that the material aspects of experience are its real aspects. Science is materialistic, not because the real is material, but because its interests are scientific. It selects the measurable aspect as the most important, because it is the aspect with which it can deal. In this it is following the natural and inevitable anthropomorphism of all human behavior. Its principle is the shoemaker's principle that there's nothing like leather.

The fact that these attitudes of mind are bound up with valuation provides us with a clue. Valuation is primarily a feature of practical activity. It is concerned originally with the necessity of choosing between possible activities. The attitudes which lie behind religion and art and science are reflective attitudes, and must themselves be derived from the common field of practical experience. Now, in ordinary life we value some things for themselves, while we value others not for themselves but for the use that we can make of them. Philosophers, therefore, have distinguished between utility value and intrinsic value. The distinction is too well known to require elaboration. Anything that we use has a utility value for us in the act of using it. On the other hand, anything that has an intrinsic value is important to us by being what it is. In action its importance is not that we use it, not that it serves our purpose, but simply that it is there for us. In action we seek to possess it or to make it our own. Now, if we turn from action to reflection, these two types of value determine two different attitudes of mind. If our reflection selects in terms of utility value, the kind of knowledge we seek is very different from the kind of knowledge we seek if our reflection is grounded in intrinsic value. In the first case, we shall find ourselves investigating things in order to find out what are the characteristics that make them useful or useable. Two consequences follow. We shall be interested in the causal properties of things and we shall endeavor to secure general knowledge. For the causal properties of anything are precisely the characters which make it useable, and our interest in it is only a general interest. I mean by this that if our only interest in a thing lies in the possibility of using it for a purpose, what we shall want to know about it is not what distinguishes it from other individuals of the same kind, but what it has in common with them. Whereas, if its value to us is intrinsic, it is precisely its unique individuality that interests us. Now, knowledge of causal properties and general characteristics is precisely the kind of knowledge which we seek and gain in science. We are driven, therefore, to the conclusion that the attitude of mind which determines the selection and organization of the field of science is defined by a valuation of experience in terms of utility. The most general characteristics of the world become central. What the data have in common takes precedence of their differences. Causal properties become all-important. The facts of science are the ordinary data of experience selected in their material aspects, since it is their material characteristics that make things useable and give them their utility value....

Question:

3. Why do scientists deal primarily with matter and its motion? Why do many people in the twentieth century think that only the material is real? (Hint: Consider the effects of science on the outlook of people in this century.) What do they leave out?

Question:

4. Distinguish between utility value and intrinsic value. Note: Macmurray's use of the word "intrinsic" is somewhat misleading. He means the value which we attribute to an object when we can enjoy (appreciate) it just because it is the way it is, and not because we intend to use it for some other purpose of ours. So perhaps understand "aesthetic value" or "enjoyment value" whenever Macmurray uses the words "intrinsic value."

Question:

5. Why is science interested in general knowledge? (Hint: What is science trying to do? If you were trying to predict and control as much of nature as possible, would you be interested in what is peculiar to each individual thing or what is common to many of them? Why?)

Reading:

What is noticeable in the progression of this scientific picture is that it moves always away from individuality toward an undistinguishable commonness. The artistic attitude, in reflection, moves in the opposite direction toward individuality and uniqueness. Bringing to experience the desire to contemplate and admire, it sees the world as a collection of unique and interesting objects. The more definite and stable they are, the more possible it is to single them out for contemplation. In reflection it passes from the concentration upon easy and superficial beauty to deeper and more difficult forms, from the obvious beauty which is evanescent and fleeting to beauties that are enduring and eternal. What distresses it most is the changeableness of the things of experience. Individuality is everywhere subject to fading and dissolution. Nothing keeps its beauty long. So the artist seeks, as we say, to immortalize what is in experience evanescent. He seeks to make what is passing a possession forever; to confer on the data of common observation an individuality which can defy time; to prevent what is unique from being wholly reabsorbed into the common dust from which it arose. The same contrast can be observed in the effect of science and art upon human activities. The effect of science is to emphasize and accelerate the processes of change. The way in which science transforms, not merely social life, but the face of the earth itself, is a commonplace among us. The effect of art upon us is the opposite. It leads to the effort to maintain and preserve, against the ravages of time, things which have for us an intrinsic value. Not merely ancient works of art, but ancient ceremonial, ancient buildings are carefully guarded and preserved; and even corners of the world which have struck man by their natural beauty, like the Yosemite Valley, are carefully and expensively preserved against the scientific attitude which would dissolve their beauty in an effort to exploit them for practical purposes.

Question:

6. Describe the activity of the artist. How does he differ from the scientist in regard to his attitude toward (a) the unique and (b) change? When we value a person for the enjoyment he gives us, are we not also "using" him then? How do the two types of use differ?

Reading:

What, then, is the field of religion? Is there a third, distinct form of valuation imposed upon common experience by the religious attitude? If there is, what does it select, and how does it organize experience?...We have seen that the artistic and the scientific attitudes are antithetical and tend to achieve opposite results both in reflection and in action. But both attitudes are common to all of us. Both forms of valuation are attitudes of one and the same person. Though at points we find an antagonism between the two in our own minds, we do not normally feel that there is any incompatibility between them. There are very many things that we value, both for their utility and for themselves. Indeed, we often look upon the failure to combine these two attitudes as a mark of barbarism. Tools have utility value primarily. They are for use. Yet a good craftsman grows to love the tools which he uses so that they acquire for him an intrinsic value, and he cares for them beyond the point which is necessary from a purely utilitarian point of view. It is an instinct with man, even from the most primitive times, to seek to combine utility and beauty. If one and the same mind, then, can adopt either of these attitudes; if men can seek for the combination of utility and intrinsic value in the things they produce or acquire, then there must be an attitude of mind which combines the two antithetical attitudes. For if there were not, human personality would be split in two and radically at war with itself. It is quite obviously characteristic of religion that it does seek this combination. Some forms of religion stress the utilitarian attitude; others, the aesthetic. Religion has always been associated with the need that men have felt for help and assistance, and part of the religious attitude has always looked upon religion as a practical means of achieving its ends. But it is equally certain that religion has always looked upon its activities as important in themselves, imbued with an intrinsic value of their own. Primitive religious ceremonial is both an expression of the sense of beauty and a means of securing the welfare of the tribe. The Lord who is to be worshiped in the beauty of holiness is also a very present help in time of trouble. Christianity has always insisted on the absolute intrinsic value of the individual. But it has also equally insisted that his value lies in doing the will of God and making himself the instrument of a divine purpose. Nor have Christians felt that there was any contradiction in this paradox. Instances of this combination in religion of the practical and the contemplative attitudes can be multiplied at will. We may therefore conclude, not merely that there must be an attitude of mind which synthesizes the two opposites, but that the activities of religion are rooted in it, and are at least one of the forms of its expression.

Question:

7. Why must there be a synthesis of the notions of utility and appreciation (of the scientific and artistic states of mind)? What is the role of religion in regard to this synthesis? (Hint: Consider the last sentence in the paragraph above.) Give concrete examples of how religion is a form of expression of this synthesis. Are there other ways of expressing this synthesis? Give some examples. (Hint: When you choose a car, a college, or a vacation date and activity, do you combine both attitudes? When a country decides its foreign policy, or how it is going to get rid of its waste materials, is there an element of both attitudes in the decision? Is religion, then, very special in synthesizing the two attitudes? Read on!)

Reading:

In describing the two attitudes which determine the scientific and the artistic field we assumed that the field of common experience was just there; standing over against us, as it were; waiting for us to impose our valuation upon it. It was there for our use or for our pleasure. On the other hand, it appeared as a matter of accident whether we adopted one attitude or the other. We had forgotten that we ourselves are part of the field of common experience. For each of us all the rest of us are data. Our situation is not completely expressed by saying, "Here is the world; how shall we value it?" It is also, "Here we are; what value have we in the world? How are we to value ourselves? And how are we to value one another?" Against the question, "What are we to make of the world?" we must set the question, "What is the world to make of us?" It is only when we take both these sides of experience together that we grasp the field of common experience as a whole. We and our attitudes of mind are part of the world. And in this complete field of experience it is we who are partial, temporary, and dependent. The attitude of mind in which we realize this, in which we set ourselves in the world as dependent creatures of it, is a very different attitude of mind from the other two that we have discussed; and the valuation which it imposes, the organization of the data which it necessitates, are very different. It is this attitude which is the attitude of religion.

If this, then, is the religious attitude of which we were in search, what is the field of common experience which it defines as the field of religion? In particular, what are the central data which become the focus of importance and round which, in relation to which, all the others are organized?

We must notice first that the religious attitude actually enlarges the scope of the field. When we agreed that the field of science was the whole range of common experience, we were in fact leaving ourselves out. We were in fact setting the world of common experience over against ourselves, and, to that extent, it was less than the whole of the data. The field of religion is therefore wider and more complete than the field of science or of art. It may be objected that science in psychology does take us and our activities in as parts of the field of science. In a sense, this is true. But it is also true that we appear as data in the field of psychological science only partially. In the field of religion, each of us appears twice, both as the source of valuation and as the object of valuation. In psychology I appear as the object that is described, analyzed, and explained; and in activity which is based upon scientific psychology, I appear as the patient who is treated or manipulated by psychological devices, such as advertisement and propaganda. But I do not appear as that which describes and analyzes, nor as that which treats me or manipulates me. But in religion I appear in both these aspects, and in both at once. When the Psalmist says, "What is Man that Thou art mindful of him, or the Son of Man that Thou visitest him?" or when he cries, "We are as the grass of the field which today is and tomorrow is cast into the oven"; when the Prophet exclaims, "Thou art God and there is none else," the essential fact about these statements is that, though they assert the nothingness of man, it is man who asserts them. It is characteristic of the religious valuation that it assigns a very high value to the human judgment that sets a very low value on its own activities, including its judgments. This is a paradox, but it is also a description of the data of ordinary human experience.

This simple fact that we are able, and indeed compelled, to pass judgment upon ourselves lies very near the center of the religious field. As pronouncing judgment we are outside the field of experience; but as judged we are inside it. In other words, we are both transcendent of experience and immanent in it. This union of transcendence and immanence is, then, the full fact about human personality. It is an empirical fact and a natural fact. We are accustomed to find it applied in theology to God, and it is usually assumed to be a peculiar and distinguishing attribute of Deity. We see now that this is a mistake. The union of immanence and transcendence is a peculiar and defining characteristic of all personality, human or divine; but it is primarily a natural, empirical fact of common human experience. Religious reflection applies it to God as a defining characteristic of universal personality because it finds it in experience as a given fact of all finite personal experience.

Question:

8. (Important question) What factor in our experience of the world have we left out of the discussion so far? Does not

psychology account for this factor? When we recognize that factor, how do we feel (what is our attitude)? Given that this is the religious attitude, can you understand why religions often include prayers expressing thanksgiving, praise, fear, and petitions? (Hint: Note that common to them all is a realization of man's dependence on other men and on nature.) Give concrete examples of how other religious rituals illustrate this attitude. Can you understand now why religions often concern themselves with ethics too? (Hint: If you recognize that you are dependent upon nature and upon others, what does that situation require of you? See how strongly this is expressed in Deuteronomy 8:1-20, especially the last nine verses.)

Question:

9. What do "immanence" and "transcendence" mean? How is human personality a union of immanence and transcendence -- i.e., when is it immanent and when is it transcendent? Why, according to Macmurray, are these characteristics applied to God? Note that he is reversing the order in the Bible where God's personality comes first and men are created in His image, and we learn whatever we know of His personality through revelation, and not through inferences based on the nature of human personality. But, in any case, note that, despite these differences, Macmurray is certainly in tune with the Biblical view in his conclusion that men share at least part of the personality structure of God.

Reading:

But this capacity for self-judgment is not quite primary. It involves an effort of reflection. There is a more primitive character of common experience of which it is the first derivative, of which, indeed, it is only an aspect. The primary fact is that part of the world of common experience for each of us is the rest of us. We are forced to value one another, and the valuation is reciprocal. It is to this point to which I must draw special attention because it is the organizing center of the field of religion. When I deal with things in the world which are not human beings, I can treat them as subject to any valuation which I like to impose. I can either use them or admire them. But, if the objects I have to deal with are other people, this is impossible, for a very simple reason. The attitude which I take up sets a value on them, no doubt; but while I am valuing them they are valuing me. While I ask myself what I am to make of them, how I am to treat them, they are asking themselves what they are to make of me, and how they will treat me. It is this that makes the relations between ourselves and other people completely different from our relations with anything else in the world. It sets the central problem of human life, and it is a religious problem....It is the fact that all personal relationships are mutual and reciprocal in their very nature.

The full significance of this can only be grasped if we see it in terms of action, not of thought and reflection. It is in action that we have to relate ourselves to the things in the world. It is the necessity of living that forces us to impose our valuation on things. Religion, the religious attitude, and the religious valuation, with the conception of the world which it organizes, are forced upon us by the necessity of entering into relation with other people if we are to live at all. We must, therefore, impose our valuation upon people, but in doing so we force them equally to impose their valuation upon us. This is, in fact, what we all do in life, whether we reflect about it or not. If, then, I adopt an attitude to another person that gives him for me a utility value merely, I say to him in effect, "You are for my use." The only possible reply that he can make is a flat denial, and if we are to work together on these terms at all, he will have to assert in turn that I am for his use, and each of us will be trying to use the other for his own ends.

The artistic attitude equally fails to establish satisfactory relations between people. The valuation it imposes would be expressed if I said to another person, "You have an intrinsic value for me. You are for my enjoyment." The kind of action to which this valuation would give rise would be that I should seek to possess the other person as an object of permanent value to myself, not for use but for enjoyment. If I could succeed I should be the owner of a priceless treasure. The other person would have value in himself for me. But this would be incompatible with his having a value in himself for himself. Along those lines, personal relationships could only become reciprocal by establishing a permanent mutual admiration society, in which each of the members sought to keep hold of the others for the emotional satisfaction of watching them with admiration.

What is required in our relations with one another, if we are to recognize in practice the essential reciprocity of the relationship, is an attitude which somehow contains both of the other two attitudes, while transcending them both. Cooperation in activity does require that I should think of other people as having a utility value, but in such a way that I also have a utility value. I cannot do this if their utility value is imposed by me. For then I should be master and they would be my servants. If we are all to have a utility value for one another, it must be imposed by all of us, or by none of us. Yet all human cooperation is necessarily on a basis of mutual service, which makes each of us a servant. Obviously, this implies that each of us values all the others for themselves. Why else should I set aside my own claim to use them in my service in order to serve them. But this involves a reference from the scientific to the artistic attitude, from a recognition of utility value to a recognition of intrinsic value. By itself, the artistic attitude would prevent me from allowing them to serve me, and would so make cooperation impossible. If, then, we are to enter into relations with one another, it has to be in terms of an attitude to one another which is able to unite these two attitudes, and so to combine utility value and intrinsic value. This attitude is a religious attitude, and it is best expressed in terms such as fellowship or communion. We have to enter into fellowship with one another and so to create community.

We have now answered our question and defined the field of religious experience. The field of religion is the whole field of common experience organized in relation to the central fact of personal relationship. It is the personal data which are central, and form the focus of attention. Everything else is seen, from the religious point of view, in its relation to personality. The personal is the fact of central importance. All other facts are valued in relation to this central value. To

put it in simpler if less exact language, the field of
religion is the field of personal relations, and the datum
from which religious reflection starts is the reciprocity
or mutuality of these. Its problem is the problem of
communion or community. Religion is about fellowship and
community, which are facts of direct, universal human
experience....

Question:

10. (Important question) What is the major fact of experience
    with which religion deals ("the organizing center of the
    field of religion")? How do religious concepts, stories,
    and laws illustrate this concern with recognizing the in-
    herent worth of <u>both</u> you and all other human beings --
    that is, the worth that you have, regardless of how useful
    or beautiful you are? Why does this lead to cooperation
    among human beings? (Note that, after question #8, and, so
    far, in question #10, you now have covered three ways in
    which religion leads to cooperation: (1) it makes us aware
    of our dependence on each other and on the world; (2) it
    makes us aware of the inherent worth of every human being;
    and (3) it gives us ritual and moral precepts by which we
    are to carry out these realizations in action.) Recall,
    now, Macmurray's previous remark that religion is both
    utilitarian and aesthetic. Why do you need both for
    cooperation -- that is, why does science alone fail to
    induce cooperation? What about art? The special business
    of religion, then, **is** (at least partially) "to establish
    satisfactory relations between people." How is this most
    often expressed? (We shall be considering several other
    functions of building a religious community in chapter 6 --
    i.e., functions besides the establishment of cooperation
    among people who recognize each other's utilitarian,
    aesthetic, <u>and</u> inherent worth.)

Question:

11. (Important question) Note that people are valued for both
    their aesthetic and utilitarian worth in many types of
    groups and not just in religion. Of course, as we have
    been discussing, there are many groups in which one type
    of valuation is much more dominant than the other (e.g.,
    in a football team or a business, where your worth to the

team or firm is measured almost solely in terms of your ability to "produce," or on the stage, where your value as an actor is measured in terms of how much people enjoy your performance). And there are some groups where both factors play a part almost equally in the way you think of others and they think of you (e.g., your neighbors probably value you both for your sociability and for the occasional favors which you might extend to them). But there are also some groups where you are (or should be) recognized for your inherent worth, too -- e.g., among your friends and, especially, within your family. Do you see now why, in Judaism especially, the family plays such a central role? But what does religion do with this need (i.e., to be recognized for your own inherent worth and to recognize others for their inherent worth) which the family does not do? (Hint: Do you live your life only within the confines of your family? Then consider the facts that religion creates a community and its celebrations; teaches an ethical code and applies social pressure to induce people to observe it; gives you a long history to be proud of; and enunciates a philosophy in its stories, laws, and books of thought which emphasize this notion of man's inherent worth. How does each of these functions of religion expand the scope of people, time, and activity over which we are reminded of this notion and induced to guide our conduct by it)?

Reading:

It is a simple commonplace that the lives of human beings are interdependent. Other people bring us into the world and other people bury us when we die, and all our life through we are dependent in a thousand ways upon other people. That is the simple fact; and it means that the structure of human experience, dependent as it is for its very existence upon the mutual relations of persons, is religious in its texture. It is this primary fact about us that gives rise to religion, and since this is a universal fact about human life, belonging to its very nature, it follows that religion is an inseparable component of human life, and always must be. To say that religion belongs to the early stages of human life and is destined to be superseded as human development goes on is to talk foolishness. That could only be true if progress reached the point when we were all hatched out by the sun on desert islands and lived and died without knowing that there was anyone else in the world but our solitary selves. A person who has no religion, or a society which has repudiated religion, has merely forgotten that humanity exists only in the relation of human beings to one another.

We are concerned now to discuss the self in its religious activity. In doing this we are trying to discover how religion, as a specific human activity, arises out of the primary facts of human relatedness. This depends primarily upon the attitude of mind in which the self deals with its experience. It is a fact that we are interdependent. But we are often unconscious of this fact. We take it for granted and concentrate our attention upon other aspects of our experience, so that they fill the field of our consciousness. The religious attitude, therefore, is that attitude of mind for which our relations to other people are central. The religious life is the life which is dominated by this belief in the centrality of personal relations. Any attitude of mind, as we have seen, imposes an order of valuation upon the world of its experience. The religious attitude sets the relationship of the self to other selves as the center of valuation and values everything else in relation to this. For such an attitude the main business of life consists in understanding, appreciating, and creating the full reality of personal relationship. The task of religion is the realization of fellowship. The religious activity of the self is its effort to enter into communion with the Other....

Question:

12. What was Marx's attitude toward the "residue theory of religion" (chapter 2, question #8)? What is Macmurray's? What reason does he give? With which (if either) do you agree? Why?

Reading:

This is precisely the function of religion. In primitive society it is quite clear that the function of religion is to create, sustain, and express the emotional relationship which unites the members of the primitive tribe. The close connection of primitive religion with ancestor worship, the tendency for religious communities to trace their descent to a common ancestor, the religious ceremonies which extend the relation of brotherhood to people who are not natural brothers, often by the symbolic mingling of their blood, and a thousand other characteristics of primitive religion, reveal very clearly that its function is to extend the sentiments which unite the members of the natural family beyond its natural limits. What is taking place is already the generalization of direct relationships of natural affection. If we look to the development of religion in history, we find that the extension of this bond of family affection to larger and larger groups of people through the acceptance of a common faith has been one of the controlling factors in the development of society. We are driven to the conclusion that the function of religion is to increase the scope and the complexity of human cooperation by creating, sustaining, and expressing the union of persons in a spiritual family or a spiritual brotherhood. It should be noticed that the term "spiritual" here means merely "not related by blood." It does not mean "not material." Without such an extension of the sense of emotional unity beyond the natural field of its instinctive expression, the development of human society would have been impossible, and the achievement of this is the work of religious reflection. We might express this shortly by saying that the task of religion is the maintenance and extension of human community.

Question:

13. Go back to question #11 and add anything which you may wish to, based upon your reading of the last few paragraphs. You will probably want to do this again after you read the Kaplan material in chapter 6. Note: Marx thought that religion deals with an illusion, and Macmurray tries to show that it deals with a very real part of our experience. Other authors claim that different parts of reality constitute the subject matter of religion -- e.g., our experience of awe and wonder (Otto, Heschel); of history (Yehudah Halevi); of revelation (Saadia Gaon); etc. But it is interesting that one of the best known twentieth century Jewish philosophers describes the subject matter of religion in much the same terms as does

Macmurray. Following, then, is a brief selection from Martin Buber:

Reading:

I and Thou
Martin Buber

To man the world is twofold, in accordance with his twofold attitude.

The attitude of man is twofold, in accordance with the twofold nature of the primary words which he speaks.

The primary words are not isolated words, but combined words.

The one primary word is the combination I-It; wherein, without a change in the primary word, one of the words He or She can replace It.

Hence the I of man is also twofold.

For the I of the primary word I-Thou is a different I from that of the primary word I-It.

Primary words do not signify things, but they intimate relations.

Primary words do not describe something that might exist independently of them, but being spoken they bring about existence.

Primary words are spoken from the being.

If Thou is said, the I of the combination I-Thou is said along with it.

If It is said, the I of the combination I-It is said along with it.

The primary word I-Thou can only be spoken with the whole being.

(cont.)

The primary word I-It can never be spoken with the whole being.

There is no I taken in itself, but only the I of the primary word I-Thou and the I of the primary word I-It.

When a man says I he refers to one or other of these. The I to which he refers is present when he says I. Further, when he says Thou or It, the I of one of the two primary words is present.

When a primary word is spoken the speaker enters the word and takes his stand in it.

The life of human beings is not passed in the sphere of transitive verbs alone. It does not exist in virtue of activities alone which have some things as their object.

I perceive something. I am sensible of something. I imagine something. I will something. I feel something. I think something. The life of human beings does not consist of all this and the like alone.

This and the like together establish the realm of It.

But the realm of Thou has a different basis.

When Thou is spoken, the speaker has no thing; he has indeed nothing. But he takes his stand in relation.

It is said that man experiences his world. What does that mean?

Man travels over the surface of things and experiences them. He extracts knowledge about their constitution from them: he wins an experience from them. He experiences what belongs to the things.

But the world is not presented to man by experiences alone. These present him only with a world composed of It and He and She and It again.

(cont.)

I experience something. If we add "inner" to "outer" experiences, nothing in the situation is changed. We are merely following the uneternal division that springs from the lust of the human race to whittle away the secret of death. Inner things or outer things, what are they but things and things!

I experience something. If we add "secret" to "open" experiences, nothing in the situation is changed. How self-confident is that wisdom which perceives a closed compartment in things, reserved for the initiate and manipulated only with the key. O secrecy without a secret! O accumulation of information! It, always It!

The man who experiences has no part in the world. For it is "in him," and not between him and the world, that the experience arises.

The world has no part in the experience. It permits itself to be experienced, but has no concern in the matter. For it does nothing to the experience, and the experience does nothing to it.

As experience, the world belongs to the primary word I-It.

The primary word I-Thou establishes the world of relation.

Question:

14. Review question #6, and note that Buber combines Macmurray's "scientific attitude" and "artistic attitude" into one "I-It" attitude, in which the "I" uses the "It," whether for prediction and control or for enjoyment. This leaves him with only one other attitude, I-Thou, which occurs when we recognize the inherent worth of the other object or individual and come into relation with it. Explain what Buber means when he says that "the I of the primary word I-Thou is a different I from that of the primary word I-It." How is he different? Why is man in the I-It relationship "self-confident," and why is it that he "has no part in the world"?

Reading:

The spheres in which the world of relation arises are three.

First, our life with nature. There the relation sways in gloom, beneath the level of speech. Creatures live and move over against us, but cannot come to us, and when we address them as Thou, our words cling to the threshold of speech.

Second, our life with men. There the relation is open and in the form of speech. We can give and accept the Thou.

Third, our life with spiritual beings. There the relation is clouded, yet it discloses itself; it does not use speech, yet begets it. We perceive no Thou, but nonetheless we feel we are addressed, and we answer -- forming, thinking, acting. We speak the primary word with our being, though we cannot utter Thou with our lips....

The Thou meets me through grace -- it is not found by seeking. But my speaking of the primary word to it is an act of my being, is indeed the act of my being.

The Thou meets me. But I step into direct relation with it. Hence the relation means being chosen and choosing, suffering and action in one; just as any action of the whole being, which means the suspension of all partial actions and consequently of all sensations of actions grounded only in their particular limitation, is bound to resemble suffering.

The primary word I-Thou can be spoken only with the whole being. Concentration and fusion into the whole being can never take place through my agency, nor can it ever take place without me. I become through my relation to the Thou; as I become I, I say Thou.

All real living is meeting.

(cont.)

The relation to the Thou is direct. No system of ideas, no foreknowledge, and no fancy intervene between I and Thou. The memory itself is transformed, as it plunges out of its isolation into the unity of the whole. No aim, no lust, and no anticipation intervene between I and Thou. Desire itself is transformed as it plunges out of its dream into the appearance. Every means is an obstacle. Only when every means has collapsed does the meeting come about....

The world of It is set in the context of space and time.

The world of Thou is not set in the context of either of these.

The particular Thou, after the relational event has run its course, is bound to become an It.

The particular It, by entering the relational event, may become a Thou.

These are the two basic privileges of the world of It. They move man to look on the world of It as the world in which he has to live, and in which it is comfortable to live, as the world, indeed, which offers him all manner of incitements and excitements, activity and knowledge. In this chronicle of solid benefits, the moments of the Thou appear as strange lyric and dramatic episodes, seductive and magical, but tearing us away to dangerous extremes, loosening the well-tried context, leaving more questions than satisfaction behind them, shattering security -- in short, uncanny moments we can well dispense with. For since we are bound to leave them and go back into the "world," why not remain in it? Why not call to order what is over against us, and send it packing into the realm of objects? Why, if we find ourselves on occasion with no choice but to say Thou to father, wife, or comrade, not say Thou and mean It? To utter the sound Thou with the vocal organs is by no means the same as saying the uncanny primary word; more, it is harmless to whisper with the soul an amorous Thou, so long as nothing else in a serious way is meant but <u>experience</u> and <u>make use of</u>.

And in all the seriousness of truth, hear this: Without It man cannot live; but he who lives with It alone is not a man....

The extended lines of relations meet in the eternal Thou.

Every particular Thou is a glimpse through to the eternal Thou; by means of every particular Thou, the primary word addresses the eternal Thou. Through this mediation of the Thou of all beings, fulfillment and non-fulfillment of relations comes to them: The inborn Thou is realized in each relation and consummated in none. It is consummated only in the direct relation with the Thou that by its nature cannot become It.

Question:

15. Describe the kinds of I-Thou relationship which we can have, according to Buber. Which is by far the most common (although difficult, nevertheless)? Why is it that "the Thou meets me through grace," that "the relation means being chosen and choosing"? (Hint: Do you decide by yourself who your friends will be? Can other people control that decision without you? Do you understand now why many religious texts talk about "the hiddenness of God" or, on the other hand, of His talking to someone "face to face"?) Why is it that "every means is an obstacle" in an I-Thou relationship?

Question:

16. What happens to most I-Thou relationships? Why does that happen? In which I-Thou relation (i.e., with which Thou) does it never happen? Why not? Explain carefully what Buber means in both clauses of the following sentence and try to decide why he says what he says: "Without It man cannot live; but he who lives with It alone is not a man."

Reading:

To this end the world of sense does not need to be laid aside as though it were illusory. There is no illusory world; there is only the world which appears to us as twofold in accordance with our twofold attitude. Only the barrier of separation has to be destroyed. Further, no "going beyond sense-experience" is necessary; for every experience, even the most spiritual, could yield us only an It. Nor is any recourse necessary to a world of ideas and values; for they cannot become presentness for us. None of these things is necessary. Can it be said what really is necessary? Not in the sense of a precept. For everything that has ever been devised and contrived in the time of the human spirit as precept, alleged preparation, practice, or meditation, has nothing to do with the primal, simple fact of the meeting. Whatever the advantages in knowledge or the wielding of power for which we have to thank this or that practice, none of this affects the meeting of which we are speaking; it all has its place in the world of It and does not lead one step, does not take the step, out of it. Going out to the relation cannot be caught in the sense of precepts being given....

In the relation with God, unconditional exclusiveness and unconditional inclusiveness are one. He who enters on the absolute relation is concerned with nothing isolated any more, neither things nor beings, neither earth nor heaven; but everything is gathered up in the relation. For to step into pure relation is not to disregard everything but to see everything in the Thou; not to renounce the world but to establish it on its true basis. To look away from the world, or to stare at it, does not help a man to reach God; but he who sees the world in him stands in His presence. "Here world, there God" is the language of It; "God in the world" is another language of It; but to eliminate or leave behind nothing at all, to include the whole world in the Thou, to give the world its due and its truth, to include nothing beside God but everything in him -- this is full and complete relation.

Men do not find God if they stay in the world. They do not find Him if they leave the world. He who goes out with his whole being to meet his Thou, and carries to it all being that is in the world, finds Him who cannot be sought.

God cannot be inferred in anything -- in nature, say, as its author, or in history as its master, or in the subject as the self that is thought in it. Something else is not "given" and God then elicited from it; but God is the Being that is directly, most nearly, and lastingly, over against us, that may properly only be addressed, not expressed.

Question:

17. Must we use illusions or something "beyond sense-experience" to have an I-Thou relationship, even with God? Can we give a recipe ("precept") for having an I-Thou relationship? Why not? (Hint: Even though there are certain things which you might do to encourage a friendship, can you, in the end, make it come about?) For example, can one arrive at an awareness of God through reasoning? Why not? What kinds of things, then, would be "things which you might do to encourage a friendship," as it were, with God? (Hint: Consider Buber's comment, "Every particular Thou is a glimpse through to the eternal Thou.")

Chapter 4

Attack on the Functions of Religion

Reading: Master Morality and Slave Morality by
Friedrich Nietzsche

In a tour through the many finer and coarser moralities which have hitherto prevailed or still prevail on the earth, I found certain traits recurring regularly together, and connected with one another, until finally two primary types revealed themselves to me, and a radical distinction was brought to light. There is master-morality and slave-morality....

Question:

1. Nietzsche claims that there are two kinds of morality. What kind of evidence does he use to make his claim?

Question:

2. Is it ever possible to agree with this kind of evidence and yet disagree with the conclusions made on the basis of this evidence? (Hint: Consider a weather forecast or a decision on what to do to settle the conflict in the Middle East.)

Question:

3. What you just discovered is an important point in general method: It is one of many principles which tell you how to carry out your thinking process. Can you formulate this principle in your own words?

Reading:

The distinction of moral values has either originated in a ruling caste, pleasantly conscious of being different from the ruled -- or among the ruled class, the slaves and dependents of all sorts. In the first case, when it is the rulers who determine the conception "good," it is the exalted, proud disposition which is regarded as the distinguishing feature, and that which determines the order of rank. The noble type of man separates from himself the beings in whom the opposite of this exalted, proud disposition displays itself. He despises them. Let it at once be noted that in this first kind of morality the antithesis "good" and "bad" means practically the same as "noble" and "despicable"; the antithesis "good" and "evil" is of a different origin. The cowardly, the timid, the insignificant, and those thinking merely of narrow utility, are despised; moreover, also, the distrustful, with their constrained glances, the self-abasing, the doglike kind of men who let themselves be abused, the mendicant flatterers, and, above all, the liars: it is a fundamental belief of all aristocrats that the common people are untruthful. "We truthful ones" -- the nobility in ancient Greece called themselves.... The noble type of man regards <u>himself</u> as a determiner of values; he does not require to be approved of; he passes the judgment: "What is injurious to me is injurious in itself"; he knows that it is he himself only who confers honor on things; he is a <u>creator of values</u>. He honors whatever he recognizes in himself; such morality is self-glorification. In the foreground there is the feeling of plentitude, of power which seeks to overflow, the happiness of high tension, the consciousness of a wealth which would fain give and bestow: the noble man also helps the unfortunate, but not -- or scarcely -- out of pity, but rather from an impulse generated by the super-abundance of power. The noble man honors in himself the powerful one, him to keep silence, and who takes pleasure in subjecting himself to severity and hardness, and has reverence for all that is severe and hard...The noble and brave who think thus are the furthest removed from the morality which sees precisely in sympathy, or in acting for the good of others, or in <u>desinteressement</u> the characteristic of the moral; faith in one's self, pride in one's self, a radical enmity and irony towards "selflessness," belong as definitely to noble morality as do a careless scorn and precaution in the presence of sympathy and the "warm heart."

Question:

4. Who forms master morality?

Question:

5. "Antithesis" means "opposite." Master morality operates on the antithesis between "noble" and "despicable," honoring the first kind of person and despising the second. Describe the "noble" man (as Nietzsche sees him), i.e., the kind of person that master morality is trying to create.

Question:

6. Try to describe what a <u>society</u> composed of such "noble" men would be like. Who would be the laborers? Who would rule? What would be the criterion (basis) to decide questions of right and wrong? In what ways would this society be better than ordinary society? What special problems would it have?

Question:

7. What would Judaism say about "master-morality?"

Reading:

It is otherwise with the second type of morality, <u>slave-morality</u>. Supposing that the abused, the oppressed, the suffering, the unemancipated, the weary, and those uncertain of themselves should moralize, what will be the common element in their moral estimates? Probably a pessimistic suspicion with regard to the entire situation of man will find expression, perhaps a condemnation of man, together with his situation. The slave has an unfavorable eye for the virtues of the powerful; he has a scepticism and distrust, a <u>refinement</u> of distrust of everything "good" that is there honored. He would fain persuade himself that the very happiness there is not genuine. On the other hand, <u>those</u> qualities which serve to alleviate the existence of sufferers are brought into prominence and flooded with light; it is here that sympathy, the kind, helping hand, the warm heart, patience, diligence, humility, and friendliness attain to honor; for here these are the most useful qualities, and almost the only means of supporting the burden of existence. Slave-morality is essentially the morality of utility. Here is the seat of the origin of the famous antithesis "good" and "evil": power and dangerousness are assumed to reside in the evil, a certain dreadfulness, subtlety, and strength, which do not admit of being despised. According to slave-morality, therefore, the "evil" man arouses fear; according to master-morality, it is precisely the "good" man who arouses fear and seeks to arouse it, while the bad man is regarded as the despicable being. The contrast attains its maximum when, in accordance with the logical consequences of slave-morality, a shade of depreciation -- it may be slight and well-intentioned -- at last attaches itself to the "good" man of this morality; because, according to the servile mode of thought, the good man must in any case be the safe man: he is good-natured, easily deceived, perhaps a little stupid, un bonhomme. Everywhere that slave-morality gains the ascendancy, language shows a tendency to approximate the significations of the words "good" and "stupid." A last fundamental difference: The desire for freedom, the instinct for happiness and the refinements of the feeling of liberty belong as necessarily to slave-morals and morality as artifice and enthusiasm in reverence and devotion are the regular symptoms of an aristocratic mode of thinking and estimation.

Question:

8. Who forms slave morality?

Question:

9. Describe the "good" man of slave morality, i.e., the kind of person that slave morality is trying to create.

Question:

10. Try to describe what a <u>society</u> composed of such "good" men would be like. Who would be the laborers? Who would rule? What would be the criterion (basis) to decide questions of right and wrong? What weaknesses would this society have? What strengths?

Question:

11. Master morality honored the "noble" man and despised the "despicable" man; slave morality, instead, honors the "good" man and despises the "evil" man. Now that you have considered each type individually, describe carefully the <u>differences</u> between these two antitheses, i.e., the differences between master and slave morality.

Reading:

By now the reader will have got some notion how readily the priestly system of valuations can branch off from the aristocratic and develop into its opposite. An occasion for such a division is furnished whenever the priest caste and the warrior caste jealously clash with one another and find themselves unable to come to terms. The chivalrous and aristocratic valuations presuppose a strong physique, blooming, even exuberant health, together with all the conditions that guarantee its preservation: combat, adventure, the chase, the dance, war games, etc. The value system of the priestly aristocracy is founded on different presuppositions. So much the worse for them when it becomes a question of war! As we all know, priests are the most evil enemies to have -- why should this be so? Because they are the most impotent. It is their impotence which makes their hate so violent and sinister, so cerebral and poisonous. The greatest haters in history -- but also the most intelligent haters -- have been priests. Beside the brilliance of priestly vengeance all other brilliance fades. Human history would be a dull and stupid thing without the intelligence furnished by its impotents. Let us begin with the most striking example. Whatever else has been done to damage the powerful and great of this earth seems trivial compared with what the Jews have done, that priestly people who succeeded in avenging themselves on their enemies and oppressors by radically inverting all their values, that is, by an act of the most spiritual vengeance. This was a strategy entirely appropriate to a priestly people in whom vindictiveness had gone most deeply underground. It was the Jews who, with frightening consistency, dared to invert the aristocratic value equations good/noble/powerful/beautiful/happy/favored-of-the-gods, and maintain, with the furious hatred of the underprivileged and impotent, that "only the poor, the powerless, are good: only the suffering, sick and ugly, truly blessed. But you noble and mighty ones of the earth will be, to all eternity, the evil, the cruel, the avaricious, the Godless, and thus the cursed and damned!...We know who has fallen heir to this Jewish inversion of values...In reference to the grand and unspeakably disastrous initiative which the Jews have launched by this most radical of all declarations of war, I wish to repeat a statement I made in a different context (<u>Beyond Good and Evil</u>), to wit, that it was the Jews who started the slave revolt in morals; a revolt with two milennia of history behind it, which we have lost sight of today simply because it has triumphed so completely..."Exploitation" does not belong to the <u>nature</u> of the living being as a primary organic function; it is a consequence of the intrinsic Will to Power, which is precisely the Will to Life. Granting that, as a theory, this is a novelty -- as a reality it is the <u>fundamental</u> fact of all history: Let us be so far honest towards ourselves!

Question:

12. For Nietzsche, is Judaism a master morality or a slave morality? Illustrate this with some concrete examples from the Bible or Talmud, i.e., Jewish laws or stories which show what kind of morality it teaches.

Question:

13. Now, then, <u>evaluate</u> Nietzsche's position. What are its strong points? Its weak points?

Question:

14. On the basis of your evaluation, <u>defend</u> Judaism as well as you can from Nietzsche's attack. How do you think Nietzsche would answer your defense?

Chapter 5

Response on the Functions of Religion I

Reading: A Faith for Moderns by Robert Gordis
Why Religion?

It is therefore clear that the extent of the revival of interest in religion in our time is both less and more than the statistical rise of congregational membership; it includes only part of the new affiliates, but also many more who have not signed any membership application.

This widely varied group of sensitive and intelligent men and women represents the saving grace of the contemporary return to religion and the ultimate hope for its genuine revival. What are the motivating factors that lead them to explore the resources of religious tradition? In a phrase, what are they seeking in religion?

First and foremost is the quest for psychological security. It is not a guarantee of personal safety they seek, but the assurance that the human adventure is no accident, destined to be wiped clean from the earth's surface. Our age had divested itself of the mantle of faith in what seemed the beginning of a perpetual springtime, only to stand shivering before the chills and blasts of an endless winter.

Let us hasten to point out that the religion which our age has lost was not the creed preached in the pulpits of church, cathedral, and synagogue. That faith had ceased to be a living and relevant reality for many modern men long before our day. At best, the pomp of ritual and the sonorities of Scripture were intended for decoration and not for use. The faith which really dominated the landscape of the Western world during the past half-century and more, and which now has crumbled, is the worship of science as the ultimate source of truth and the fountain of all good. The cornucopia of scientific discovery and technological advance made it easy not only for the unreflective masses, but for the intellectual leaders of the age as well, to look to science as the great god from whom all blessings flow. Whatever was not known science would disclose; whatever was lacking science would grant.

In our day, the tide of blessings has continued to flow, but it is dwarfed by a greater inundation of catastrophe, generated in the same kind of scientific laboratories. An earlier generation, perhaps more naive than ours, would have stood in silent awe before the miracle of the discovery of nuclear energy and would have seen in it a manifestation of the Divine. Had not the first words flashed across the telegraph by its inventor, Samuel F. B. Morse, been, "What hath God wrought?" Instead, the birth of the atomic age was heralded by no paeans of thanksgiving, but by the horrors of Hiroshima and Nagasaki. Even the sense of wonder has been dwarfed by abject, helpless terror. It is noteworthy that the destructive capacities of atomic energy have been explored far more successfully and exploited far more effectively than have its peaceful uses, which are still largely in the blueprint stage.

This is no criticism of the scientific process or of its practitioners. By its very nature, science is concerned solely with disinterested quest after truth, and not with the application of its results to human life. By the same token, it is not within its function or capacity to determine the goals of life, or to offer any assurance that they will be attained.

Through the ages, men have found that religious faith alone could bring to them this security, this sense of the permanent behind the flux of life, this assurance of the triumph of the ideal. In the words of the Psalmist, "The Lord is my light and my life; whom shall I fear? The Lord is the fortress of my life; of whom shall I be afraid?"

Confronted by fears unimagined by the Psalmist, modern intelligent people are therefore led to ask themselves whether faith in God is possible for them. Such a faith becomes more than a distant hope, once men disabuse themselves of the error of believing that only that which can be weighed and measured is real. The crucial step is to recognize that what counts in life usually cannot be counted.

Question:

1. In what sense have we lost our faith in science? That is, we no longer believe that science can do what? Why?

Question:

2. In what sense, then, do we believe in science?

Question:

3. What is it that we feel secure about as a result of religion? How does religion try to give us this security? What questions still have to be answered if it is going to succeed in this task?

Question:

4. Why is it important both for the individual and society to feel secure in regard to this matter? In other words, why is religion performing a valuable function if it gives us this security -- or is it?!

Reading:

A second goal impels men to turn to religion -- the deeply felt need for a satisfying philosophy of life. They are beginning to discover, after a long period of neglect and even of scorn, that the insights of religion are indispensable for a world-view by which they can live. It should not be necessary to argue that, in building one's vision of reality, the conclusions and methods of science play a basic role, so that any religious system which turns its back on science, however emotionally satisfying it may appear to be, will ultimately prove stultifying and self-defeating. It is, however, important to understand both the functions and the limitations of science. For the purpose of mastering the complexities of the universe, science divides the world into distinct areas, such as astronomy, geology, physics, chemistry, biology, and many others. After decades and centuries of dedicated and brilliant investigation in his chosen field, the scientist is able to point to a substantial body of information. This material, however, is not of uniform value. Much of it is undoubtedly true, some is doubtful, while other elements, now accepted as valid, will turn out to be mistaken. Finally, there is a considerable area where the scientist still stands on the frontier and has not succeeded in bringing it into the domain of law and order. As scientific progress continues, the contents within each category, the known, the doubtful, the erroneous, and the unknown, continue to change, but the categories themselves remain permanent features of the landscape. This is true, because each new scientific discovery solves some problem, to be sure, but opens up new, previously unsuspected vistas of the unknown. Not only is _ignoramus_, "we do not know," a constant of the human situation, but also "_ignorabimus_," "we shall not know," the conviction that the totality of the universe will continue to elude man's intellectual grasp.

That is not all. The necessary specialization of science, without which its progress would be impossible, exacts a heavy price. One of the great problems of our time is the fact that the various disciplines find it increasingly difficult to communicate with one another. This creates scientific problems of the first magnitude, and efforts are therefore being made to bridge the gaps by means of "frontier sciences" like biochemistry and biophysics. Yet each of these new disciplines, valuable as it is, simply becomes another unit in the seemingly endless series of research specialties that amass details in the portrait of the universe, but complicate the task of seeing the total pattern. The result is that man, who is an integral and organic unit, finds himself confronted by a plethron of knowledge and dearth of wisdom. Life must be lived in the world as a whole, not in the limited area of biology or physics or psychology, into which the scientist must divide reality for purposes of analysis. At best, science can supply the bricks for the edifice of a world-view; it cannot serve as the architect.

Finally, each man living in the here and now must achieve an outlook on life that will encompass chaos as well as cosmos, tragedy as well as joy. He must evolve an approach to life which will make it possible for him not only to accept the elements of the world that "make sense" because they are rational and pleasant, but also to come to terms with those aspects which are negative and painful, impossible to grasp, and all but impossible to bear. Living beings cannot always be drinking of the cup of self-fulfillment and joy; frustration, suffering, and death are universal elements in experience. Indeed, for most men the shadows linger longer than the sunlight.

In sum, the facts supplied by science constitute a necessary, but not a sufficient, condition for constructing a world-view. In other words, after the scientist has completed his work, each man, scientist and layman alike, is faced by the task of evolving his personal philosophy of life. The problems posed by the mutual relationship of science, philosophy, and religion will be elucidated below. Let it be noted here that increasing numbers of men and women today are asking whether the insights of religious tradition, in whole or in part, cannot help to create a philosophy by which they can live, work, and hope, in the face of the chaos and peril of the age.

Question:

5. Give three reasons why "the facts supplied by science constitute a necessary but not a sufficient condition for constructing a world-view." Would Marx agree? How do you think he (or someone else holding his view) would answer Gordis?

Question:

6. Why is it important to have a "philosophy of life?"

Reading:

Perhaps the most powerful motivation for the religious quest today lies in the desire to find a firm basis for ethical standards. Immorality, in all its protean forms, is no modern invention, but, in the past, the generality of man, including the sinners themselves, knew right from wrong, and thus had a firm basis for holding themselves and their neighbors accountable in judgment. One of the hallmarks of the modern age is the increase in the number of men who lack any moral convictions, any belief in the existence of ethical standards, by which they could evaluate the acts of individuals and of nations. To expect science to discover ethical standards betrays anew a failure to comprehend the character of science. Its function is fulfilled in the elucidation of reality, which includes both the natural world and the data of human experience. To achieve its purpose, science must be morally neutral in its approach. Many scientists, as we know, have been stricken with remorse at their contribution to the development of nuclear weapons and the wholesale destruction that has been wrought. Their emotions are understandable, yet the guilt is not theirs. The physicist, in his work on the atomic bomb, is not a whit more immoral than the biologist seeking a cure for cancer. What society does with the results of scientific discovery is not the responsibility of science, which is governed by only one moral principle: loyalty to the truth. To demand that science be held responsible for the uses to which its results are put by society is as fatuous as to demand that music stipulate moral behavior, that poetry advance social reform, and that arithmetic make men honest.

The amoral character of science, however, makes it a superb servant but a dangerous master. It is like a high-powered automobile that can bring us swiftly where we wish to go, but obviously cannot determine where we wish it to go. Which goals in life are worthwhile? What is the ideal man? What traits are to be cultivated in men, and which are to be redirected or restricted? What are the qualities of the ideal society, and what means shall be adopted for approaching the goal? On all these questions, science, qua science, can have no answer.

Where shall a basis for ethical behavior be sought? Looking upon the collapse of international morality and the wholesale decline of moral standards at home, men are beginning to discover that there is nothing innate about the so-called basic human virtues. Elementary decency, love of justice, devotion to the truth, consideration for the weak, a sense of personal honor, a hatred of cruelty, a respect for human personality, opposition to vandalism and genocide -- these and similar qualities had long been taken for granted as inborn in all men. The tragic history of the twentieth century has shown that, far from being "self-evident" or "natural," these ethical norms represent the precious distillation of the religious ideals cherished by past generations. Our modern age has been the spendthrift heir of virtuous, hard-working ancestors, who created the heritage that their children have now all but squandered. All the decencies of human nature today were nurtured by the creeds of yesterday. Justice, mercy, and truth became human imperatives, because they were felt to be the attributes of God, whom men were commanded to imitate. Ethical culture is possible only in a soil rendered fertile earlier by religious faith.

Question:

7. Why does science fail as a standard for ethics? What about "natural law" (i.e., that a knowledge of basic moral distinctions is part of nature and is inborn in us)? What about national standards (specifically, say, the American secular code)? Why does religion have a better chance to succeed as a standard for ethics? Would Nietzsche agree? How would Gordis answer him?

Question:

8. As a result of the thoughts expressed in chapter 5, describe the proper domain of science and the proper domain of religion. Give an example which illustrates when science oversteps its bounds, and then do the same thing for religion -- specifically, Judaism.

Chapter 6

Response on the Functions of Religion II

Reading: Between God and Man by Abraham J. Heschel
Religion in Modern Society

The insecurity of freedom is a bitter fact of historic experience. In times of unemployment, vociferous demagogues are capable of leading the people into a state of mind in which they are ready to barter their freedom for any bargain. In times of prosperity, hidden persuaders are capable of leading the same people into selling their conscience for success. Unless a person learns how to rise daily to a higher plane of living, to care for that which surpasses his immediate needs, will he in a moment of crisis insist upon loyalty to freedom?

The threat to freedom lies in the process of reducing human relations to a matter of fact. Human life is not a drama any more, it is a routine. Uniqueness is suppressed, repetitiveness prevails. We teach our students how to recognize the labels, not how to develop a taste. Standardization corrodes the sense of ultimate significance. Man to his own self becomes increasingly vapid, cheap, insignificant. Yet without the sense of ultimate significance and ultimate preciousness of my own existence, freedom becomes a hollow phrase.

The central problem of this generation is emptiness in the heart, the decreased sensitivity to the imponderable quality of the spirit, the collapse of communication between the realm of tradition and the inner world of the individual. The central problem is that we do not know how to think, how to pray, how to cry, or how to resist the deceptions of the silent persuaders. There is no community of those who worry about integrity.

One of the chief problems of contemporary man is the problem: What to do with time? Most of our life we spend time in order to gain space, namely, things of space. Yet, when the situation arrives in which no things of space may be gained, the average man is at a loss as to what to do with time.

With the development of automation, the number of hours to be spent professionally will be considerably reduced. The four-day week may become a reality within this generation. The problem will arise: What to do with so much leisure time? The problem will be <u>too much</u> time rather than too little time. But too much time is a breeding ground for crime. Idleness is unbearable, and the most popular method to solve the problem of time is to kill time. Yet time is life, and to kill time is to murder.

The average man does not know how to stand still, how to appreciate a moment, an event, for its own sake. When witnessing an important event or confronted with a beautiful sight, all he does is take a picture. Perhaps this is what our religious traditions must teach the contemporary man: to stand still and to behold, to stand still and to hear.

Judaism claims that the way to nobility of the soul is the art of sanctifying time. Moral dedications, acts of worship, intellectual pursuits are means in the art of sanctification of time. Personal concern for justice in the marketplace, for integrity in public affairs and in public relations, is a prerequisite for our right to pray.

Acts of worship counteract the trivialization of existence. Both involve the person, and give him a sense of living in ultimate relationships. Both of them are ways of teaching man how to stand alone and not be alone, of teaching man that God is a refuge, not a security.... Religion's major effort must be to counteract the deflation of man, the trivialization of human existence.

<u>Question</u>:

1. The "freedom" that Heschel is talking about is not only physical freedom but, rather, the "freedom" and "integrity"

to be one's self, to think and act according to one's set of standards rather than according to the dictates of a real tyrant or the equally tyrannical social pressure. What threatens our freedom? How does religion help to secure our integrity and freedom? (Hint: Consider Heschel's statement: "Perhaps this is what our religious tradition must teach the contemporary man: to stand still and behold, to stand still and hear." How does this lead to "nobility of the soul" and "counteract the trivialization of existence"?) How would Nietzsche respond to this? How would Heschel reply? (Hint: Recall the distinction developed in the Macmurray reading between treating a person as a useful object, as opposed to treating him as having intrinsic worth. Then consider the last paragraph in the Heschel reading.)

Question:

2. Is "integrity" important? Why, or why not? (If it is, of course, religion will again be performing a significant role and will therefore be worth our bother.)

Reading: The Future of the American Jew by Mordecai M. Kaplan

An awareness of peoplehood, or ethnic consciousness, plays as important a role in the lives of human beings as does the awareness of one's ego, of one's family, and of one's community. The question is, does the sense of peoplehood make for the best interests of the individual in whom it inheres, and of the group which is its object? The answer calls for an examination of the conditions under which the sense of peoplehood functions.

The sense of peoplehood is the awareness which an individual has of being a member of a group that is known, both by its own members and by outsiders, as a people. Neither those within nor those without, as a rule, give much thought to the question of what makes the group into a people. Those within are satisfied with the "we-feeling", which they have with regard to all who belong to their people. That "we-feeling" is more inclusive than the "we-feeling" of family, clan, or tribe, and yet definitely excludes others who have a like feeling about their own people. Everyone yearns to be a member of some people, and deems it a catastrophe to have no people to which to belong.

Why is it a catastrophe? Because, as human beings, there are two states or conditions we cannot do without. We cannot do without being needed, and without something of which we are proud. This is why we need this "we-feeling" to embrace a group inclusive enough in time and space, inclusive of a sufficient number of generations to render certain that our being desired or needed is not ephemeral, and that all of us, no matter how commonplace, can recall some person, event, or achievement we can be proud of. To be sure, one's own family might be of a kind which could provide these two conditions. But it would have to be a very exceptional family, one with an ancient pedigree, and with many a hero and great achievement to its credit. Very few people are that lucky. The average person requires a whole chain of families to be linked together into a social unit, for him to satisfy these essential needs. This is the psychological aspect of peoplehood as a humanizing force in the life of the average individual. If he lacks it, he feels rootless and nameless. The American-Jew is in the awkward position of having, as it were, but half his personality fulfilled -- the American half. As for the Jewish half, that is in a chaotic state because it misses both being needed and having something of which to be proud. As an American, he rejoices in his "we-feeling"; as a Jew, he often feels trapped.

As a matter of principle, we may be convinced of the legitimacy of Jewish peoplehood in a democratic society. Nevertheless, we may find it difficult to fit such a status into the actual frame of American life and democracy. Jewish peoplehood finds expression in a tradition, in a way of life, in a milieu and in specific sights and sounds. If Judaism is to be more than a memory of ancient glory, or more than a way of speaking, it must consist of things that are visible, audible, and tangible. The sum of all that is recognizable as belonging to Judaism makes of it a civilization.

A civilization, as modern nationalism might define it, is looking and acting like others. But as a humanizing process, a civilization is the cumulative heritage of knowledge, experience and attitudes acquired by the successive generations of a people in its striving to achieve salvation. That heritage links the generations together into a continuing unity. It consists of a variety of elements; memories of the people's past and hopes concerning its future; a particular language and literature; specific laws, morals, customs, and folkways; evaluations of life and an assortment of art forms. Various items are chosen from each of these elements and are made the object of special regard and reverence; they are treated as sacred. Taken in their entirety, those items constitute the religion, or the religious aspect, of the civilization.

To grasp, however, the essence of a civilization, we must do more than recognize the organic unity of all of its elements. We must learn to appreciate its interrelated functions which have one basic purpose, namely, that all who live by that civilization should feel the need of one another. Only in that way can they get the most out of life and give their maximum to it. The precept, "Thou shalt love thy neighbor as thyself" is not some fantastic aspiration, too good to be practicable. It is nothing more than an elementary requirement that those who belong to the same civilization shall want and welcome one another, and not regard one another as rivals and as a thorn in each other's side. By the same token, the precept, "Thou shalt love the Lord thy God" means experiencing a need for and welcoming God. It means so to accept life that for its sake we are prepared to be and do our utmost and even willing to bear the worst that may befall us. Whenever we say, "Blessed art Thou, O Lord our God," we, in effect, welcome God on those terms. This is what makes Judaism a religious civilization.

Accordingly, our answer to the challenge of modern nationalism should be: We Jews depend upon Judaism and the fellowship of the Jewish people for that feeling of being needed and welcomed, without which we can neither live a normal, healthy life, nor possess the essential ingredients that go into the making of **worthy** character and personality. We need Judaism to help us maintain our human dignity and achieve our salvation. Almost ten percent of the American people declare themselves anti-Semites, and harbor the criminally insane sentiment of wishing to destroy us. Twice that number are ready to join them upon the flimsiest provocation. In the country as a whole, Jews at best are tolerated, but neither desired nor welcomed. Our best friends will forgive us our being Jews, but can seldom forget it. This is presently true of all democracies.

The fact that our non-Jewish neighbors are not glad to receive us should not make us resentful or bitter. They belong, after all, to a part of the human race that has been indoctrinated for over two thousand years with a vicious hatred toward our people. They have had it drilled into them that we are the incarnation of evil. We should not expect them to overcome, in the course of one or two generations, the effects of such persistent propaganda of hate. In the meantime, however, we and our children and our children's children are entitled to our share of happiness, for which being needed and welcomed is an indispensable prerequisite. Eretz Yisrael Jews need and welcome their fellow-Jews. That is the way we Jews in the United States should feel toward one another. We need that feeling of comradeship, if we are to be integrated, self-respecting and fearless human beings. Surely, the United States can benefit but little from citizens who live broken, self-hating, and fear-ridden lives.

Question:

3. Have you ever felt the "we-feeling" toward other Jews that Kaplan describes? What made you feel that way? Were you proud of that feeling, disturbed by it, or indifferent to it? Why?

Question:

4. Why must a person belong to a civilization, for Kaplan? Now, review question #11 in chapter 3.

Question:

5. Why is it that the American Jew rejoices in his "we-feeling" as an American, but "as a Jew, he often feels trapped"? What remedy does Kaplan suggest?

Reading:

The function of a religion is to enable those who live by it to achieve salvation, or life abundant. To be sure, salvation would not consist, as it did in the past for all Jews, in a feeling of confidence in the coming of a personal Messiah, who would gather all Jews back to Eretz Yisrael, and in eternal bliss to be enjoyed by each Jew in the hereafter. It would consist, rather, in the cultivation of basic values, like faith, patience, inner freedom, humility, thankfulness, justice, and love, which enable a man to be and do his best, and to bear uncomplainingly the worst that may befall him. A religio-cultural community that can help its members achieve that kind of salvation is invaluable to a democratic state, whose strength consists in a citizenry of self-reliant and self-respecting men and women. Whatever values American life itself begets are at present lacking in that religious character and function. This is why it looks to the religious cultures, which its various historic groups have brought with them, to give the individual citizen the moral stamina and sense of responsibility which are indispensable to national survival and health. Judaism looks to the religio-cultural heritage which Jews have brought with them to accomplish this for its Jewish citizens. That expectation is a challenge to us Jews, not only to retain our group life in this country, but also to achieve a religious orientation that might prove of great value to the religiously starved mankind of our day.

Question:

6. What is "salvation" for Kaplan? Give concrete examples of Jewish laws, customs, or stories, which try to bring us to "salvation."

Question:

7. (Important question) Earlier, Kaplan said that "we need Judaism to help us maintain our human dignity and achieve our salvation." What does he mean? Why does he say this? Do you agree?

Question:

8. Which of the following is true, and why?

   a. Being a good American means forgetting and hiding my Jewishness as much as possible.

   b. To be a good American I must be as committed to my Judaism -- in word, deed, and knowledge -- as possible.

   c. Being a good Jew is totally irrelevant to my being a good American.

Question:

9. Can you think of what it would be like not to have a sense of peoplehood? That may be hard for Jews to imagine, but do try. Then consider the following brief reading as an example of people who do not have what you take for granted.

   Reading: Black Power by Carmichael and Hamilton

   Black people must redefine themselves, and only they can do that. Throughout this country, vast segments of black communities are beginning to recognize the need to assert their own definitions, to reclaim their history, their culture; to create their own sense of community and togetherness. There is a growing resentment of the word "Negro," for example, because this term is the invention of our oppressor; it is his image of us that he describes. Many blacks are now calling themselves Afro-Americans, African-Americans, or black people, because that is our image of ourselves. When we begin to define our own image, the stereotypes -- that is, lies -- that our oppressor has developed will begin in the white community, and end there. The black community will have a positive image of itself that it has created. This means we will no longer call ourselves lazy, apathetic, dumb, good-timers, shiftless, etc. Those are words used by white America to define us. If we accept these adjectives, as some of us have in the past, then we see ourselves only in a negative way, precisely the way white America wants us to see ourselves. Our incentive is broken and our will to fight is surrendered. From now on we shall view ourselves as African-Americans and as black people who are, in fact, energetic, determined, intelligent, beautiful, and peace-loving.

There is a terminology and ethos peculiar to the black community of which black people are beginning to be no longer ashamed. Black communities are the only large segments of this society where people refer to each other as brother -- soul brother, soul sister. Some people may look upon this as <u>ersatz</u>, as make-believe, but it is not that. It is real. It is a growing sense of community. It is a growing realization that black Americans have a common bond, not only among themselves, but with their African brothers. In <u>Black Man's Burden</u>, John O. Killens described his trip to ten African countries as follows:

> Everywhere I went, people called me <u>brother</u>....
> "Welcome, American brother." It was a good feeling
> for me, to be in Africa. To walk in a land for
> the first time in your entire life, knowing within
> yourself that your color would not be held against
> you. No black man knows this in America (p. 160).

More and more black Americans are developing this feeling. They are becoming aware that they have a <u>history</u> which pre-dates their forced introduction to this country. African-American history means a long history, beginning on the continent of Africa, a history not taught in the standard textbooks of this country. It is absolutely essential that black people know this history, that they know their roots, that they develop an awareness of their cultural heritage. Too long have they been kept in submission by being told that they had no culture, no manifest heritage, before they landed on the slave auction blocks in this country. If black people are to know themselves as a vibrant, valiant people, they must know their roots. And they will soon learn that the Hollywood image of man-eating cannibals waiting for, and waiting on, the Great White Hunter is a lie.

With redefinition will come a clearer notion of the role black Americans can play in this world. This role will emerge clearly out of the <u>unique common experiences</u> of Afro-Asians.

Killens concludes:

> I believe furthermore that the American Negro can be the bridge between the West and Africa-Asia. We black Americans can serve as a bridge to mutual understanding. The one thing we black Americans have in common with the other colored peoples of the world is that we have all felt the cruel and ruthless heel of white supremacy. We have all been "niggerized" on one level or another. And all of us are determined to "deniggerize" the earth. To rid the world of "niggers" is the Black Man's Burden; human reconstruction is the grand objective (p. 176).

Only when black people fully develop this <u>sense of community</u> of themselves can they begin to deal effectively with the problems of racism in <u>this</u> country. This is what we mean by a new consciousness; this is the first vital step.

<u>Question</u>:

10. What is the black man looking for, according to this article? Can you give some concrete examples of that search? When and/or where does a Jew feel that "Everywhere I went people called me brother"? (Note that while Israel is a striking parallel to this, Jews feel somewhat "at home" in any group of Jews anywhere. Give some examples. Have any of you ever visited a synagogue away from home?)

Question:

11. What good effects can a sense of community have, as outlined in this reading? Compare Kaplan's account. When does a sense of community become a bad thing? (Hint: What happens when a people ceases to recognize the worth of other human beings? Give some examples of such groups, large and small, present and past.) What, then, should be our attitude toward any community of which we are a part -- that is, what shall we look for and appreciate, and what shall we seek to avoid? Now, apply your conclusion in analyzing your connections to the Jewish community.

Question:

12. In review, now, briefly list the arguments presented against, and for, religion in this unit. Can you add others (on either side)? If so, be sure to bring them up during the course of your group's discussion.

UNIT II

THE SPECIAL FUNCTIONS OF JUDAISM

If religion does have a place in society, it must deal with some important aspects of reality or achieve certain goals which people consider valuable. In Unit I we discussed several of those aspects and goals and the reasons why religion can account for them where other agents fail. But any religion does those things, at least to some extent. Why, then, bother to be Jews? After all, it is much easier to be a Christian, especially in a predominantly Christian society; so if we do not accomplish any more by being Jewish, why not choose the easier method of Christianity to reach our goals? Of course, the answer is that Judaism presents a view of man and the world, which differs from that of all other religions in essential ways, and it promotes certain goals which no other religion does in the same manner, and therefore, if we agree with its viewpoint, and value those goals, we must be Jewish. Although we hardly have space or time to make an exhaustive study of distinctively Jewish views and values, we will now discuss at least some of them that appear in just one of the institutions of Judaism, the Shabbat. (Note that the first question is to be answered before you read the source material.)

PREVIEW QUESTIONS to Unit II, Chapters 7-9

1. Why is it important to be a good Jew if you are already a good American -- or is it?

2. Can you think of any Jewish values which are qualitatively different from American values?

3. Can you think of any values which the Jewish and American societies share, but which one emphasizes more than the other?

Chapter 7

Jewish Values Distinctive in Degree

Question:

1. <u>Before reading Heschel's article</u>, answer this question: if you could have whatever you wanted, what would you ask for? <u>Jot down</u> your list so that you will not forget it. Include about five items in your list. Now read Heschel before answering the following questions.

Reading: <u>The Sabbath</u> by Abraham Joshua Heschel

Technical civilization is man's conquest of space. It is a triumph frequently achieved by sacrificing an essential ingredient of existence, namely, time. In technical civilization, we expend time to gain space. To enhance our power in the world of space is our main objective. Yet to have more does not mean to be more. The power we attain in the world of space terminates abruptly at the borderline of time. But time is the heart of existence....

We are all infatuated with the splendor of space, with the grandeur of things of space. "Thing" is a category that lies heavy on our minds, tyrannizing all our thoughts. Our imagination tends to mold all concepts in its image. In our daily lives we attend primarily to that which the senses are spelling out for us: to what the eyes perceive, to what the fingers touch. Reality to us is thinghood, consisting of substances that occupy space; even God is conceived by most of us as a thing....

Question:

2. How many of the items on your list were things rather than times? How much, then, are you dominated by concerns for "thinghood"? What about the civilization in which we live? Give concrete examples to support or refute Heschel's claim that "reality to us is thinghood."

Reading:

To gain control of the world of space is certainly one of our tasks. The danger begins when, in gaining power in the realm of space, we forfeit all aspirations in the realm of time. There is a realm of time where the goal is not to have but to be, not to own but to give, not to control but to share, not to subdue but to be in accord. Life goes wrong when the control of space, the acquisition of things of space, becomes our sole concern....

The result of our thingness is our blindness to all reality that fails to identify itself as a thing, as a matter of fact. This is obvious in our understanding of time, which, being thingless and insubstantial, appears to us as if it had no reality....

Is the joy of possession an antidote to the terror of time which grows to be a dread of inevitable death? Things, when magnified, are forgeries of happiness; they are a threat to our very lives; we are more harassed than supported by the Frankensteins of spatial things.

It is impossible for man to shirk the problem of time. The more we think the more we realize: we cannot conquer time through space. We can only master time in time.

<u>The higher goal of spiritual living is not to amass a wealth of information, but to face sacred moments.</u> In a religious experience, for example, it is not a thing that imposes itself on man, but a spiritual presence. What is retained in the soul is the moment of insight rather than the place where the act came to pass. A moment of insight is a fortune, transporting us beyond the confines of measured time. Spiritual life begins to decay when we fail to sense the grandeur of what is eternal in time.

Our intention here is not to deprecate the world of space. To disparage space and the blessing of things of space is to disparage the works of creation, the works which God beheld and saw "it was good." The world cannot be seen exclusively sub specie temporis. Time and space are interrelated. To overlook either of them is to be partially blind. What we plead against is man's unconditional surrender to space, his enslavement to things. We must not forget that it is not a thing that lends significance to a moment; it is the moment that lends significance to things....

Question:

3. Is our concern for the control of space in itself bad? When does it become bad? Why is it then bad?

Reading:

Judaism is a religion of time aiming at the sanctification of time. Unlike the space-minded man to whom time is unvaried, iterative, homogeneous, to whom all hours are alike, qualitiless empty shells, the Bible sees the diversified character of time. There are no two hours alike. Every hour is unique and the only one given at the moment, exclusive and endlessly precious.

Judaism teaches us to be attached to holiness in time, to be attached to sacred events, to learn how to consecrate sanctuaries that emerge from the magnificent screen of a year. The Sabbaths are our great cathedrals; and our Holy of Holies is a shrine that even apostasy cannot easily obliterate: the Day of Atonement. According to the ancient rabbis, it is not the observance of the Day of Atonement, but the Day itself, the "essence of the Day," which, with man's repentance, atones for the sins of man.

Jewish ritual may be characterized as the art of significant forms in time, as architecture of time. Most of its observances -- the Sabbath, the New Moon, the festivals, the Sabbatical and the Jubilee Year -- depend on a certain hour of the day or season of the year. It is, for example, the evening, morning, or afternoon that brings with it the call to prayer. The main themes of faith lie in the realm of time. We remember the day of the exodus from Egypt, the day when Israel stood at Sinai; and our Messianic hope is the expectation of a day, of the end of days....

It is, indeed, a unique occasion at which the distinguished word _qadosh_ is used for the first time in the Book of Genesis at the end of the story of creation. How extremely significant is the fact that it is applied to time: "And God blessed the seventh _day_ and made it _holy_." There is no reference in the record of creation to any object in _space_ that would be endowed with the quality of holiness.

This is a radical departure from accustomed religious thinking. The mythical mind would expect that, after heaven and earth have been established, God would create a holy place -- a holy mountain or a holy spring -- whereupon a sanctuary is to be established. Yet, it seems as if to the Bible it is _holiness in time_, the Sabbath, which comes first.

When history began, there was only one holiness in the world, holiness in time. When, at Sinai, the word of God was about to be voiced, a call for holiness in _man_ was proclaimed: "Thou shalt be unto me a holy people." It was only after the people had succumbed to the temptation of worshipping a thing, a golden calf, that the erection of a tabernacle, of holiness in _space_, was commanded. The sanctity of time came first, the sanctity of man came second, and the sanctity of space last. Time was hallowed by God; space, the Tabernacle, was consecrated by Moses....

The meaning of the Sabbath is to celebrate time rather than space. Six days a week we live under the tyranny of things of space; on the Sabbath we try to become attuned to _holiness in time_. It is a day on which we are called upon to share in what is eternal in time, to turn from the results of creation to the mystery of creation; from the world of creation to the creation of the world.

Question:

4. What, then, does the _Jewish_ religious experience of the Sabbath come to teach us?

Does Christianity or the American secular code teach the same lesson as effectively?

(Note that both Christianity and the United States <u>do</u> have hallowed times. Name some for each. But also note that each has many holy places as well. Again, name some for each. On the other hand, in Judaism, while many places may be memorable, only one is called "holy." What is it? On the other hand, how many times in Judaism are holy? Where is the overwhelming emphasis?)

<u>Question</u>:

5. In answering question 4, you discovered a difference in <u>degree</u>: Christianity, the United States, and Judaism all have the same <u>kind</u> of time sanctification, but they differ radically in the degree to which they emphasize this difference. Now, then, lest you think that a difference in degree is a very meager contribution for Judaism to make, consider the importance of degree in the following situations:

   a. The amount of studying that you do if your goal is to learn the material and get a high grade.

   b. The amount of seasoning that you add to food if your goal is to make it taste good.

   c. The amount of strength which you use when you pass a football if your goal is to complete the pass.

As you see, a difference in degree often determines whether or not you achieve your goal at all. Therefore, when Judaism differs from Christian and secular society in the degree to which it emphasizes **time** sanctification, this is a major difference indeed. (In fact, most civilizations, in one way or another, talk about roughly the same kind of values, and what differentiates religions and civilizations is quite often, not a difference in kind, but rather a difference in the relative degrees of emphasis that they put on the various values -- in other words, how they balance the various values.)

Reading:

...According to the Stagirite (Aristotle), "we need relaxation because we cannot work continuously. Relaxation, then, is not an end"; it is "for the sake of activity," for the sake of gaining strength for new efforts. To the biblical mind, however, labor is the means toward an end, and the Sabbath, as a day of rest, as a day of abstaining from toil, is not for the purpose of recovering one's lost strength for the forthcoming labor. The Sabbath is a day for the sake of life. Man is not a beast of burden, and the Sabbath is not for the purpose of enhancing the efficiency of his work. "Last in creation, first in intention," the Sabbath is "the end of the creation of heaven and earth."

The Sabbath is not for the sake of the weekdays; the weekdays are for the sake of the Sabbath. It is not an interlude but the climax of living....

Call the Sabbath a delight: a delight to the soul and a delight to the body. Since there are so many acts which one must abstain from doing on the seventh day, "you might think I have given you the Sabbath for your displeasure; I have surely given you the Sabbath for your pleasure." To sanctify the seventh day does not mean: Thou shalt mortify thyself, but, on the contrary: Thou shalt sanctify it, with all thy heart, with all thy soul, and with all thy senses. "Sanctify the Sabbath by choice meals, by beautiful garments; delight your soul with pleasure and I will reward you for this very pleasure."

Question:

6. Explain what Heschel means when he says that "The Sabbath is not for the sake of the weekdays; the weekdays are for the sake of the Sabbath." What concrete acts does a Jew do in preparation for the Sabbath, and during that day, which illustrate this? Consider the remark of Eleazar b. Hananiah b. Hezekiah b. Garon in the Mekhilta (Tractate Bahodesh): "Remember the day of the Sabbath to keep it holy: that is, keep it in mind from the first day of the week on, so that if something good happens to come your way, fix it up for the Sabbath."

Chapter 8

Jewish Values Distinctive in Kind

Reading: *The Meaning of God in Modern Jewish Religion*
by Mordecai M. Kaplan

An artist cannot be continually wielding his brush. He must stop at times in his painting to freshen his vision of the object, the meaning of which he wishes to express on his canvas. Living is also an art. We dare not become absorbed in its technical processes and lose our consciousness of its general plan....The Sabbath represents those moments when we pause in our brush-work to renew our vision of this object. Having done so, we take ourselves to our painting with clarified vision and renewed energy. This applies alike to the individual and to the community. For the individual, the Sabbath becomes thereby an instrument of social salvation....

Question:

1. Define what Kaplan means by "salvation." (Hint: Look at the last sentence in the source reading from Kaplan in this chapter.) How does this differ from the Christian concept of salvation as you understand it?

Question:

2. "Having done so, we take ourselves to our painting with clarified vision and renewed energy." Is Kaplan thereby disagreeing with Heschel when the latter says, "The Sabbath is not for the sake of the weekdays; the weekdays are for the sake of the Sabbath"? Or is he just describing a *result* of Sabbath observance?

Reading:

The Sabbath implies an affirmation that the world is so constituted as to afford man the opportunity for salvation. But what is there in the world that gives us this assurance? In what aspects of life do we recognize the Power that makes for salvation? The answer to these questions is to be found in the three leading motifs enunciated in the Torah and developed by the Sages in their interpretation of the Sabbath. The first of these is the idea of creativity, for the Sabbath is associated in Jewish tradition with the completion of the task of creation, when God surveyed all that He had made and found it "very good" (Gen. 1:31). The second is the idea of holiness. The reference to the Sabbath in the Decalogue bids us "Remember the Sabbath day to keep it holy" (Exodus 20:8); and the prophetic passage from the book of Isaiah, quoted at the beginning of this chapter, calls the Sabbath "the holy of the Lord" (Isaiah 58:13). The third is the idea of covenantship which regards the Sabbath as a sign of God's covenant with Israel (Exodus 31:16,17). These three leading ideas, associated with observance of the Sabbath, play an important part in Jewish religion generally. They therefore make the Sabbath the symbol of the most significant elements in the Jewish conception of God.... <u>The moral implication of the traditional teaching that God created the world is that creativity, or the continuous emergence of aspects of life not prepared for or determined by the past, constitutes the most divine phase of reality</u>....The Sabbath is regarded in Jewish tradition as celebrating the creation of the world. The modern equivalent of that interpretation of the day would be the use of it as a means of accentuating the fact that we must reckon with creation and self-renewal as a continuous process. The liturgy speaks of God as "renewing daily the works of creation." By becoming aware of that fact, we might gear our own lives to this creative urge in the universe and discover within ourselves unsuspected powers of the spirit.

The belief in God as a creator, or its modern equivalent, the conception of the creative urge as the element of godhood in the world, is needed to fortify the yearning for spiritual self-regeneration. That yearning dies down unless it is backed by the conviction that there is something which answers to it in the very character of life as a whole. <u>There can hardly be any more important function for religion than to keep alive this</u>

<u>yearning for self-renewal and to press it into the service of human progress</u>. In doing that, religion will combat the recurrent pessimism to which we yield whenever we misjudge the character of the evil in the world. It will teach us to live without illusion and without despair about the future, with clear recognition of the reality of evil and creative faith in the possibility of the good.

We should not minimize in the least the pain, the agony, the cruelty, and the destruction that deface the world. But we should not go to the extent to which the ancients and moderns have gone when they interpreted all that evil as inherent and eternal in the very constitution of the world. Of what avail to strive to improve the conditions of life when we know beforehand that life must ever remain the same? Koheleth's conclusion, "all is vanity," derives from the premise, "there is nothing new under the sun." Religion should indicate to us some way whereby we can transform the evils of the world, if they are within our control, and transcend them, if they are beyond our control. If we give heed to the creative impulse within us, which beats in rhythm with the creative impulse of the cosmos, we can always find some way of making our adjustment to evil productive of good. It is not given to us, with our necessarily limited vision and understanding, to know how the effects of the creative adjustment can withstand the ravages of time. It is enough that in the art of achieving such adjustment we experience self-fulfillment, as though that act were eternal and an end itself....

<u>Question</u>:

3. "The Sabbath is associated in Jewish tradition with the completion of creation." So what? That is, how does the fact that God finished creation on the seventh day give me any new insight about how I should live my life? What laws connected with the Jewish Shabbat convey this lesson of the completion of creation? Does the Christian Sabbath involve these <u>laws</u>? Does it, then, succeed in conveying this lesson? (Be careful!)

Reading:

As the Sabbath serves to save the Jewish people from pessimism by emphasizing the idea that God manifests Himself in creativity, so it serves to save them from cynicism by emphasizing the idea that God manifests Himself in holiness. It represents not only the affirmation that life is not evil, but also the affirmation that it is not vain or futile, but supremely worthwhile.

The term "holy" is not frequently on people's lips in modern times. But we must not leap to the hasty conclusion that holiness represents a concept that has no valid meaning for our day. Words are frequently subject to peculiar vicissitudes of fortune. In an earlier generation, there was no higher praise for a man than to be called holy; today the expression is more likely to be used with a tinge of contemptuous sarcasm. That is doubtless due to the fact that the term "holy" or "sacred" has so frequently been applied by interested individuals or organizations to outworn institutions which they wished to protect from destructive criticism. But when a Communist, even though he may belong to the "League of the Godless," fights for the possession of the red flag, that to him is the symbol of revolution, he is, in effect, declaring it to be holy. When he observes Lenin's birthday, or pays a pilgrimage to his tomb, he is, to all intents and purposes, making a saint of him.

If we consider all the various objects, institutions, and persons that have been declared holy, not only by the Jewish religion but by any of the other religions, both those of antiquity and of modern times, we find that they are the objects, institutions, and persons that particular groups felt to be of supreme importance to them. Many of these objects may, from our particular point of view, be unimportant, and the ascription of holiness to them may appear absurd. We cannot today thrill to the worship of "sacred cows." Doubtless that is one reason why the term "sacred" has fallen into disrepute. It has been applied to too many objects that are not sacred to us at all. But there are objects to which we react with that same degree of reverence. The distinction between the holy and the profane, the sacred and secular, is essentially the same as the distinction between the valuable and the worthless, the important and the trivial, the significant and the meaningless. Holiness is that quality by virtue of which an object is felt to be of transcendent importance to us. Every civilization recognizes the existence of such sancta, or transcendently important objects. The Constitution of the United States, the Declaration of Independence, the Liberty Bell, the national cemetery at Arlington, the Stars and Stripes, are but a few of the sancta that have been hallowed by America in the course of its history. The Sefer Torah, the Sabbaths and Festivals, Zion, the Hebrew language, are a few of the Jewish sancta that the history of Israel has hallowed.

But the value or sacredness of such holy objects is not inherent in them. The flag is but a piece of colored cloth, the Sefer Torah is a piece of parchment with ink marks on it. It is life, or the relationship to those purposes, that spell life's meaning for us, that gives value to these objects. Their holiness is derivative, and depends on our faith in the supreme value of life itself, in the holiness of life. If life itself is worthless, no object on earth can have any value. When religion ascribes holiness to God, it is saying, in effect, that life as a whole, the life of the universe of which our lives are but a part, is the supreme value from which all others are derived. The criterion for the sacredness of any object is its contribution to the enhancement of life, to our sense of its worth and importance....

Question:

4. What does "holy" mean, according to Kaplan? Give a synonym. How does the Shabbat represent "not only the affirmation that life is not evil, but also the affirmation that it is not vain or futile, but supremely worthwhile?" (Hint: "Remember the Sabbath day to keep it holy"; thus the Sabbath is holy just as God is holy, and, as Kaplan says, "When religion ascribes holiness to God...")

Question:

5. Give examples of "holy" objects in other societies. Why does almost every society have sancta? That is, what function do they serve in a society? Why is that an important function?

Question:

6. Why is it necessary to observe the "holy" occasions and honor the "holy" objects of both the American and Jewish societies? That is, why is it that neither set of sancta by itself can fulfill the functions of both?

Reading:

In all that has been said, it is assumed that the Jew is committed to the quest of salvation, to the service of the Power in the world that, manifesting itself in life's creativity and holiness, makes it possible for him to fulfill the possibilities for good that are latent in his personality. But there are many today who question the validity of this or any other Jewish commitment. The question frequently takes a form somewhat like this: How can the fact that I was born a Jew impose any obligations upon me? It was a mere accident, in regard to which I was not consulted. I accept responsibility for my own individual acts and will stand committed by any obligations I have voluntarily assumed. But I deny the right of my ancestors to assume obligations for me. My religion is a personal matter between me and the individuals with whom I have personal relations.

The Jewish answer to this attitude is the idea of covenantship. This is the third of those ideas which are associated by tradition with the Sabbath, and which enable it to function as a means of salvation. The Sabbath has always been regarded as a sign of God's covenant with Israel. On other days of the week, the observant Jew, when he says his prayers, wears the tefillin as a "sign of the covenant," but not on the Sabbath. For the Sabbath itself is considered a sufficient token of the covenant to require no further visual reminder. In the liturgy of the day, the idea of the Sabbath as a symbol of the covenant finds frequent expression....

It is not so much our duty to our fathers that makes it important for us to maintain the continuity of our tradition as it is our duty to our children. All human progress has been achieved by the fact that each generation begins its career where its predecessors left off, availing itself of the accumulated knowledge and wisdom of past ages. But we cannot expect the Chinese people, for example, to preserve the heritage of Hebrew literature and make it available for the world, any more than we are ready or able to assume responsibility for preserving the Chinese classics and elaborating their implications for our day.

This is the answer to those who object to any specific commitments by reason of their being Jews. Such commitments are inherent in the very structure of society and civilization. Mankind is not all of one piece, and, in the task of preserving and developing the spiritual heritage of the human race, the various historic groups have to assume responsibility, each one for the maintenance of its own identity as a contributor to the sum of human knowledge and experience...

If we regard God as the Life of the universe, the Power that evokes personality in men and nations, <u>then the sense of the nation's responsibility for contributing creatively to human welfare and progress in the light of its own best experiences becomes the modern equivalent of the covenant idea</u>. In it is implied that reciprocity between God and the nation that the term covenant denotes. For the life of the nation is not lived in a void but in the world. It is dependent on, and conditioned by, its geographic and social environment. It thus owes all the values which it develops to the fact that God, the Life of the universe, is such as to call forth these values. They can be realized only to the extent that the nation conforms to the highest ethical standards that express God's will, of which it is aware. At the same time the nation is an active agent in developing these ethical standards, and not merely a passive instrument. In this sense, God still governs the nation, and the nation still establishes His kingdom, in collaboration, of course, with all other nations.

If the Sabbath, which is still observed, at least to some extent, by great masses of Jews, were utilized to the full to emphasize the implications of the traditional ideals associated with it, it would contribute immeasurably to the achievement of this goal. If its ritual and all Jewish activities connected with it stressed the view that emphasizes the creative aspect of life, as against the view that life is meaningless and futile, if it thrilled us with an appreciation of the role Israel has played, and will continue to play, in the history of mankind, the Sabbath would unquestionably be experienced as an occasion for delight in the Lord. For through our observances of the Sabbath we shall come to know God as the source of salvation, of that state of being in which all our powers are harmoniously employed in the achievement of worthwhile aims.

<u>Question</u>:

7. "How can the fact that I was born a Jew impose any obligations upon me?" Judaism tries to answer this question through the notion of the covenant:

   a. What is the covenant idea? Formulate it in ancient and modern terms.

   b. Where does God fit into the idea? Does the notion of the covenant require you to believe in any specific type of God? Explain.

   c. Give examples of how the United States uses the covenant idea. Why do modern Jews have more trouble accepting the authority of the Jewish covenant than they do accepting that of the American covenant? Does that make the Jewish covenant any less binding?

   d. How does the covenant idea attempt to answer the question at the beginning of 7? Does it succeed as an answer? Why, or why not?

<u>Question</u>:

8. Note that the three themes of creation, holiness (at least as Judaism defines it), and the covenant, all serve to point up one of the major differences between Judaism and Christianity: for Judaism this life is extremely important, and therefore, Judaism emphasizes involvement in this world. For Christianity, on the other hand, this world is only an unpleasant interim

before the "real" world after death; consequently, these aspects of the Jewish Shabbat are played down in Christianity. Give examples of Christian doctrines and practices which demonstrate this. Contrast these with comparable doctrines and practices in Judaism. Judaism's attitude toward this life, then, definitely represents a difference in _kind_, and your choice of religion will, at least in part, depend on where you stand in regard to these differences, in outlook, value, and practice.

Chapter 9

Jewish Values Distinctive in Degree and Kind

Reading: The Forgotten Language by Eric Fromm

To the modern mind, there is not much of a problem in the Sabbath institution. The idea that man should rest from his work one day every week sounds to us like a self-evident, social-hygenic measure intended to give man the physical and spiritual rest and relaxation he needs in order not to be swallowed up by his daily work. No doubt, this explanation is true as far as it goes -- but it does not answer some questions which arise if we pay closer attention to the Sabbath law of the Bible, and particularly to the Sabbath ritual as it developed in the post-biblical tradition.

Why is this social-hygienic law so important that it is placed among the Ten Commandments, which otherwise stipulate only the fundamental religious and ethical principles? Why is it explained with God's rest on the seventh day, and what does this "rest" mean? Is God pictured in such anthropomorphic terms as to need a rest after six days of hard work? Why, in the second version of the Ten Commandments, is the Sabbath explained in terms of freedom rather than of God's rest? What is the common denominator of the two explanations? Moreover -- and this is perhaps the most important question -- how can we understand the intricacies of the Sabbath ritual in the light of the modern social-hygienic interpretation of rest? In the Old Testament, a man who "gathers sticks" (Num. 4:32 ff.) is considered a violator of the Sabbath law, and punished by death. In the later development, not only work, in our modern sense, is forbidden, but activities like the following: making any kind of fire, even if it is for convenience's sake and does not require any physical effort; pulling a single grass blade or flower from the soil; carrying anything, even something as light as a handkerchief, on one's person. All this is not work in the sense of physical effort; its avoidance is often more of an inconvenience and discomfort than the doing of it would be. Are we dealing here with extravagant and compulsive exaggerations of an originally "sensible" ritual, or is our understanding of the ritual perhaps faulty and in need of revision?

A more detailed analysis of the symbolic meaning of the Sabbath ritual will show that we are dealing, not with obsessional over-strictness, but with a concept of work and rest which is different from our modern concept.

Question:

1. Fromm begins with a "self-evident" explanation of the Sabbath. What is it? What problems does he encounter with this explanation? Why are these problems? That is, why can he not retain this original explanation of the Sabbath despite these problems? What, then, is the relation between the philosophy of Judaism and Judaism's primary sources (the Bible, Talmud, etc.), or, for that matter, between any philosophy and its subject matter? What practical implication does this have in terms of your studying of primary Jewish texts?

Question:

2. After Fromm runs into problems with his first explanation, what does he do? What other plan of action is logically open to him? Why does he choose the path that he does? Give comparable examples of this method of investigation in science, literature, or history.

Reading:

To begin with, the essential point -- the concept of work underlying the Biblical and the later Talmudic concept -- is not simply that of physical effort, but can be defined thus: "Work" is any interference by man, be it constructive or destructive, with the physical world. "Rest" is a state of peace between man and nature. Man must leave nature untouched, not change it in any way, neither by building nor by destroying anything; even the smallest change made by man in the natural process is a violation of "rest." The Sabbath is a violation of "rest." The Sabbath is the day of peace between man and nature; work is any kind of disturbance of the man-nature equilibrium. On the basis of this general definition, we can understand the Sabbath ritual. Indeed, any heavy work like plowing or building is work, in this as well as in our modern sense. But lighting a match and pulling up a grass blade, while not requiring effort, are symbols of human interference with the natural process, are a breach of peace between man and nature. On the basis of this principle, we understand also the Talmudic prohibition of carrying something of even little weight on one's person. In fact, the carrying of something as such is not forbidden. I can carry a heavy load within my house or my estate without violating the Sabbath ritual. But I must not carry even a handkerchief from one domain to the other, for instance, from the private domain of the house to the public domain of the street. This law is an extension of the idea of peace from the natural to the social realm. Just as man must not interfere with or change the natural equilibrium, he must refrain from changing the social order. That means not only not to do business, but also the avoidance of that most primitive form of transference of property, namely, its local transference from one domain to the other.

The Sabbath symbolizes a state of complete harmony between man and nature and between man and man. By not working -- that is to say, by not participating in the process of social and natural change -- man is free from the chains of nature and from the chains of time, although only for one day a week.

Question:

3. What _is_ the concept of work behind the Sabbath, as Fromm sees it? Does this concept explain the Sabbath laws that the first, "self-evident" concept did? Does it explain any more of the Sabbath laws which the first concept could not explain? (Give examples.) Do you see, then, why the second is considered a more adequate explanation?

Reading:

The full significance of this idea can be understood only in the context of the Biblical philosophy of the relationship between man and nature. Before Adam's "fall" -- that is, before man had reason -- he lived in complete harmony with nature; the first act of disobedience, which is also the beginning of human freedom, "opens his eyes," he knows how to judge good and evil, he has become aware of himself and of his fellows, the same and yet unique, tied together by bonds of love and yet alone. Human history has begun. He is cursed by God for his disobedience. What is the curse? Enmity and struggle are proclaimed between man and animals ("And I will put enmity between thee (the serpent) and the woman, and between thy seed and her seed; it shall bruise thy head, and thou shalt bruise his heel"), between man and the soil ("Cursed is the ground for thy sake; in sorrow shalt thou eat of it all the days of thy life; thorns also and thistles shall it bring forth to thee; and thou shalt eat the herb of the field; in the sweat of thy face shalt thou eat bread, till thou return unto the ground"), between man and woman ("And thy desire shall be to thy husband, and he shall rule over thee"), between woman and her own natural function (In sorrow thou shalt bring forth children"). The original, pre-individualist harmony was replaced by conflict and struggle.

What, then, is -- in the prophetic view -- the goal of man? To live in peace and harmony again with his fellow men, with animals, with the soil. The new harmony is different from that of paradise. It can be obtained only if man develops fully in order to become truly human, if he knows the truth and does justice, if he develops his power of reason to a point which frees him from the bondage of man and from the bondage of irrational passions. The prophetic descriptions abound with symbols of this idea. The earth is unboundedly fruitful again, swords will be changed into plowshares, lion and lamb will live together in peace, there will be no war any more, women will bear children without pain (Talmudic), the whole mankind will be united in truth and in love. This new harmony, the achievement of which is the goal of the historical process, is symbolized by the figure of the Messiah.

On this basis we can understand fully the meaning of the Sabbath ritual. The Sabbath is the anticipation of the Messianic time, just as the Messianic period is called the time of "continuous Sabbath." In fact, the Sabbath is not only the symbolic anticipation of the Messianic time, but is considered its real precursor. As the Talmud puts it, "If all of Israel observed the Sabbath fully only once, the Messiah would be here."

Resting, not working, then, has a meaning different from the modern meaning of relaxation. In the state of rest, man anticipates the state of human freedom that will be fulfilled eventually. The relationship of man and nature and of man and man is one of harmony, of peace, of noninterference. Work is a symbol of conflict and disharmony; rest is an expression of dignity, peace, and freedom.

In the light of this understanding some of the previously raised questions find an answer. The Sabbath ritual has such a central place in the Biblical religion because it is more than a "day of rest" in the modern sense; it is a symbol of salvation and freedom. This is also the meaning of God's rest; this rest is not necessary for God because he is tired; but it expresses the idea that, great as creation is, a greater and crowning creation is peace; God's work is condescension; he must "rest," not because he is tired, but because he is free and fully God only when he has ceased to work. So is man fully man only when he does not work, when he is at peace with nature and his fellow men; that is why the Sabbath commandment is at one time motivated by God's rest, and at the other by the liberation from Egypt. Both mean the same and interpret each other: rest is freedom.

Question:

4. What is the Jewish view of the Messianic era? What values are involved in it?

Question:

5. How does the Shabbat symbolize that era and its values? What value does such a symbol have for our own daily lives?

Question:

6. Is the lesson of the Shabbat, then, that work and involvement in life is bad? (Hint: the Torah also commands, "Six days shalt thou labor...").

Question:

7. Does the American secular code teach this lesson? If yes, how? And does it do the job as effectively? Does Christianity teach this value? If yes, how? And does it do the job as effectively? (Be careful: what do Judaism, Christianity, and the American secular code each mean by "freedom"?) Do we have, then, a difference in degree or kind or both?

UNIT III

THE NEED FOR LAW

In the last unit we discussed briefly some of the values which Judaism strives to realize, pointing out that they were in many ways distinctive to Judaism in kind or degree, so that simply being a good American will not attain those values. But that still does not prove that we have to encumber ourselves with the many obligations of Judaism in order to attain Jewish values. In fact, the basic claim of Christianity -- and, incidentally, of many modern Jews -- is that, while the values of Judaism may be extremely desirable, the legal methods are unnecessary. In other words, while Judaism claims that we must <u>act</u> accordingly to <u>law</u> in order to attain Jewish values, Christianity and many modern Jews claim that the burdensome law is completely superfluous. For modern Jews often maintain that we need only do what is "right," determining what "right" is through our moral conscience (our "heart"); and when we use our moral conscience, we find that some of the ethical norms of Judaism are too petty to bother with, and almost all of the rituals are meaningless and useless, so observing Jewish law is simply unnecessary in order to be a "good" man. And Christians go even further: the Law is not only useless, but actually detrimental, to the accomplishment of our ethical goals. For, according to Paul, Law increases the consciousness of sin and thus contributes to the sinfulness of man. In this unit, then, we shall discuss Judaism's claim that acting according to Jewish law is an absolute necessity in order to attain Jewish values.

PREVIEW QUESTIONS for Unit III:

1. What do the laws of a society do? Do they in any way help to accomplish the goals of the society? How?

2. What happens to the society and its goals if the laws are abrogated or disobeyed?

3. In what way do the laws of a society sometimes hinder the accomplishing of its goals? Is there any way to make sure that the law does not become perverse in this way?

Chapter 10

Attack on Law

Reading: The New Testament, The Letter of Paul to the Romans, 7:1-8:8; 9:30-33

Do you not know, brethren -- for I am speaking to those who know the law -- that the law is binding on a person only during his life? Thus, a married woman is bound by law to her husband as long as he lives; but if her husband dies, she is discharged from the law concerning the husband. Accordingly, she will be called an adulteress if she lives with another man while her husband is alive. But if her husband dies, she is free from that law, and if she marries another man, she is not an adulteress.

Likewise, my brethren, you have died to the law through the body of Christ, so that you may belong to another, to him who has been raised from the dead, in order that we may bear fruit for God. While we were living in the flesh, our sinful passions, aroused by the law, were at work in our members to bear fruit for death. But now we are discharged from the law, dead to that which held us captive, so that we serve not under the old written code but in the new life of the Spirit.

Question:

1. Paul says that we are "dead to the Law." What does he mean? What analogy does he use to prove his point? Now, apply the analogy to our present situation, as Paul sees it, to see how he intends his analogy to prove that we are dead to the Law.

Reading:

What, then, shall we say? That the law is sin? By no means! Yet, if it had not been for the law, I should not have known sin. I should not have known what it is to covet if the law had not said, "You shall not covet." But sin, finding opportunity in the commandment, wrought in me all kinds of covetousness. Apart from the law, sin lies dead. I was once alive apart from the law, but when the commandment came, sin revived and I died; the very commandment which promised life proved to be death to me. For sin, finding opportunity in the commandment, deceived me, and by it, killed me. So the law is holy, and the commandment is holy and just and good.

Did that which is good, then, bring death to me? By no means! It was sin, working death in me through what is good, in order that sin might be shown to be sin, and through the commandment might become sinful beyond measure. We know that the law is spiritual; but I am carnal, sold under sin. I do not understand my own actions. For I do not do what I want, but I do the very thing I hate. Now if I do what I do not want, I agree that the law is good. So then it is no longer I that do it, but sin which dwells within me. For I know that nothing good dwells within me, that is, in my flesh. I can will what is right, but I cannot do it. For I do not do the good I want, but the evil I do not want is what I do. Now if I do what I do not want, it is no longer I that do it, but sin which dwells within me.

So I find it to be a law that when I want to do right, evil lies close at hand. For I delight in the law of God, in my inmost self, but I see in my members another law at war with the law of my mind, and making me captive to the law of sin which dwells in my members. Wretched man that I am! Who will deliver me from this body of death?

Thanks be to God through Jesus Christ our Lord! So then, I of myself serve the law of God with my mind, but with my flesh I serve the law of sin.

Question:

2. Is the Law bad in itself? Does _it_ make human beings evil? What does? What part does the law play in making us evil? What part does our human nature play in making us evil?

Reading:

There is therefore now no condemnation for those who are in Christ Jesus. For the law of the Spirit of life in Christ Jesus has set me free from the law of sin and death. For God has done what the law, weakened by the flesh, could not do; sending his own Son in the likeness of sinful flesh and for sin, he condemned sin in the flesh, in order that the just requirement of the law might be fulfilled in us, who walk not according to the flesh, but according to the Spirit. For those who live according to the flesh set their minds on the things of the flesh, but those who live according to the Spirit set their minds on the things of the Spirit. To set the mind on the flesh is death, but to set the mind on the Spirit is life and peace. For the mind that is set on the flesh is hostile to God; it does not submit to God's law, indeed it cannot; and those who are in the flesh cannot please God.

Question:

3. What, then, does Jesus do in order to deliver us from sin? What happens to the Law?

Reading: The Letter of Paul to the Galatians, 5:16-26

But I say, walk by the Spirit, and do not gratify the desires of the flesh. For the desires of the flesh are against the Spirit, and the desires of the Spirit are against the flesh; for these are opposed to each other, to prevent you from doing what you would. But if you are led by the Spirit you are not under the law. Now, the works of the flesh are plain: immorality, impurity, licentiousness, idolatry, sorcery, enmity, strife, jealousy, anger, selfishness, dissension, party spirit, envy, drunkenness, carousing, and the like. I warn you, as I warned you before, that those who do such things shall not inherit the kingdom of God. But the fruit of the Spirit is love, joy, peace, patience, kindness, goodness, faithfulness, gentleness, self-control; against such there is no law. And those who belong to Christ Jesus have crucified the flesh with its passions and desires.

If we live by the Spirit, let us also walk by the Spirit. Let us have no self-conceit, no provoking of one another, no envy of one another.

Question:

4. What does Paul want to substitute for the Law?

Question:

5. Can you describe some concrete obligations that a person living by the Spirit would have?

Question:

6. How do you -- or how could a Christian -- know that what you have described are really obligations of Spiritual living? (Hint: Consider the possibility of learning precept by example, and remember that the New Testament is full of accounts of Jesus' deeds.)

Question:

7. But even if you can describe what a Spiritual person should do, how can you hold him to the pattern of living that you have described? (Note that one answer, the answer of the Catholic Church, is death and/or excommunication for extreme cases of disobedience. But, then, is the Catholic really living "spiritually"? Or is he, rather, living under the obligations of the Church, which are perhaps a different and more relaxed set of legal obligations from those of Judaism, but which are legal obligations nevertheless, since they involve punishment for their transgression? In other words, it appears that you must either give up enforcing the pattern of living toward which you aim, and perhaps give up the aim in the process, or otherwise you must reconcile yourself to enforcing legal obligations.)

Chapter 11

The Need for Law I

Reading: Sociology and Philosophy by Emile Durkheim

Civilization is the result of the cooperation of men in association through successive generations; it is essentially a social product. Society made it, preserves it, and transmits it to individuals. Civilization is the assembly of all the things to which we attach the highest price; it is the congregation of the highest human values. Because it is at once the source and the guardian of civilization, the channel by which it reaches us, society appears to be an infinitely richer and higher reality than our own. It is a reality from which everything that matters to us flows. Nevertheless, it surpasses us in every way, since we can receive from this storehouse of intellectual and moral riches, of which it is the guardian, at most a few fragments only. The more we advance in time, the more complex and immense does our civilization become, and, consequently, the more does it transcend the individual consciousness, and the smaller does the individual feel in relation to it. Each of the members of an Australian tribe carries in himself the integrated whole of his civilization, but of our present civilization each one of us can only succeed in integrating a small part.

Question:

1. What is "civilization" for Durkheim? Who makes it? What does it do? Why is it "an infinitely richer and higher reality than our own"?

Reading:

However small it may be, we do nevertheless always integrate in ourselves a part, and thus, while society transcends us, it is immanent in us, and we feel it as such. While it surpasses us, it is within us, since it can only exist by and through us. It is ourselves or, rather, the best part of us, since a man is only a man to the degree that he is civilized. That which makes us real human beings is the amount that we manage to assimilate of this assembly of ideas, beliefs and precepts for conduct that we will call civilization. As Rousseau showed long ago: deprive man of all that society has given him, and he is reduced to his sensations. He becomes a being more or less indistinct from an animal. Without language, essentially a social thing, general or abstract ideas are practically impossible, as are all the higher mental functions. Left to himself, the individual would become dependent upon physical forces. If he has been able to escape, to free himself, to develop a personality, it is because he has been able to shelter under a sui generis force; but an intelligent and moral force capable, consequently, of neutralizing the blind and amoral forces of nature. This is the collective force. The theoretician may demonstrate that man has the right to liberty, but, whatever the value of these demonstrations, it is certain that this liberty can become a reality only in and through society.

Thus, to love society is to love both something beyond us and something in ourselves. We could not wish to be free of society without wishing to finish our existence as men. I do not know whether civilization has brought us more happiness, and it is of no consequence; what is certain is that from the moment that we are civilized we can only renounce civilization by renouncing ourselves. The only question that a man can ask is, not whether he can live outside society, but in what society he wishes to live. I recognize very wittingly the right of the individual to live in the society of his choice, provided that he is not bound to the society of his birth by previously contracted duties....

Question:

2. What is the relationship of the civilization of a society to the individual? "A man is only a man to the degree that he is civilized." Why? Why, then, would one want to be civilized?

Question:

3. Why does civilization require a society? Or, in other words, why must you be part of a society in order to be civilized?

Question:

4. Can you choose to renounce society completely? Why not? What right does Durkheim recognize? One of the men who fled to Canada to avoid the draft was quoted by Life (December 9, 1966) magazine as saying the following: "There are rights and privileges in any society, also obligations. If I'm willing to give up the rights and privileges, I should be able to give up the obligations." (page 42). Would you agree? Would Durkheim? Why, or why not?

Reading:

This outline may be helpful in understanding society, which for me is the source and the end of morality. I have often been accused of giving moral activity a very mediocre objective, as well as a limited arena. Certainly, if one sees in society only the group of individuals that compose it, and their dwelling place, the accusation is justified without difficulty. But society is different; it is, above all, a composition of ideas, beliefs, and sentiments of all sorts, which realize themselves through individuals. Foremost of these ideas is the moral ideal which is its principal raison d'etre. To love one's society is to love this ideal, and one loves it so that one would rather see society disappear as a material entity than renounce the ideal which it embodies. Society is the field of an intense intellectual and moral life with a wide range of influence. From the actions and reactions between its individuals arises an entirely new mental life which lifts our minds into a world of which we could have not the faintest idea had we lived in isolation. This we observe best at those signal epochs of crises when some great collective movement seizes us, lifts us above ourselves, and transfigures us. If, in the course of ordinary life, we feel its action less keenly because it is less violent and sharp, it does not for that reason cease to be real....

Society is qualified to play the part of legislator because in our eyes it is invested with a well-founded moral authority. The term "moral authority" is opposed to material authority or physical supremacy. Moral authority is a psychic reality, a higher and richer conscience than our own, one upon which we feel that our own depends. I have shown how society presents this characteristic because it is the source and seat of all the intellectual benefits that constitute civilization. From society we derive all the essentials of our mental life. Our individual reason is, and has the same value as, that collective and impersonal reason called science, which is, both in its constitution and in its processes, preeminently a social thing. Our aesthetic faculties, the fineness of our taste, derive from art, which is again a social thing. It is to society that we owe the power over matter which is our glory. It is society that has freed us from nature. Is it not then to be expected that we think of it as a mental being higher than ourselves from which our mental powers emanate? This explains why it is that when it demands of us those sacrifices, great or small, that make up our moral life, we bow before its demands with deference.

The Believer bows before his God, because it is from God that he believes that he holds his being, particularly his mental being, his soul. We have the same reasons for experiencing this feeling before the collective....

Question:

5. Durkheim pictures society as a force by means of which we can and do conquer nature. What kind of force is it? Physical? Where does this force of society receive its power? (Important question) Why is it that "liberty can become a reality only in and through society"?

Question:

6. To be part of a society requires commitment to its ideals. "To love one's society is to love this ideal, and one loves it so that one would rather see society disappear as a material entity than renounce the ideal which it embodies." Why can't you be part of a society without being

committed to its ideals, at least tacitly? (Hint: Consider what would happen to the society if there were many within its midst who acted to the detriment of its goals -- for example, Russian spies in the United States.)

Question:

7. Why does commitment to a society's ideals involve at least obedience to its laws? (Hint: Again, consider what would happen to a society whose laws were disobeyed.)

Question:

8. What attitude toward society is then required of us? Durkheim uses reverence for society as a substitute for what? Is he justified in making this substitution? To answer that, consider the following:

   a. What functions does the God-concept traditionally serve in a God-centered society?

   b. What functions does society serve, as Durkheim sees it?

   c. Where do the two sets of functions overlap, so that one could be substituted for the other? Where do they fail to overlap?

   d. What problems, then, do you think Durkheim's substitution will encounter? What advantages does it have over holding society together and directing it by means of a God-concept?

   e. If we were to adopt Durkheim's substitution, then, what would we have to add in order to make it a viable philosophy of Jewish law? (In the following selection, Durkheim will attempt to fill one of these deficiencies.)

Reading: The Division of Labor in Society by Emile Durkheim

Everybody knows that there is a social cohesion whose cause lies in a certain conformity of all particular consciences to a common type which is none other than the psychic type of society. In these conditions, not only are all the members of the group individually attracted to one another because they resemble one another, but also because they are joined to what is the condition of existence of this collective type; that is to say, to the society that they form by their union. Not only do citizens love each other and seek each other out in preference to strangers, but they love their country. They will it as they will themselves, hold to it durably and for prosperity, <u>because, without it, a great part of their psychic lives would function poorly</u>. Inversely, society holds to what they present in the way of fundamental resemblances because that is a condition of its cohesion. There are in us two consciences; one contains states which are personal to each of us and which characterize us, while the states which comprehend the other are common to all society. The first represents only our individual personality and constitutes it; the second represents the collective type, and consequently, society, without which it would not exist. When it is one of the elements of this latter which determines our conduct, it is not in view of our personal interest that we act, but we pursue collective ends. Although distinct, these two consciences are linked one to the other, since, in sum, they are only one, having one and the same organic substratum. They are thus solidary....

It is this solidarity which repressive law expresses, at least whatever there is vital in it. The acts that it prohibits and qualifies as crimes are of two sorts. Either they directly manifest very violent dissemblance between the agent who accomplishes them and the collective type; or else they offend the organ of the common conscience. In one case as in the other, the force that is offended by the crime and which suppresses it is thus the same. It is a product of the most essential social likenesses, and it has for its effect the maintenance of the social cohesion which results from these likenesses. It is this force which penal law protects against all enfeeblement, both in demanding from each of us a minimum of resemblances, without which the individual would be a menace to the unity of the social body, and in imposing upon us the respect for the <u>symbol</u> which expresses and summarizes these resemblances at the same time that it guarantees them.

We thus explain why acts have been so often reputed criminal and punished as such, without, in themselves, being evil for society; that is, just like the individual type, the collective is formed from very diverse causes, and even from fortuitous combinations. Produced through historical development, it carries the mark of circumstances of every kind which society has gone through in its history. It would be miraculous, then, if everything that we find there were adjusted to some useful end. But it cannot be that elements more or less numerous were there introduced without having any relation to social utility. Among the inclinations and tendencies that the individual has received from his ancestors, or which he has formed himself, many are certainly of no use, or cost more than they are worth. Of course, the majority are not harmful, for being, under such conditions, does not mean activity. But there are some of them remaining without any use, and those whose services are most incontestable often have an intensity which has no relation to their utility, because it comes to them, in part, from other causes. The case is the same with collective passions. All the acts which offend them are not dangerous as they are made out to be. <u>But, the reprobation of which these acts are the object still has reason for existing, whatever the origin of the sentiments involved, once they are made part of a collective type, and especially if they are essential elements, everything which contributes to disturb them, at the same time disturbs social cohesion and compromises society.</u> It is not at all useful for them to be born, but once they have endured, it becomes necessary that they persist in spite of their irrationality. That is why it is good, in general, that the acts which offend them be not tolerated. Of course, reasoning in the abstract, we may well show that there is no reason for a society to forbid the eating of such and such meat, in itself inoffensive. But once the horror of this has become an integral part of the common conscience, it cannot disappear without a social link being broken, and that is what sane consciences obscurely feel.

<u>Question</u>:

9. Why must one also obey the society's ritual laws in order to be part of the society, even if those laws now <u>appear</u> useless to the preservation of the society? (A very important question. Hint: explain the last two sentences

of Durkheim which are quoted, noting especially the concept and importance of the "common conscience" or "collective type." To understand the significance of this factor, note that while both Sweden and the United States share many of the same democratic goals, many relationships which are considered promiscuous here are perfectly legitimate there, and, even though such sexual behavior manifestly has not endangered the survival of Sweden, <u>we punish that behavior here</u> because our "common conscience" has been offended. In other words, to remain part of American society we must obey its purely ritual law or we are excluded from the society by imprisonment; that we must obey Jewish ritual law to remain Jewish should not be so surprising then.) To what extent does it boil down to a question of "United we stand, divided we fall"?

<u>Reading</u>: <u>The World of the Talmud</u> by Morris Adler

The supremely significant place which Halacha occupies in the economy of Judaism has helped give currency to the charge that it is a faith dominated by legalism and a legalistic spirit. That this spurious allegation is repeated by a variety of sources and has endured for centuries proves once again that an error is often both contagious and sturdy. The truth of the Rabbinic statement that the sage has, ever since prophecy ceased in Israel, inherited the mantle of the prophet is attested to by more objective and more recent students. The prophets' passion for righteousness, their abhorrence of injustice, their universal outlook, their vision of a day "when the earth will be filled with the knowledge of the Lord as the waters cover the sea," and "nation shall not lift up sword against nation," inform and elevate Rabbinic legislation. R. Travers Herford, who has devoted many years of a long life to study of Rabbinic Judaism, concludes that "nothing is farther from the truth than to say that Pharisaism made the Jewish religion, the religion of the prophets, into a hard and barren formation, with no spiritual value in it. The truth, rather, is that the Pharisees took up the religion of the prophets and brought it to bear upon the lives of the people in a way and to an extent which the prophets had never been able to accomplish. And, paradoxical though it may sound, it is not far from the truth to say that if it had not been for the Pharisees and what they did, the prophets would never have been heard of. Be this as it may, the Pharisees certainly developed their ideas of the unwritten Torah, and the Halacha based on it, with a clear and conscious reference to the teachings of the prophets." Legalism implies that the law becomes its own end and that the mass of legal technicality and procedure obscures the end to which the law is properly a means. The legalist does in the realm of law what the fanatic, according to Santayana, does in the sphere of life, namely, redouble his efforts as he forgets his aim. In every legal system great attention is of necessity paid to methodology, to precedent, to correct procedure. For the law seeks to bring order into man's life, guiding and liberating it by rule and code. Proper procedure is, in a society of law, the best safeguard of the rights of man. Law at its best has its eyes upon a purpose beyond itself, namely, the improvement of the lot and the advancement of the welfare of the people for whom it legislates....

What worship does sporadically on festive occasions the Rabbis sought to achieve as a constant influence. Service of God was for them not only the utterance of the lips in moments of exaltation, but the faith by which we normally live, expressed through act, effort, deed. Religion is not a matter of living on the "peaks" of experience. That is for the saint and the mystic. More fundamentally, <u>religion must mean transposing to a higher level of spiritual awareness and ethical sensitivity the entire plateau of daily living by the generality of men</u>. Idolatry is defeated, not by recognition of its intellectual absurdity alone, but by a life that expresses itself in service to God. Selfishness and greed are overcome, not by professions of a larger view, but by disciplines that direct our energies, our wills, and our actions, outward and upward. Study and learning are not to be left to the happenstance of leisure or to the occasional upsurge of interest or curiosity, but are to be made part of the daily regimen of religious activity.

The law was therefore no meaningless and dull burden for the Jew, since it was both opportunity and privilege. The traditional Jew through the ages would not have comprehended such judgments as "the curse of the Law," "the dead weight of the Law," "the letter that killeth the spirit." He spoke of "simha shel mitzvah," the joy of personal fulfillment that comes from observing the Law. God in his love of Israel multiplied commandments. The Law not only linked the Jew to God, but likewise integrated him in a community. It filled his life with festive occasions and exalted moments and provided him with a redeeming and blessed instrument by which to rise above the routine and prosiness of daily existence. To this day the morning worship service includes the words, "Happy are we! How goodly is our portion, how pleasant our lot and how beautiful our heritage."

The aims of the prophets guided the rabbis in their work. One of the greatest students of Rabbinic Judaism decries the "misunderstanding (which) has arisen regarding the nature of the transition from the Prophets to the Scribes, from biblical Judaism to rabbinical Judaism." He goes on to say, "The intellectual endeavors of the Scribes are apt to be considered as a degeneration and decline from the idealism which pervades the conception of life laid down in the Scriptures. The truth is that the Scribes succeeded where the Prophets had failed. Through them the teachings proclaimed in the schools of the Prophets became the common property of the whole people."

The purpose of the laws of the Torah, declared a noted sage, is to refine man. Another outstanding legal scholar stated, "He whose wisdom exceeds his deeds, to what may he be compared? To a tree of many branches but few roots, which the wind can easily pluck up and overturn. But he whose deeds exceed his wisdom, to what may he be compared? To a tree of few branches but many roots, which, even though the strongest wind blow upon it, will not be moved."

The Rabbis saw the prescriptive law as the best means of introducing, through discipline and daily obligations, higher motivations and loftier purposes into the consciousness of man. Through deed, the will is mobilized and fortified. Even if one do a good act out of an unworthy motive, says an ancient teacher, he will, if he persists, come to be governed by a right motive. An admiring nonbeliever once said to Pascal, "I wish that I had your faith so that I might lead a life like yours." Pascal replied, "Lead my life and you will acquire my faith."

Question:

10. What is legalism? Why is it a danger?

Question:

11. For all its concern with law, is rabbinic Judaism legalistic? To answer this, describe what the rabbis of the Talmud (who were Pharisees) did when they formed law, and describe also the relationship of their law to Prophetic ideals.

Question:

12. What is the aim of Talmudic law?

Question:

13. "Religion <u>must</u> mean transposing to a higher level of spiritual awareness and ethical sensitivity the entire plateau of daily living by the generality of men. Idolatry is defeated, not by recognition of its intellectual absurdity alone, but by a life that expresses itself in service to God." Why is this so?

Question:

14. Besides concretizing goals which we already have, what other purpose does law serve?

Chapter 12

The Need for Law II

Reading: Between God and Man by Abraham J. Heschel
Religion and Law

The claim of Judaism that religions and law are inseparable is difficult for many of us to comprehend. The difficulty may be explained by modern man's conception of the essence of religion. To the modern mind, religion is a state of the soul, inwardness; feeling rather than obedience, faith rather than action, spiritual rather than concrete. To Judaism, religion is not a feeling for something that is, but an _answer_ to Him who is asking us to live in a certain way. It is in its very origin a consciousness of total commitment; a realization that all of life is not only man's but also God's sphere of interest.

"God asks of the heart." Yet does he ask for the heart only? Is the right intention enough? Some doctrines insist that love is the sole condition for salvation (Sufi, Bhakti-marga), stressing the importance of the inwardness of love, faith, to the exclusion of good works.

Paul waged a passionate battle against the power of law and proclaimed instead the religion of grace. Law, he claimed, cannot conquer sin, nor can righteousness be attained through works of law. A man is justified "by faith without the deeds of the law."

That salvation is attained by faith alone was Luther's central thesis. The antinomian tendency resulted in the overemphasis of love and faith to the exclusion of good works.

The Formula of Concord of 1580, still valid in Protestantism, condemns the statement that good works are necessary to salvation and rejects the doctrine that they are harmful to salvation. According to Ritschl, the doctrine of the merit of good deeds is an intruder in the domain of Christian theology; the only way of salvation is justification by faith. Barth, following Kierkegaard, voices Lutheran thoughts, when he claims that man's deeds are too sinful to be good. There are fundamentally no human deeds which, because of their significance in this world, find favor in God's eyes. God can be approached through God alone.

Those who have only paid attention to the relation of man to the ideals, disregarding the relation of the ideals to man, have in their theories seen only the motive but not the purpose of either religion or morality. Echoing the Paulinian doctrine that man is saved by faith alone, Kant and his disciples taught that the essence of religion, or morality, would consist in an absolute quality of the soul or the will, regardless of the actions that may come out of it or the ends that may be attained. Accordingly, the value of a religious act would be determined wholly by the intensity of one's faith or by the rectitude of one's inner disposition. The intention, not the deed, the how, not the what, of one's conduct, would be essential, and no motive other than the sense of duty would be of any moral value. Thus, acts of kindness, when not dictated by the sense of duty, are no better than cruelty, and compassion or regard for human happiness as such is looked upon as an ulterior motive. "I would not break my word even to save mankind!" exclaimed Fichte. His salvation and righteousness were apparently so much more important to him than the fate of all men that he would have destroyed mankind to save himself. (1) Does not such an attitude illustrate the truth of the proverb, "The road to hell is paved with good intention"? Should we not say that a concern with one's own salvation and righteousness that outweighs the regard for the welfare of other human beings cannot be qualified as a good intention?

Question:

1. How does the "modern" mind characterize religion, according to Heschel? From what source in the Catholic tradition does this notion of religion come? How did the Protestants carry on this notion? How do they change it? How do Kant and his disciples formulate it?

Question:

2. What is the first thing (1) that Heschel finds wrong with this notion of religion? Do you agree? Why or why not? (Give concrete examples to support your position.)

Reading:

The dichotomy of faith and works which presented such an important problem in Christian theology was never a problem in Judaism. To us, the basic problem is neither what is the right action nor what is the right intention. The basic problem is: what is right living? And life is indivisible. The inner sphere is never isolated from outward activities. Deed and thought are bound into one. (2a) All a person thinks and feels enters everything he does, and all he does is involved in everything he thinks and feels.

Spiritual aspirations are doomed to failure when we try to cultivate deeds at the expense of thoughts, or thoughts at the expense of deeds. Is it the artist's inner vision or his wrestling with the stone that brings about a work of sculpture? Right living is like a work of art, the product of a vision and of a wrestling with concrete situations.

Judaism is averse to generalities, averse to looking for meaning in life detached from doing, as if the meaning were a separate entity. Its tendency is to make the ideas convertible into deeds, to interpret metaphysical insights as patterns for action, to endow the most sublime principles with bearing upon everyday conduct. In its tradition, the abstract became concrete, the absolute historic. By enacting the holy on the stage of concrete living, we perceive our kinship with the divine, the presence of the divine. What cannot be grasped in reflection we comprehend in deeds.

(3) The world needs more than the secret holiness of individual inwardness. It needs more than sacred sentiments and good intentions. God asks for the heart because He needs the lives. It is by lives that the world will be redeemed, by lives that beat in concordance with God, by deeds that outbeat the finite charity of the human heart.

Man's power of action is less vague than his power of intention. And an action has intrinsic meaning; its value to the world is independent of what it means to the person performing it. The act of giving food to a helpless child is meaningful, regardless of whether or not the moral intention is present. God asks for the heart, and we must spell our answer in terms of deeds.

(2b) It would be a device of conceit, if not presumption, to insist that purity of the heart is the exclusive test of piety. Perfect purity is something we rarely know how to obtain or how to retain. No one can claim to have purged all the dross even from his finest desire. The self is finite, but selfishness is infinite.

God asks for the heart, but the heart is oppressed with uncertainty in its own twilight. God asks for faith, and the heart is not sure of its own faith. It is good that there is a dawn of decision for the night of the heart; deeds to objectify faith, definite forms to verify belief.

The heart is often a lonely voice in the marketplace of living. Man may certainly entertain lofty ideals and behave like the ass that, as the saying goes, "carries gold and eats thistles." The problem of the soul is how to live nobly in an animal environment; how to persuade and train the tongue and the senses to behave in agreement with the insights of the soul.

Question:

3. What does Heschel want to substitute for the "modern" notion of religion?

Question:

4. The first reason (1) that Heschel gave for making this substitution had to do with the results of good intention alone. His second reason (2) deals with the intentions themselves. Why, according to Heschel, do we need to transform our intentions into actions in order to preserve the integrity of the intentions themselves? (Hint: Consider (2a) and especially this sentence of his: "What cannot be grasped in reflection we comprehend in deeds.") Why else? (Consider 2b.)

Question:

5. On the other hand, (3) "an action has an intrinsic meaning." Why? Given this, formulate Heschel's third objection to the "modern" conception of religion in your own words.

Reading:

The integrity of life is not exclusively a thing of the heart; it implies more than consciousness of the moral law. The innermost chamber must be guarded at the uttermost outposts. Religion is not the same as spiritualism; what man does in his concrete, physical existence is directly relevant to the divine. Spirituality is the goal, not the way, of man. In this world music is played on physical instruments, and, to the Jew, the mitzvot are the instruments on which the holy is carried out. If man were only mind, worship in thought would be the form in which to commune with God. But man is body and soul, and his goal is so to live that both "his heart and his flesh should sing to the living God."

But how do we know what the right deeds are? Is the knowledge of right and wrong derived from reason and conscience alone?

There are those who are ready to discard the message of the divine commands and call upon us to rely on our conscience. Man, we are told, is only under obligation to act in conformity with his reason and conscience, and must not be subjected to any laws except those which he imposes upon himself. Moral laws are attainable by reason and conscience, and there is no need for a lawgiver. God is necessary merely as a guarantee for the ultimate triumph of the moral effort.

The fallacy of the doctrine of autonomy is in equating man with "the good drive," and all of his nature with reason and conscience. Man's capacity for love and self-denial ("the good drive") does not constitute the totality of his nature. He is also inclined to love success, to adore the victors, and to despise the vanquished. Those who call upon us to rely on our inner voice fail to realize that there is more than one voice within us, that the power of selfishness may easily subdue the pangs of conscience. The conscience, moreover, is often celebrated for what is beyond its ability. The conscience is not a legislative power, capable of teaching us what we ought to do, but rather, a preventive agency; a brake, not a guide; a fence, not a way. It raises its voice after a wrong deed has been committed, but often fails to give us direction in advance of our actions.

The individual's insight alone is unable to cope with all the problems of living. It is the guidance of tradition on which we must rely, and whose norms we must learn to interpret and to apply. We must learn not only the ends but also the means by which to realize the ends; not only the general laws but also the particular forms.

Judaism calls upon us to listen <u>not only</u> to the voice of the conscience but also to the norms of a heteronomous law. The good is not an abstract idea but a commandment, and the ultimate meaning of its fulfillment is in its being <u>an answer</u> to God.

<u>Question</u>:

6. "Spirituality is the goal, not the way, of man." Explain.

<u>Question</u>:

7. Why does our "moral conscience" fail as the measuring stick of what is "good"? How <u>should</u> we determine what is "good," according to Heschel? Why is that a better indicator?

<u>Reading</u>:

<u>Law and Life</u>: Does Judaism glorify outward action, regardless of intention and motive? Is it action it calls for rather than devotion? Is a person to be judged by what he <u>does</u> rather than by what he <u>is</u>? Is conduct alone important? Have the mitzvot nothing to say to the soul? Has the soul nothing to say through the mitzvot? We are commanded to carry out specific rituals, such as reciting twice a day "Hear O Israel..." or setting of the tefillin on arm and head. Are we merely commanded <u>to recite</u> "Hear O Israel...

God is One," and not _to hear_? Is one's setting of the tefillin on the head and arm merely a matter of external performance?

No religious act is properly fulfilled unless it is done with a willing heart and a craving soul. You cannot worship Him with your body if you do not know how to worship Him in soul. The relationship between deed and inner devotion must be understood, as we shall see, in terms of polarity.

Jewish observance, it must be stressed, takes place on two levels. It consists of acts performed by the body in a clearly defined and tangible manner, and of acts of the soul carried out in a manner that is neither definable nor ostensible; of the right intention and of putting the right intention into action. Both body and soul must participate in carrying out a ritual, a law, an imperative, a mitzvah. Thoughts, feelings, ensconced in the inwardness of man, deeds performed in the absence of the soul, are incomplete.

Judaism stresses the importance of a fixed pattern of deeds as well as that of spontaneity of devotion, quantity as well as quality of religious living, actions as well as kavvanah. A good deed consists not only in _what_ but _how_ we do it. Even those mitzvot which require for their fulfillment a concrete object and an external act call for inner acknowledgment, participation, understanding, and the freedom of the heart.

It is true that the law speaks always of external performance and rarely of inner devotion. It does not rigorously insist upon kavvanah. There is wisdom in this reticence. The rabbis knew that man may be commanded to act in a certain way, but not to feel in a certain way; that the actions of man may be regulated, but not his thoughts or emotions.

There are therefore no detailed laws of kavvanah, and kavvanah may, indeed, run dry in the mere halakhah. To maintain the flow of kavvanah we must keep alive the sense of the ineffable, that which lies beyond kavvanah.

Question:

8. What, then, is the place of kavvanah in the Law? Describe the polarity of deed and inner devotion. Why, then, does the Law regulate man's actions and not his intentions?

Question:

9. In review of chapters 10, 11, and 12, why must society transform its ideals into laws? That is, (a) why is agreement with a society's goals not sufficient? And (b) what functions does law serve that society needs? Apply this now to Jewish Law in particular: (c) Why is a religion of the heart not sufficient? (d) What functions do the Jewish ethical laws serve for Judaism? What about the ritual laws? Give examples of each. What about ritual laws which are not directly connected with a given value -- what function do they serve? (Review Durkheim.) (e) What, then, is the place of kavvanah (intention) in Jewish Law? (f) To what extent, then, is the following claim true? "Christianity is a religion of love, Judaism a religion of law."

Reading: Franz Rosenzweig, "The Builders: Concerning the Law," from On Jewish Learning, N. N. Glatzer, ed.

To Martin Buber

Dear Friend:

...You point to a new principle of selection, through which the vast subject matter of learning (Lernstoff) you unfurl can again become a teaching (Lehre), a principle more trustworthy than anyone has attempted to set up. You introduce the concept of inner power. For inner power is what you demand when you ask him who learns to stake his whole being for the learning, to make himself a link in the chain of tradition and thus become a chooser, not through his will but through his ability...

But in this wise, the teaching ceases to be something that can be learned, something "knowable" in the sense that it is an already existing "something," some definite subject matter. The subject matter must indeed be learned and known, and in a far wider sense than either the representatives of "Judaism on one foot" or those of traditional erudition and learning ever demanded. For now the outside books, the books from beyond the pale, and the "women's books" that were considered beneath the dignity of that classical form of learning, are both included in the subject matter to be learned, included as equals. But all this that can and should be known is not really knowledge! All this that can and should be taught is not teaching! Teaching begins where the subject matter ceases to be subject matter and changes into inner power...

Question:

10. Rosenzweig gives a very different reason to our question about why Judaism needs law. In this selection, he is responding to eight lectures given by Martin Buber ("Lectures on Judaism") at Frankfort in 1923, in which Buber outlined a new approach to Jewish education and Jewish law. In Buber's approach to education, is study of the simple facts in Jewish history, law, literature, etc., necessary? What, then, is the new and crucial notion which Buber introduces?

Reading:

And so it is all the more curious that after liberating us and pointing the way to a new teaching, your answer to the other side of the question, the question concerning the Law: "What are we to do?" -- that your answer should leave this Law in the shackles put upon it -- as well as upon the teachings -- by the nineteenth century. For is it really Jewish law with which you try to come to terms? and, not succeeding, on which you turn your back only to tell yourself and us who look to you for answer that our sole task must be to take cognizance of the Law with reverence -- a reverence which can effect no practical difference in our lives or to our persons? Is that really Jewish law, the law of millenia, studied and lived, analyzed and rhapsodized, the law of everyday and of the day of death, petty and yet sublime, sober and yet woven in legend; a law which knows both the fire of the Sabbath candle and that of the martyr's stake? The law Akiba planted and fenced in, and Aher trampled under, the cradle Spinoza hailed from, the ladder on which the Baal Shem ascended, the law that always rises beyond itself, that can never be reached -- and yet has always the possibility of becoming Jewish life, of being expressed in Jewish faces? Is the Law you speak of not rather the Law of the Western orthodoxy of the past century?

...For did any Jew prior to this really think -- without having the question put to him -- that he was keeping the Law, and the Law him, only because God imposed it upon Israel at Sinai? Actually faced by the question, he might have thought of such an answer; and the philosophers to whom the question has been put because they were supposedly "professional" thinkers, have always been fond of giving this very reply...

And can we really fancy that Israel kept this Law, this Torah, only because of the one "fact which excluded the possibility of delusions," that the six hundred thousand heard the voice of God on Sinai? <u>This "fact" certainly does play a part, but no greater part than all we have mentioned before, and all that our ancestors perceived in every "today" of the Torah</u>: that the souls of all generations to come stood on Sinai along with those six hundred thousand, and heard what they heard...for a miracle does not constitute history, a people is not a juridical fact, martyrdom is not an arithmetical problem, and love is not social. We can reach both the teachings and the Law only by realizing that we are still on the first lap of the way, and by taking every step upon it, ourselves.

Question:

11. What is Buber's approach to Jewish Law, as described by Rosenzweig? Why does Rosenzweig object to it?

Question:

12. Why does Rosenzweig reject the claim that we should obey the law simply because God commanded Israel to do so at Sinai? What does Rosenzweig want to substitute as a motivation for observing the law?

Reading:

But what is this way to the Law? What was it in the case of the teachings? It was a way that led through the entire realm of the knowable, but really <u>through</u> it; a way that was not content to touch upon a few heights which yielded a fine view, but struggled along where former eras had not thought it even worth while to blaze a trail and yet would not give him who had traveled its whole length the right to say that he had now arrived at the goal...

(For) our people, the only one that did not originate from the womb of nature that bears nations, but -- and this is unheard of! -- was led forth "a nation from the midst of another nation" (Deuteronomy 4:34) -- our people was decreed a different fate. Its very birth became the great moment of its life, its mere being already harbored its destiny. Even "before it was formed," it was "known," like Jeremiah its prophet. And so only he who remembers this determining origin can belong to it; while he who no longer can, or will, utter the new word he has to say "in the name of the original speaker," who refuses to be a link in the golden chain, no longer belongs to his people. And that is why this people must learn what is knowable as a condition for learning what is unknown, for making it his own.

All this holds also for the Law, for doing...There the way led through all that is knowable; here it leads through all that is doable. And the sphere of "what can be done" extends far beyond the sphere of the duties assumed by orthodoxy. As in the teaching, the rigid difference between the essential and the non-essential, as outlined by liberalism, should no longer exist, so in the sphere of what can be done the difference between the forbidden and the permissible, as worked out, not without precedent, yet now for the first time with so much consequence and efficiency by Western European orthodoxy of the 19th century, must cease to exist. The separation of the forbidden from the permissible had instituted a Jewish sphere within one's life; whatever remained outside of this sphere, whatever was extra-Jewish, was released, or, in legal terms, was made "permissible"; whatever remained within constituted the Jewish sphere with its commandments and prohibitions. The method of basing "allowances" on the text of the law permitted an extension of the realm of the permissible as long as the norms valid for the inner sphere were observed; this procedure, recognized through the ages as legitimate, had only in modern times been made into a system. Only in earlier periods where the security of Jewish life had been at stake, had that boundary been recognized and its temporary extension been accepted as its necessary complement.

Only in modern times, when Jewish survival was considered perpetually at stake, was this treatment of the law given a permanent status. The future must no longer recognize that boundary, that method, nor even the general distinction described above. As in the sphere of the Law, there should be nothing *a priori* "permissible." Exactly those things, generally rendered permissible by orthodoxy, must be given a Jewish form. Outside of the Jewish sphere is the domain that should be formed by the "custom," i.e., by a positive principle, instead of merely the negative concept of "permissible." Where Judaism was alive, this had always been true; but whereas previously this fact had been treated with criticism or with slight irony, it will in the future have to be treated with seriousness. Not one sphere of life ought to be surrendered. To give one example for each of the two possibilities I have in mind: for those who eat Jewish dishes all the traditional customs of the menu as handed down from mother to daughter must be as irreplaceable as the separation of meat and milk; and he who refrains from opening a business letter on the Sabbath must not read it even if somebody else has opened it for him. Everywhere the custom and the original intention of the law must have the same rank of inviolability as the law itself.

Even what is within that sphere of demarcations, within that inner realm of Judaism, will be influenced by the fact that it is no longer separated from the realm of the merely "permissible." By contrast to the "permissible" it was essentially a sphere dominated by the term "forbidden." Even the positive commandment had somehow received a negative character. The classical Hebrew term for fulfilling one's duty, an expression which may be rendered by "discharging one's obligation," had a fateful implication, which it could not have where leaving the sphere of one obligation meant entering the sphere of another -- an implication which, however, it had to adopt when all around the province of the Jewish duty lay the domain of a Jewishly formless "permissible." As in the sphere of *teaching* where, after the non-essential has become essential, the essential itself receives some of the characteristics of the non-essential, so, in the sphere of the Law, after customs have clothed themselves with the dignity of law, the law will share the positive character of the custom. Not the negative but the positive will be dominant in the

Law. Even the prohibitions may now reveal their positive character. One refrains from working on the Sabbath because of the positive commandment concerning rest; when refraining from eating forbidden food one experiences the joy of being able to be Jewish even in the every-day and generally human aspects of one's material existence. Even an act of refraining becomes a positive act.

And again we have to realize that with this unifying and broadening of the Jewishly do-able, nothing has really been done. Whatever can and must be done is not yet deed, whatever can and must be commanded is not yet commandment. Law (Gesetz) must again become commandment (Gebot) which seeks to be transformed into deed at the very moment it is heard. It must regain that living reality (Heutigkeit) in which all great Jewish periods have sensed the guarantee for its eternity. Like teaching, it must consciously start where its content stops being content and becomes inner power, our own inner power. Inner power which in turn is added to the substance of the law. For even if one should wish to do "everything" possible, he would still not fulfill the Law -- he would not fulfill it in a way by which law would become commandment; a commandment which he must fulfill, simply because he cannot allow it to remain unfulfilled, as it was once expressed in Akiba's famous parable of the fishes. Thus, what counts here, too, is not our will, but our ability to act. Here, too, the decisive thing is the selection which our ability -- without regard to our will -- makes out of the wealth of the possible deeds. <u>Since this selection does not depend on the will but on our ability, it is a very personal one; for while a general law can address itself with its demands to the will, ability carries in itself its own law</u>; there is only my, your, his ability, and, built on them, ours; not everybody's. Therefore, whether much is done, or little, or maybe nothing at all, is immaterial in the face of the one and unavoidable demand; that whatever is being done, shall come from that inner power. As the knowledge of everything knowable is not yet wisdom, so the doing of everything do-able is not yet deed. The deed is created at the boundary of the merely do-able, where the voice of the commandment causes the spark to leap from "I must" to "I can." The Law is built on such commandments, and only on them.

For this is what we felt was lacking in the law presented to us by its new observers: that the old law was not at the same time the new. This lack of actuality, of living reality, was recognized when the line of demarcation I mentioned made today's life "permissible." Thereby the law had been denied actuality. Moses' bold words, spoken to the generation who had not experienced the event of Mount Sinai (Deuteronomy 5:3), "The Lord made not this covenant with our fathers, but with us, even us, who are all of us alive this day," -- those words (the paradox of which was keenly felt by ancient commentators) had fallen into oblivion. It is upon us to accept the challenge of this boldness...In the words of the Talmud, we have only to be sons, in order to become builders.

Question:

13. Explain what Rosenzweig means when he says that "only he who remembers this determining origin can belong to it; while he who no longer can or will utter the new word he has to say 'in the name of the original speaker'...no longer belongs to his people." How does Rosenzweig apply this remark, made in regard to Jewish intellectual activity, to Jewish law? Your answer should make clear Rosenzweig's distinction between <u>Gesetz</u> and <u>Gebot</u>. In sum, then, why should you observe Jewish law according to Rosenzweig? What experience is behind such observance?

Question:

14. Carefully distinguish Rosenzweig's reason for observing Jewish law from Durkheim's. What place does the nation (or people) have in each conception? the individual?

Question:

15. If you are observant because you feel that the Laws are your own personal commandments, as Rosenzweig would want you to do, what happens to the attitude which you have toward the Laws? The number of Laws and customs which you observe? The attitude which you have towards the observance or non-observance of other people?

Reading:

Turning back, recapturing what has remained behind, is here a permanent and life necessity. For we must be able to _live_ in our eternity. The protecting wall of the instincts, sufficient for the nations of the world, who are endangered only occasionally, does not suffice for us. We need stronger safeguards than our instincts. These safeguards stem from what we found before to be ultimately decisive: the measure of our ability to act. Referring oneself to such a court of appeal is not flippancy, it is extremely serious when re-interpreting Israel's free acceptance of God's word "under" Mount Sinai into a compelled acceptance, compelled by -- God. "He lifted up the mountain like a basket, until they accepted," the Sages say. We may do what is in our power to remove obstacles; we can and should make free our ability and power to act. But the last choice is not within our will; it is entrusted to our ability.

A decision based on ability cannot err, since it is not choosing, but listening, and therefore, only accepting. For this reason no one can take another person to task, though he can and should teach him; because only _I_ know what _I_ can do; only my own ear can hear the voice of my own being which I have to reckon with. And perhaps another's non-ability does more for the upbuilding of both teaching and law than my own ability. We only know that we all have potential abilities to act. For what may be a hard task for the other nations, that is to turn back in the on-rushing stream of life -- because they consider themselves united by time and space, and only on festive days and in hours of destiny do they feel as members in a chain of generations -- this is just the very basis of our communal and individual life: the feeling of being our fathers' children, our grandchildren's ancestors. Therefore we may rightly expect to find ourselves again, at some time, somehow, in our fathers' every word and deed; and also that our own words and deeds will have some meaning for our grandchildren. For we are, as Scripture puts it, "children"; we are, as tradition reads it, "Builders."

Question:

16. How does Rosenzweig try to insure that anyone who accepts his philosophy will not simply decide that he need observe no Jewish laws whatsoever? Your answer should include an explanation of the distinction between acting according to will and acting according to ability. Has Rosenzweig succeeded in meeting this difficulty? Do you find any other difficulties in his approach? What are its strengths?

UNIT IV

THE PROCESS OF AMERICAN LAW

Chapter 13

Early Sources on Segregation

Now that we have seen why law is a necessary part of Judaism, we shall turn to the processes by which Jewish law is formed and changed (Unit V). But before we do, we shall consider an example of how American law developed, so that we can see clearly where Jewish law is unusual and where it follows common patterns of development used in at least one other legal system (the American code). So, throughout Units IV and V, have this question in the back of your mind: Is Jewish law totally unusual, and perhaps even archaic, in its methods? Where is it that way? Why? Where is it not that way?

Reading: The Constitution of the United States: Amendment XIV (Proposed in 1866, adopted in 1868)

Section I: All persons born or naturalized in the United States, and subject to the jurisdiction thereof, are citizens of the United States and of the State wherein they reside. No State shall make or enforce any law which shall abridge the privileges or immunities of citizens of the United States; nor shall any State deprive any person of life, liberty, or property, without due process of law; nor deny to any person within its jurisdiction the equal protection of the laws.

Question:

1. Who made this law? What was the source of their authority? Who can, then, legally change it? How do they go about it?

Question:

2. Who has the power of determining what acts are permitted and what acts are prohibited under this law? What is the source of their authority? What happens if a given citizen disagrees with them?

Reading: <u>Plessy V. Fergusen</u> (Decided May 18, 1896)

Mr. Justice Brown, after stating the case, delivered the opinion of the court.

This case turns upon the constitutionality of an act of the General Assembly of the State of Louisiana, passed in 1890, providing for separate railway carriages for the white and colored races. Acts 1890, No. 111, p.152.

The first section of the statute enacts "that all railway companies carrying passengers in their coaches in this State, shall provide equal but separate accommodations for the white and colored races, by providing two or more passenger coaches for each passenger train, or by dividing the passenger coaches by a partition so as to secure separate accommodations: <u>Provided</u>, That this section shall not be construed to apply to street railroads. No person or persons shall be admitted to occupy seats in coaches other than the ones assigned to them on account of the race they belong to."

By the second section it was enacted "that the officers of such passenger trains shall have power, and are hereby required, to assign each passenger to the coach or compartment used for the race to which such passenger belongs; any passenger insisting on going into a coach or compartment to which, by race, he does not belong, shall be liable to a fine of twenty-five dollars, or, in lieu thereof, to imprisonment for a period of not more than twenty days in the parish prison, and any officer of any railroad insisting on assigning a passenger to a coach or compartment other than the one set aside for the race to which said passenger belongs, shall be liable to a fine of twenty-five dollars, or, in lieu thereof, to imprisonment for a period of not more than twenty days in the parish prison; and should any passenger refuse to occupy the coach or compartment to which he or she is assigned by the officer of such railway, said officer shall have power to refuse to carry such passenger on his train, and, for such refusal, neither he nor the railway company which he represents shall be liable for damages in any of the courts of this State."

The information filed in the criminal District Court charged, in substance, that Plessy, being a passenger between two stations within the State of Louisiana, was assigned by officers of the company to the coach used for the race to which he belonged, but he insisted upon going into a coach used by the race to which he did not belong. Neither in the information nor plea was his particular race or color averred.

The constitutionality of this act is attacked upon the ground that it conflicts both with the Thirteenth Amendment of the Constitution, abolishing slavery, and the Fourteenth Amendment, which prohibits certain restrictive legislation on the part of the States.

1. That it does not conflict with the Thirteenth Amendment, which abolishes slavery and involuntary servitude, except as a punishment for crime, is too clear for argument...

A statute which implies merely a legal distinction between the white and colored races -- a distinction which is founded in the color of the two races, and which must always exist so long as white men are distinguished from the other race by color -- has no tendency to destroy the legal equality of the two races, or reestablish a state of involuntary servitude. Indeed, we do not understand that the Thirteenth Amendment is strenuously relied upon by the plaintiff in error in this connection.

2. By the Fourteenth Amendment, all persons born or naturalized in the United States, and subject to the jurisdiction thereof, are made citizens of the United States,

and of the State wherein they reside; and the States
are forbidden from making or enforcing any law which
shall abridge the privileges or immunities of citizens
of the United States, or shall deprive any person of
life, liberty, or property without due process of law,
or deny to any person within their jurisdiction the
equal protection of the laws.

The object of the amendment was undoubtedly to enforce the
absolute equality of the two races before the law, but,
in the nature of things, it could not have been intended
to abolish distinctions based upon color, or to enforce
social, as distinguished from political, equality, or a
commingling of the two races upon terms unsatisfactory
to either. Laws permitting, and even requiring their
separation in places where they are liable to be brought
into contact, do not necessarily imply the inferiority
of either race to the other, and have been generally,
if not universally, recognized as within the competency
of the State legislatures in the exercise of their pol-
ice power. The most common instance of this is
connected with the establishment of separate schools
for white and colored children, which has been held to
be a valid exercise of the legislative power, even by
courts of States where the political rights of the
colored race have been longest and most earnestly enforced.

One of the earliest of these cases is that of <u>Roberts
vs. City of Boston</u>. 5 Cush. 198, in which the Supreme
Judicial Court of Mass. held that the general school
committee of Boston had power to make provision for the
instruction of colored children in separate schools
established exclusively for them, and to prohibit their
attendance upon the other schools. "The great principle," said Chief Justice Shaw, p.206, "advanced by
the learned and eloquent advocate for the plaintiff"
(Mr. Charles Sumner), "is, that by the Constitution
and laws of Massachusetts, all persons, without distinction of age or sex, birth or color, origin or
condition, are equal before the law...But, when this
great principle comes to be applied to the actual and

various conditions of persons in society, it will not warrant the assertion that men and women are legally clothed with the same civil and political powers, and that children and adults are legally to have the same functions and be subject to the same treatment; but only that the rights of all, as they are settled and regulated by law, are equally entitled to the paternal consideration and protection of the law for their maintenance and security." It was held that the powers of the committee extended to the establishment of separate schools for children of different ages, sexes, and colors, and that they might also establish special schools for poor and neglected children, who have become too old to attend the primary school, and yet have not acquired the rudiments of learning, to enable them to enter the ordinary schools. Similar laws have been enacted by Congress under its general power of legislation over the District of Columbia, Rev. Stat. D.C., paragraphs 281, 282, 283, 310, 319, as well as by the legislatures of many of the States, and have been generally, if not uniformly, sustained by the courts. State vs. McCann, 21 Ohio St. 198; Lehew vs. Drummall, 15 S. W. Rep. 765; Ward vs. Flood, 48 California, 36; Bartonneau v. School Directors, 3 Woods, 177; People v. Gallagher, 93 N. Y. 438; Cory v. Carter, 48 Indiana, 327; Dawson v. Lee, 83 Kentucky, 49.

So far, then, as a conflict with the Fourteenth Amendment is concerned, the case reduces itself to the question whether the statute of Louisiana is a reasonable regulation, and with respect to this there must necessarily be a large discretion on the part of the legislature. In determining the question of reasonableness, it is at liberty to act with references to the established usages, customs, and traditions of the people, and with a view to the promotion of their comfort, and the preservation of the public peace and good order. Gauged by this standard, we cannot say that a law which authorizes or even requires the separation of the two races in public conveyances is unreasonable, or more obnoxious to the Fourteenth Amendment than the acts of Congress requiring separate schools for colored children in the District of Columbia, the constitutionality of which does not seem to have been questioned, or the corresponding acts of State legislatures.

We consider the underlying fallacy of the plaintiff's argument to consist in the assumption that the enforced separation of the two races stamps the colored race with a badge of inferiority. If this be so, it is not by reason of anything found in the act, but solely because the colored race chooses to put that construction upon it. The argument necessarily assumes that if, as has been more than once the case, and is not unlikely to be so again, the colored race should become the dominant power in the State legislature, and should enact a law in precisely similar terms, it would thereby relegate the white race to an inferior position. We imagine that the white race, at least, would not acquiesce in this assumption. The argument also assumes that social prejudices may be overcome by legislation, and that equal rights cannot be secured to the Negro except by an enforced commingling of the two races. We cannot accept this proposition. If the two races are to meet upon terms of social equality, it must be the result of natural affinity, a mutual appreciation of each other's merits, and a voluntary consent of individuals. As was said by the Court of Appeals of New York in People v. Gallagher, 93 N. Y. 438, 448, "this end can neither be accomplished nor promoted by laws which conflict with the general sentiment of the community upon whom they are designed to operate. When the government, therefore, has secured to each of its citizens equal rights before the law and equal opportunities for improvement and progress, it has accomplished the end for which it was organized and performed all the functions respecting social advantages with which it is endowed." Legislation is powerless to eradicate racial instincts or to abolish distinctions based upon physical differences, and the attempt to do so can only result in accentuating the difficulties of the present situation. If the civil and political rights of both races be equal, one cannot be inferior to the other, civilly or politically.

If one race be inferior to the other socially, the Constitution of the United States cannot put them upon the same plane.

It is true that the question of the proportion of colored blood necessary to constitute a colored person, as distinguished from a white person, is one upon which there is a difference of opinion in the different States, some holding that any visible admixture of black blood stamps the person as belonging to the colored race (State v. Chavers, 5 Jones(N. C.), 1, p. 11); others that it depends upon the preponderance of blood (Gray v. State, 4 Ohio, 354; Monroe v. Collins, 17 Ohio St. 665); and still others that the predominance of white blood must only be in the proportion of three fourths (People v. Dean, 14 Michigan, 406; Jones v. Commonwealth, 80 Virginia, 538). But these are questions to be determined under the laws of each State and are not properly put in issue in this case. Under the allegations of his petition, it may undoubtedly become a question of importance whether, under the laws of Louisiana, the petitioner belongs to the white or colored race.

The judgment of the court below is, therefore,

Affirmed

Mr. Justice Harlan dissenting.

Question:

1. Describe the Louisiana statute involved. What did Plessy do?

Question:

2. Plessy forced the Supreme Court to interpret the Fourteenth Amendment. What general principle of interpretation do they enunciate? What two specific examples do they give of applying this principle?

Question:

3. What supporting evidence does the Supreme Court bring for its decision? If it had no such evidence, or if the

evidence were incorrect, would that affect the authority of the decision in any way? Why, or why not? What function does the evidence serve, then?

Question:

4. How do "the established usages, customs, and traditions of the people" relate to the law? Discuss the quotation brought from People v. Gallagher in this regard. Now explain why the Supreme Court did not rule on the proportion of blood which defines a Negro.

Question:

5. The decision is followed by Mr. Justice Harlan's dissent and his reasons for it. What authority does it have in terms of law? Why is it, then, included?

Question:

6. How is this decision enforced? How does it differ in its authority and/or enforcement from a law made by Congress -- if it does? Why?

Question:

7. In this decision, the Constitution of the United States, that of several States, and some State laws are involved. They are put in a hierarchy of authority. Which laws supersede which? Why is such a hierarchy necessary?

Reading: Brown v. Board of Education. Appeal from the U. S. District Court for the District of Kansas. Briggs v. Elliott, Appeal from the U. S. District Court for the Eastern District of South Carolina. Davis v. County School Board, Appeal from the U. S. District Court for the Eastern District of Virginia. Gebhart v. Bolton, Certioriari to the Supreme Court of Delaware.

BROWN V. BOARD OF EDUCATION (1954)

Mr. Chief Justice Warren delivered the opinion of the Court.

128

These cases came to us from the States of Kansas, South Carolina, Virginia, and Delaware. They are premised on different facts and different local conditions, but a common legal question justifies their consideration together in this consolidated opinion.

In each of the cases, minors of the Negro race, through their legal representatives, seek the aid of the courts in obtaining admission to the public schools of their community on a non-segregated basis. In each instance, they had been denied admission to schools attended by white children under laws requiring or permitting segregation according to race. This segregation was alleged to deprive the plaintiffs of the equal protection of the laws under the Fourteenth Amendment. In each of the cases other than the Delaware case, a three-judge federal district court denied relief to the plaintiffs on the so-called "separate but equal" doctrine announced by this Court in Plessy v. Ferguson, 163 U. S. 537. Under that doctrine, equality of treatment is accorded when the races are provided substantially equal facilities, even though these facilities be separate. In the Delaware case, the Supreme Court of Delaware adhered to that doctrine, but ordered that the plaintiffs be admitted to the white schools because of their superiority to the Negro schools.

The plaintiffs contend that segregated public schools are not "equal" and cannot be made "equal," and that hence they are deprived of the equal protection of the laws. Because of the obvious importance of the question presented, the Court took jurisdiction. Argument was heard in the 1952 Term, and reargument was heard this Term on certain questions propounded by the Court.

Reargument was largely devoted to the circumstances surrounding the adoption of the Fourteenth Amendment in 1868. It covered exhaustively consideration of the Amendment in Congress, ratification by the States, then-existing practices in racial segregation, and the views of proponents and opponents of the Amendment. This discussion and our own investigation convince us that, although these sources cast some light, it is not enough to resolve the problem with which we are faced. At best, they are inconclusive. The most avid proponents of the post-War Amendments undoubtedly intended them to remove all legal distinctions known, "all persons born or naturalized in the United States." Their opponents, just as certainly, were antagonistic to both the letter and the spirit of the Amendments and wished them to have the most limited effect. What others in Congress and the State legislatures had in mind cannot be determined with any degree of certainty.

An additional reason for the inconclusive nature of the Amendment's history, with respect to segregated schools, is the status of public education at that time. In the South, the movement toward free common schools, supported by general taxation, had not yet taken hold. Education of white children was largely in the hands of private groups. Education of Negroes was almost nonexistent, and practically all of the race were illiterate. In fact, any education of Negroes was forbidden by the law in some States. Today, in contrast, many Negroes have achieved outstanding success in the arts and sciences as well as in the business and professional world. It is true that public school education at the time of the Amendment had advanced further in the North, but the effect of the Amendment on Northern States was generally ignored in the congressional debates. Even in the North, the conditions of public education did not approximate those existing today. The curriculum was usually rudimentary; ungraded schools were common in rural areas; the school term was but three months a year in many States; and compulsory school attendance was virtually unknown. As a consequence, it is not surprising that there should be so little in the history of the Fourteenth Amendment relating to its intended effect on public education.

In the first cases in this Court construing the Fourteenth Amendment decided shortly after its adoption, the Court interpreted it as proscribing all State-imposed discriminations against the Negro race. The doctrine of "separate but equal" did not make its appearance in this Court until 1896 in the case of Plessy v. Ferguson, supra, involving not education but transportation. American courts have since labored with the doctrine for over half a century. In this Court, there have been six cases involving the "separate but equal" doctrine in the field of public education. In Cumming v. County Board of Education,

175 U. S. 528, and Gong Lum v. Rice, 275 U. S. 78, the validity of the doctrine itself was not challenged. In more recent cases, all on the graduate school level, inequality was found in that specific benefits enjoyed by white students were denied to Negro students of the same educational qualifications. Missouri ex rel. Gaines v. Canada, 305 U. S. 337; Sipual v. Oklahoma, 332 U. S. 631; Sweatt v. Painter, 339 U. S. 629; McLaurin v. Oklahoma State Regents, 339 U. S. 637. In none of these cases was it necessary to re-examine the doctrine to grant relief to the Negro plaintiff. And in Sweatt v. Painter, supra, the Court expressly reserved decision on the question whether Plessy v. Ferguson should be held inapplicable to public education.

In the instant cases, that question is directly presented. Here, unlike Sweatt v. Painter, there are findings below that the Negro and white schools involved have been equalized, or are being equalized, with respect to buildings, curricula, qualifications, and salaries of teachers, and other "tangible" factors. Our decision, therefore, cannot turn on merely a comparison of these tangible factors in the Negro and white schools involved in each of the cases. We must look instead to the effect of segregation itself on public education.

In approaching this problem, we cannot turn the clock back to 1868 when the Amendment was adopted, or even to 1896 when Plessy v. Ferguson was written. We must consider public education in the light of its full development and its present place in American life throughout the nation. Only in this way can it be determined if segregation in public schools deprives these plaintiffs of the equal protection of the laws.

Today, education is perhaps the most important function of State and local governments. Compulsory school attendance laws and the great expenditures for education both demonstrate our recognition of the importance of education to our democratic society. It is required in the performance of our most basic public responsibilities, even service in the armed forces. It is the very foundation of good citizenship. Today it is a principal instrument in awakening the child to cultural values, in preparing him for later professional training, and in helping him to adjust normally to his environment. In these days, it is doubtful that any child may reasonably be expected to succeed in life if he is denied the opportunity of an education. Such an opportunity, where the State has undertaken to provide it, is a right which must be made available to all on equal terms.

We come, then, to the question presented: Does segregation of children in public schools solely on the basis of race, even though the physical facilities and other "tangible" factors may be equal, deprive children of the minority group of equal educational opportunities? We believe that it does.

In <u>Sweatt v. Painter, supra</u>, in finding that a segregated law school for Negroes could not provide them equal educational opportunities, this Court relied in large part on "those qualities which are incapable of objective measurement but which make for greatness in a law school." In <u>McLaurin v. Oklahoma State Regents, supra</u>, the Court, in requiring that a Negro admitted to a white graduate school be treated like all other students, again resorted to intangible considerations: "...his ability to study, to engage in discussions and exchange views with other students, and, in general, to learn his profession." Such considerations apply with added force to children in grade and high schools. To separate them from others of similar age and qualifications solely because of their race generates a feeling of inferiority as to their status in the community that may affect their hearts and minds in a way unlikely ever to be undone. The effect of this separation on their educational opportunities was well stated by a finding in the Kansas case by a court which nevertheless felt compelled to rule against the Negro plaintiffs:

> "Segregation of white and colored children in public schools has a detrimental effect upon the colored children. The impact is greater when it has the sanction of the law; for the policy of separating the races is usually interpreted as denoting the inferiority of the Negro group. A sense of inferiority affects the motivation of a child to learn. Segregation with the sanction of law, therefore, has a tendency to (retard) the educational and mental development of Negro children and to deprive them of some of the benefits they

would receive in a racial(ly) integrated school system."

Whatever may have been the extent of psychological knowledge at the time of Plessy v. Ferguson, this finding is amply supported by modern authority. Any language in Plessy v. Ferguson contrary to this finding is rejected.

We conclude that in the field of public education the doctrine of "separate but equal" has no place. Separate educational facilities are inherently unequal. Therefore, we hold that the plaintiffs and others similarly situated for whom the actions have been brought are, by reason of the segregation complained of, deprived of the equal protection of the laws guaranteed by the Fourteenth Amendment. This disposition makes unnecessary any discussion whether such segregation also violates the Due Process Clause of the Fourteenth Amendment.

Because these are class actions, because of the wide applicability of this decision, and because of the great variety of local conditions, the formulation of decrees in these cases presents problems of considerable complexity. On reargument, the consideration of appropriate relief was necessarily subordinated to the primary question -- the constitutionality of segregation in public education. We have now announced that such segregation is a denial of the equal protection of the laws. In order that we may have the full assistance of the parties in formulating decrees, the cases will be restored to the docket, and the parties are requested to present further argument on Questions 4 and 5 previously propounded by the Court for the reargument this Term. The Attorney General of the United States is again invited to participate. The Attorneys General of the States requiring or permitting segregation in public education will also be permitted to appear as amici curiae upon request to do so by September 15, 1954, and submission of briefs by October 1, 1954.

It is so ordered.

Question:

8. What legal doctrine is referred to? Where does it come from? Is it a law or an interpretation of a law? Is the

plaintiffs' claim, then, that the Fourteenth Amendment is unconstitutional or that a previous interpretation of it is bad? Which is easier to change? Why?

Question:

9. In interpreting the Fourteenth Amendment, what source of information did the Supreme Court first try to use? Why did they find it uninformative? How did they know this information?

Question:

10. Why did the Supreme Court mention previous cases? Why is it concerned to differentiate the question at issue now from the questions at issue in the previous cases?

Question:

11. Note carefully the paragraph beginning "In approaching this problem..." What has changed since Plessy v. Ferguson -- the empirical (social) situation, or the legal principles? Why does this change make a difference? If this distinction carries over into Jewish law (and it does, to a surprising degree), what would constitute a good reason for changing a legal practice? (You will see an example of this in Chapter 16.)

Question:

12. The change noted in question 11 leads to a change in the "separate but equal" doctrine. But note carefully: is this a Constitutional principle? Where did it come from? What has not changed, even after the Brown decision?

Chapter 14

Subsequent Developments on Segregation

Reading: Congressional Record, July 2, 1964, House of Representatives -- CIVIL RIGHTS ACT OF 1964

MR. MADDEN. Mr. Speaker, by direction of the Committee on Rules, I call up House Resolution 789 and ask for its immediate consideration.

The Clerk read the resolution, as follows:

> Resolved, that immediately upon the adoption of this resolution the bill (H.R.7152) to enforce the constitutional right to vote, to confer jurisdiction upon the district courts of the United States to provide injunctive relief against discrimination in public accommodations, to authorize the Attorney General to institute suits to protect constitutional rights in public facilities and public education, to extend the Commission on Civil Rights, to prevent discrimination in federally assisted programs, to establish a Commission on Equal Employment Opportunity, and for other purposes, with the Senate amendment thereto, be, and the same is hereby taken from the Speaker's table, to the end that the Senate amendment be, and the same is, hereby agreed to.

MR. MADDEN. Mr. Speaker, I yield 30 minutes to the gentleman from Ohio (Mr. Brown).

Civil Rights has been debated in the Congress, pro and con, for weeks, months, and for years. Had the "skim milk" civil rights bill enacted in 1957 dealt with this problem as comprehensively, factually, and completely as the bill now under consideration, we would have been saved from a lot of embarrassing situations like Little Rock, Birmingham, Jacksonville, and so forth. This bill will be effective and amply provides to make all sections of our Constitution a reality to all American citizens.

Presidents and American statesmen for generations knew in their own minds that civil rights legislation for all citizens had to be enacted some day. When this bill is signed into law it will be our first official start to aid in extending voting equality, educational equality, public facilities equality and citizenship equality to all American citizens. The issue we vote upon today has been neglected and postponed by lack of courage on the part of generations of American statesmen and leaders. Presidents Franklin D. Roosevelt, Truman, Eisenhower, Kennedy, and now President Johnson have pressed the Congress for action on effective civil rights legislation for a period covering almost 30 years.

The comment had been made that a precedent was broken when the Rules Committee voted that a committee member in favor of the resolution should present it to the House.

I want it to be understood that the members of the Rules Committee, in my judgment, were displaying no disregard or lack of confidence in the integrity of our chairman. The majority of our members decided that it was time to call a termination to some of the shenanigans and delays to which the progress of this legislation has been a victim.

I personally felt that our good chairman, by reason of his known and admitted intense opposition to this legislation, could not enthusiastically file the report that this resolution be considered and also bring it up on the floor of the House for debate. Possibly he could have accomplished this task, but not with jubilation or enthusiasm and with any hop-skip-and-jump hilarity. I firmly believe that down in his heart, our good chairman was very happy to let the committee confer this task upon somebody who was enthusiastic and in support of this legislation.

The time limit for debate on this resolution is 1 hour. I have extended 30 minutes to the minority member of the Rules Committee, the gentleman from Ohio, Congressman Brown, and 30 minutes at my disposal. I am extending one-half or 15 minutes of my time to the chairman of the Rules Committee, the gentleman from Virginia (Mr. Smith), and he can advise me as to how he wishes it allotted.

The support of the American public opinion is necessary for the success of civil rights legislation. Progress in the first months, and possibly first few years, of this legislation will determine its effectiveness. It is my earnest hope that some members long experienced in legislative processes over the years will devote their time to meeting with and extending advice and counsel to the leaders of well-meaning civil rights organizations and groups on how to best secure and maintain public opinion and support on this important task to secure civil rights equality for all citizens.

It is my thought that the leaders of the Congress primarily responsible for the passage of this legislation, to wit: Speaker McCormack, Congressmen Halleck, Albert, Celler, McCulloch; Senators Dirksen, Mansfield, Humphrey, and Kuchel, would be glad to sit and confer with leaders of any civil rights organizations and groups who have been active in bringing about this legislation and in civil rights activities. The exchange of thoughts and recommendations at a meeting, or meetings, with these legislative leaders might be the determining factor on the immediate success or failure of this great legislative adventure, which is admittedly difficult, and all advice and suggestions possible are needed for its success.

In conclusion, let me say that President Johnson last week gave this important message on civil rights:

> We are going on from this civil rights bill to give every American citizen, of every race and color, the equal rights which the Constitution commands and justice directs. This will not be a simple task. No law can instantly destroy the differences shaped over centuries. And there is a law more hallowed than the civil rights bill, or even the Constitution of the United States. That law commands every man to respect the life and dignity of his neighbor -- to treat others as he would be treated. That law asks not only obedience in our action, but understanding in our heart. May God grant us that understanding.

Question:

1. What, according to Mr. Madden, is this bill supposed to do that the 1957 bill failed to do? What, then, is the relationship of this bill to the Constitution? What do you think will be the corresponding feature in Jewish law?

Question:

2. What effect is the mentioning of Presidents Roosevelt, Truman, Eisenhower, and Kennedy supposed to have? Can you think of a parallel in Jewish law?

Question:

3. Why is Mr. Madden concerned to justify the fact that he is presenting the bill to the House, and not the chairman of the Rules Committee. Give other examples of precedents and rules of procedure in the reading. Why are such rules necessary?

Question:

4. "The support of the American public opinion is necessary for the success of civil rights legislation." Why? What about other kinds of legislation? (Hint: Consider what would happen if such support were lacking.) Does law ever serve an educative function, contrary to public opinion? (Consider the South's reaction to this bill, or decrees of benevolent dictators contrary to general practice, but also note President Johnson's remark that "No law can instantly destroy the differences shaped over centuries.") To sum up, then, what is the relationship of the law to those for whom it is made?

Question:

5. Mr. Madden notes that the Chairman of the Rules Committee is against the bill. How did that affect discussion of the bill? Is opinion contrary to the Speaker's stifled? What is the relationship of Representatives who have opposing views? Check these features when we discuss the President of the Sanhedrin and the Rabbis.

Question:

6. Note that Mr. Madden is careful to note the names of the people chiefly responsible for the bill. Why? The same feature occurs in Jewish law, but for a different reason: note it carefully when we get to Unit V.

Reading:

MR. MADDEN. Mr. Speaker, I yield 6 minutes to the gentleman from Virginia (Mr. Smith).

MR. SMITH of Virginia. Mr. Speaker, I ask unanimous consent to revise and extend my remarks and include certain extraneous matter. Mr. Speaker, under the exercise of raw, brutal power of the majority of both the Democrats and Republicans, the opponents of the civil rights bill on this side are given only 15 minutes to debate a bill that has never been before the Judiciary Committee of the House or before the House itself before today. This is not the bill the House passed. It is the substitute bill of the Senate with some 80-odd new and different provisions. Under the rule, there is no opportunity for the House to consider or amend the Senate bill. When the roll is called, you will vote this monstrous invasion of the civil and constitutional rights of all the 180 million people of this country into the law of the land. It will contain implements of oppression upon the people of this country unmatched in harshness and brutality and raw dictatorship never before witnessed since the tragic days of reconstruction following the War between the States.

The history of this legislation is one of heedless trampling upon the rights of American citizens from the time the first bill was introduced, marching ruthlessly through the Judiciary Committee with every opportunity denied to members to either discuss the measure or offer amendments. You will recall that the only committee hearings held upon the bill upon which the House voted were those which I insisted upon in the Rules Committee, over strenuous opposition, at which hearing only members of the Congress were permitted to be heard.

You have sowed the wind. Now an oppressed people are to reap the whirlwind. King, Martin Luther, not satisfied with what will then be the law of the land, has announced his purpose, with the backing of the executive department, to begin a series of demonstrations inevitably to be accompanied by mob violence, strife, bitterness, and bloodshed. Already the second invasion of carpetbaggers of the Southland has begun. Hordes of beatniks, misfits, and agitators from the North, with the admitted aid of the Communists, are streaming into the Southland on mischief bent, backed and defended by other hordes of federal marshals, federal agents, and federal power.

Be forewarned that the agents and leaders of the NAACP can never permit this law to be gradually and peacefully accepted because that means an end to their well-paid activities. Let us still hope for a peaceful and gradual solution of this problem that has brought this country, north, east, west, and south, closer to disaster than anything that has confronted us in the past 100 years. With all allowable disrespect to the Supreme Court of the United States, may I still be permitted in this hall to utter the pious and prayerful words, "God save the United States of America."

Mr. Speaker, I include with my remarks the following newspaper articles:

Point of View: Civil Rights in History

President Johnson vetoed the civil rights bill. In his veto message to Congress, he spoke his mind:

"In all our history no such system as that contemplated by the details of this bill has ever before been proposed or adopted. They establish for the security of the colored race safeguards which go infinitely beyond any that the general government has ever provided for the white race. In fact, the distinction of race and color is, by the bill, made to operate in favor of the colored and against the white race. They interfere with the municipal regulations of the States, with the relations existing exclusively between a State and its citizens, or between inhabitants of the same State -- an absorption and assumption of power by the general government which, if acquiesced in, must sap and destroy our federative system of limited powers, and break down the barriers which preserve the rights of the States. It is another step, or rather, stride, to centralization and the concentration of all legislative power in the national government."

Does this sound like Lyndon Johnson? Well, no. This commentator is quoting, of course, the words of President Andrew Johnson, with reference to the civil rights bill of 1866. But they seem apropos.

Question:

7. Contrary opinion is tolerated, but what is not tolerated? Why? Why, then, is contrary opinion tolerated?

Question:

8. Give examples of humor in the discussion of the law.

Reading:

MR. MADDEN. Mr. Speaker, I yield 6 minutes to the chairman of the Committee on the Judiciary, the gentleman from New York (Mr. Celler), to close debate.

MR. CELLER. Mr. Speaker and members of the House, it is my fervent hope that all of the United States shall unite and work with patience and with harmony to achieve the objectives of this legislation. Let all of us of all regions, of all faiths, of all races, move forward together to redeem the American pledge of equality of opportunity for all. No exhortation of mine should be necessary to bring this performance to a close. Further delay, I will say, would be fatal.

Cervantes once said, "By the street of by and by you reach the house of never."

MR. CORMAN. Mr. Speaker, will the gentleman yield?

MR. CELLER. I yield to the gentleman from California.

MR. CORMAN. I would like to ask my chairman, what is the meaning of "pattern or practice" as it is used to limit the Attorney General's power to initiate suit under titles II and VII?

MR. CELLER. A pattern or practice of resistance would exist, for example, where there is discrimination by several concerns in the same industry or line of business, where a chain of motels or restaurants discriminated in all or part of its branches, or where a single company regularly refused to treat Negroes without discrimination. There would be authority for the Attorney General to sue a single firm for an isolated or sporadic act of discrimination. The words, "resistance to enjoyment of the rights" under the act; that is, engaging in any prohibited discrimination. There is no requirement that the pattern or practice be pursuant to a conspiracy or a concert of action, and the Attorney General is authorized under titles II and VII to join in a single lawsuit all or some of the persons or companies whose conduct amounts to a pattern or practice, whether or not joinder would otherwise be appropriate.

MR. SPEAKER. I shall outline the substance of changes made by the Senate to the House version of H.R. 7152.

TITLE IV (DISCRIMINATION UNDER PUBLIC EDUCATION)

HOUSE

Title IV of the House bill authorizes the Attorney General to initiate and intervene in public school desegregation cases where students or parents are unable to institute and maintain legal proceedings. It provides for federal technical and financial assistance when requested by school boards and communities to assist in the desegregation of their schools.

SENATE

The Senate amendment proposes several language changes to clarify the intent of this title. It provides that the Attorney General must receive a complaint that is meritorious prior to initiating action. The Attorney General must give notice to a complaint to the appropriate school board or college authority and give them a reasonable time to correct the situation. It deletes authorization for dependents' allowances when school personnel attend special training sessions. A new section 410 states that nothing in this title is intended to prohibit classification and assignment of school children for reasons other than race, color, religion, or national origin.

Mr. Speaker, I hope that we will have an overwhelming vote for this bill; that that vote will reverberate throughout the length and breadth of the land so that it can be said that Congress hearkens unto the voice of Leviticus, "proclaiming liberty throughout the land to all the inhabitants thereof."

THE SPEAKER. The time of the gentleman from New York (Mr. Celler) has expired. All time has expired.

MR. MADDEN. Mr. Speaker, I move the previous question on the resolution.

The previous question was ordered.

THE SPEAKER. The question is on the resolution.

MR. SMITH OF VIRGINIA. Mr. Speaker, on that I demand the yeas and nays.

The yeas and nays were ordered. The question was taken; and there were -- yeas, 289; nays, 126; answered "present," 1; not voting, 15, as follows: (Roll No. 179)...

So the resolution was agreed to.

Question:

9. Give examples of the use of general literature in the discussion. Why is it used?

10. What is Mr. Corman's question? This question is very common in the Talmud, although the answers are not always as readily available. Why is it important to know this?

Question:

11. The new Senate version has a few "language changes." Why are these important? Try to describe why these would have even greater importance with reference to Talmudic law.

Reading: Congressional Record, July 2, 1964, Senate

MESSAGE FROM THE HOUSE

A message from the House of Representatives, by Mr. Hackney, one of its reading clerks, announced that the House had agreed to the amendment of the Senate to the bill (H.R. 7152) to enforce the constitutional right to vote, to confer jurisdiction upon the district courts of the United States to prove injunctive relief against discrimination in public facilities and public education, to extend the Commission on Civil Rights, to prevent discrimination in federally assisted programs, to establish a Commission on Equal Employment Opportunity, and for other purposes.

CIVIL RIGHTS -- ENROLLED BILL SIGNED

The message also announced that the Speaker had affixed his signature to the enrolled bill (H.R. 7152) to enforce the constitutional right to vote, to confer jurisdiction upon district courts of the United States to provide injunctive relief against discrimination in public accommodations, to authorize the Attorney General to institute suits to protect constitutional rights in public facilities and public education, to extend the Commission on Civil Rights, to prevent discrimination in federally assisted programs, to establish a Commission on Equal Employment Opportunity, and for other purposes, and it was signed by the President pro tempore.

Question:

12. How does the Senate learn of the House's action on the bill? How, do you imagine, did the schools of Babylonia learn of the legal discussions in Israel, and vice versa? Why is such information important?

Question:

13. The <u>Record</u> repeats the content of the bill several times. Why? Does this become more or less important if the decisions are kept only in oral form?

Reading: <u>CIVIL RIGHTS ACT (H.R. 7152) -- TITLE IV</u>

S 401 <u>Definitions</u>
As used in this subchapter:

(A) "Commissioner" means the Commissioner of Education.

(B) "Desegregation" means the assignment of students to public schools and within such schools without regard to their race, color, religion, or national origin, but "desegregation" shall not mean the assignment of students to public schools in order to overcome racial imbalance.

(C) "Public school" means any elementary or secondary educational institution, and "public college" means any institution of higher education or any technical or vocational school above the secondary school level, provided that such public school or public college is operated by a State, subdivision of a State, or governmental agency within a State, or operated by a State wholly or predominantly from or through the use of governmental funds or property, or funds or property derived from a governmental source.

(D) "School board" means any agency or agencies which administer a system of one or more public schools and any other agency which is responsible for the assignment of students to or within such system.

S 402 <u>Survey and Report of Educational Opportunities</u>

The Commissioner shall conduct a survey and make a report to the President and the Congress, within two years of July 2, 1964, concerning the lack of availability of equal educational opportunities for individuals by reason of race, color, religion, or natural origin in public educational institutions at all levels in the United States, its territories and possessions, and the District of Columbia.

S 403 <u>Technical Assistance in Preparation, Adoption, and Implementation of Plans for Desegregation of Public Schools</u>

The Commissioner is authorized, upon the application of any school board, State, municipality, school district, or other governmental unit legally responsible for operating a public school or schools, to render technical assistance to such applicant in the preparation, adoption, and implementation of plans for the desegregation of public schools. Such technical assistance may, among other activities, include making available to such agencies information regarding effective methods of coping with special educational problems occasioned by desegregation, and making available to such agencies personnel of the Office of Education or other persons specially equipped to advise and assist them in coping with such problems.

S 408 <u>Liability of United States for Costs</u>

In any action or proceeding under this subchapter the United States shall be liable for costs, the same as a private person.

S 409 <u>Personal Suits for Relief Against Discrimination in Public Education</u>

Nothing in this subchapter shall affect adversely the right of any person to sue for or obtain relief in any court against discrimination in public education.

S 410 <u>Classification and Assignment</u>

Nothing in this subchapter shall prohibit classification and assignment for reasons other than race, color, religion, or national origin.

Question:

14. In the statement of the law, does the vote appear? Do the reasons for it appear? The reasons against it? The general literature and jokes that we found in The Congressional Record? The names of the proponents of the law? The institution in whose name the law is being made? (Be careful!) What does appear? How, then, does a law code differ from accounts of the reasons, positions, and personalities behind the laws? What is the relationship between the two? Which has final legal authority? What, then, is the value of the other? (Hint: Consider the evidence that the Supreme Court first tried to use in the Brown case.)

UNIT V

THE PROCESS OF JEWISH LAW

Chapter 15

Historical Survey

Having established the uniqueness and importance of Jewish values and the need for embodying them in law in order to attain them, we are now going to confront the massive body of Jewish Law that we have found to be necessary. In this unit we are simply going to take a brief look at how Jewish law developed, continuing to use our example of Shabbat, and in the following Unit we will discuss the three modern reactions to this body of Law by the Orthodox, Reform, and Conservative Movements.

You should not expect this chapter to challenge your mental powers as much as the previous readings did or the following readings will; it is primarily historical in nature. But we cannot talk sensibly <u>about</u> Jewish Law if we have no acquaintance with the subject about which we are talking! In other words, this chapter represents a bit of the less glamorous, but absolutely essential, work that real scholarship requires. So master it well.

Reading: <u>The World of the Talmud</u> by Morris Adler

At the center of Judaism is the tradition or, if you will, a Book; in Christianity, it is the figure of a man. A Christian scholar suggested this significant difference when he wrote, "Pharisaism is a religion of ideals, Christianity of an ideal person." If we substitute for the word "Pharisaism" the more inclusive term "Judaism," it stands as an essentially true description of a basic contrast.

This fundamental diversity between the two faiths helps explain the different paths each faith followed in its development. The centrality of the Book in Judaism gave rise to the formation of the vast literature which grew up about the Bible and of which the Talmud is the most important example.

On the return from the Babylonian exile in the middle of the fifth century B.C.E., Ezra and his associates consciously elevated the Torah to primacy in the economy of the Jewish life they hopefully desired to reestablish.

They did not stumble upon such an emphasis accidentally. It was implicit in the nature of the tradition almost from the onset. It is to Ezra's enduring credit that he recognized this in-dwelling characteristic of his people's faith and that he set about with determination to make the Book the foundation of the community's life and the chart of individual behavior. "For Ezra had set his heart to seek the law of the Lord, and to do it, and to teach in Israel statutes and ordinances" (Ezra 7:10). In this verse from Ezra, the Hebrew word here translated "to seek" is "lidrosh" which may also be rendered "to interpret." It suggests the method by which the Torah was to be made a functioning force relevant and applicable in the midst of the changes to which men are subject. The Torah was to be enlarged by interpretation, and the Hebrew word for this process is derived from the root of the word Ezra employed. The process is "Midrash" -- interpretation.

A group of teachers arose to teach and interpret the law. This new class of Interpreters and Expounders was known as Soferim, generally translated as Scribes. The term Scribes has become a judgment word and is heavily freighted with negative evaluations. In the New Testament it appears by the side of the word "hypocrites," and reiteration for many centuries has made them all but synonyms in many minds. Hebrew scholars, however, point out that a more correct rendition of the title "Soferim" by which these teachers became known is "Bookmen" or "Men of the Book," rather than Scribes.

A great convocation was held and Ezra brought out the Torah before the assembled multitude and he read its words before them. The Biblical account of this occasion declares, "and they read in the book, in the law of God, distinctly and they gave the sense and caused them to understand the reading" (Nehemiah 8:8).

The first task of the Men of the Book was to make its words known. They sought to teach its contents to the people. They wished to have it serve as the textbook of the community. But their aspirations went far beyond that. The Book might have been accepted as a classic: its words entering popular speech; its poetry embellishing the rhetoric of speaker and writer, and nothing more. Their purpose, however, was to make of the Book the primary guide to action and belief; its words and teachings the motivation of good attitudes and habit, the inspiration to good life and noble character. They strove for nothing less than that the book function as the vital and effective central authority in communal and personal life.

In a sense, their aim was revolutionary and precipitated a struggle that was to last for several centuries. If the Book was to be the greatest source of authority, the power of the Temple and its priesthood would inevitably contract. The center of influence would shift from the priestly class that inherited religious position and privilege, to teachers and expounders drawn from all strata of society. Religious knowledge would no longer remain the esoteric possession of a caste -- as it was in all ancient religions -- but become, quite literally, an open book for the entire community. The period of the Soferim heralded a democratic religious and cultural revolution in the life of the Jewish people.

Question:

1. What was Ezra's major contribution? How did his work and the work of the Soferim affect the position and power of the priesthood?

Reading:

When the Men of the Book attempted to translate their intention into reality, they were confronted by difficulties. The Book was regarded as divine in origin and character. It was the record of a historic revelation of God's will and law. Philo was to describe this view centuries later in these words: "The provisions of this law alone, stable, unmoved, unshaken, as it were stamped with the seal of nature itself, remain in fixity from the day they were written until now, and we expect them to abide through all time as immortal, so long as the sun and moon and the whole heaven and the world exist." The Book represented for the Men of the Book no transitory legal system born of the passing conditions of one era, limited in its scope, confined in its authority, standing in constant need of revision and correction. This was not man-made jurisprudence, partial and incomplete, written in terms of the prevailing needs and circumstances, outdated by changing circumstances. This was a final book, all-embracing, adequate for every contingency. No future, however distant and revolutionary, could possibly render it antiquated. The words of a later sage pithily expressed what was in their mind, "Leaf it (the Book) and leaf it yet again, for everything is in it."

This was the conception that governed the Men of the Book, and the premise upon which their approach to the Book was predicated. However, in seeking to effect the transition from the word to the act, the Soferim soon found themselves confronted by palpable difficulties. The content of the Book did not always lend itself to ready implementation. Divine in origin and character, it was nonetheless obscure in some places. Its words did not always yield clear directions as to conduct. There were passages of uncertain intent and words whose connotation was not known. Frequently a law or institution was cited in so general a way that the lack of the detailed prescription did not indicate the procedure to be followed in its observance. Some laws were rehearsed several times in the Bible and the reason for the repetition was unexplained in the text. Nor was the Book entirely free from apparent contradictions.

In a divine book, these obscurities and difficulties could not be attributed to lapses by the author. They could be explained only as resulting from insufficient study and inadequate comprehension on the part of its mortal readers. Even as nature, fashioned by the same hand that wrote the Book, does not reveal at first glance the laws by which it functions, the Book does not yield its full meaning at first reading. The intent, hidden beneath surface discrepancies and perplexities, will be brought to light through exploration, patient study, diligent and dedicated probing. Its implementation depended upon the determination of its meaning through proper interpretation. This method, to which allusion has already been made, was called Midrash -- the seeking out, through interpretation, of the actual intent of the Biblical doctrine and statute. Indeed, the Men of the Book did not feel that they were originating this method of exploration. Since the Torah was a law of life whose words were meant to be translated into belief and action, many supplementary, oral interpretations were said to have been transmitted to Moses simultaneously with the written text. From the outset, the Book was fringed by supplement and commentary. The Torah could be understood and practiced only in terms of its doctrines and narrations. The Men of the Book and their successors did not believe that they were adding to the text but that they were educing from and reading out of the Bible the meanings which, from the very beginning, had been enclosed within it. And at no time were they reading into the text what was not meant to be there. There were signs all through the Torah by which its intention could be established. There were rules of interpretation which, if followed, would help students elicit from the text its true purport wherever the words themselves were unclear. Theirs was a work of discovery, not of innovation. They saw themselves, where the Torah was concerned, as interpreters, not legislators.

The Men of the Book had a good reason for their belief that the Written Law of Moses was supplemented by oral explanation from the outset. Already in their observances, customs were in vogue among Jews for which the Torah, literally understood, offered no warrant. There also was a popular lore which was obviously an extension of the narratives of the Bible. Only through oral interpretation could the Torah become operative in every phase of the life of the community. To develop the interpretation adequate to this purpose was the function of the Men of the Book...

The inevitability of a commentary or an extension of the written text is probably best illustrated by the laws governing the Sabbath. In unmistakable language the Israelites are enjoined from labor on the Sabbath. Its sanctity is related to the very creation of the world, "And

God blessed the seventh day, and hallowed it; because in it He rested from all His work which God in creating had made" (Genesis 2:3). In the Ten Commandments the seventh day is explicitly ordained as a day of rest. Indeed, Scripture ordains capital punishment for a violation of the prohibition to work on the Sabbath: "Six days shall work be done, but on the seventh day there shall be to you a holy day, a Sabbath of solemn rest to the Lord; whosoever doeth any work therein shall be put to death" (Exodus 35:2). Yet there is no enumeration of the forbidden types of labor. What constitutes work is a question crucial to the institution of the Sabbath, yet no answer is provided. The kindling of fire is prohibited (Exodus 35:3). Work was forbidden even during the season of plowing and harvesting (Exodus 34:21). The cryptic injunction, "Let no man go out of his place on the seventh day"(Exodus 16:29) is another specific instance of the general principle establishing the Sabbath as a day of rest. These few particular definitions of labor on the Sabbath were not meant to exhaust the list of forbidden work. The admonition to refrain from work is so strongly worded, and the reference to it so recurring and emphatic, that it becomes clear that the Sabbath was meant to be marked by a more complete cessation of work than the few and meagre specific designations would indicate. Somewhere in the Scripture there must be a guide to its intent with regard to Sabbath rest. Indeed, even before the days of the Men of the Book, other types of work were traditionally classified as forbidden, despite the absence of clear instruction in the Torah. The prophet Isaiah admonishes the people that doing business on the Sabbath, or indeed, even talking about it, constitutes a desecration (Isaiah 58:13). Jeremiah censures those who bear burdens on the day of rest (Jeremiah 17:21). Amos indicates that trading on the Sabbath is not permitted (Amos 8:5). As Moore points out: "These are plainly only casual instances of a much more comprehensive customary law, which was probably extended in the course of time to meet changing conditions." The Written Law, it was believed, was meant to be understood in the context of an oral commentary which accompanied it.

The shapers of the Oral Law found authorization for their activity of interpretation and elucidation in the Sacred Writ itself. The reasoning of the Rabbis is illustrated by the following example. The Bible declares: "If there arise a matter too hard for thee in judgment, between blood and blood, between plea and plea, and between stroke and stroke, even matters of controversy within thy gates; then shalt thou arise, and get thee up unto the place which the Lord thy God shall choose. And thou shalt come unto the priests and Levites, and unto the judge that shall be in those days; and thou shalt inquire; and they shall declare unto thee the sentence of judgment" (Deuteronomy 17:8,9). The Rabbis pointedly comment on the phrase: "That shall be in those days." They ask: "Could we have possibly thought that one would go to a judge other than in one's day?" The meaning is that one should have recourse to the judges of one's own time and accept their judgment, and thus fulfill the verse in Ecclesiastes which declares: "Say not how was it that the former days were better than these." On the same page of the Talmud they declare that the humblest and most ungifted judge is to be regarded in his age as Moses or Aaron or Samuel were in theirs.

This process was not a deliberately planned one, nor was it as consciously pursued as our description might suggest. The Men of the Book and those who followed them felt that in studying and re-examining the Book they would find in the text itself the answers to their needs. The divine Book, they believed, was and always will remain the source of instruction and guidance in all circumstances to the end of time...

Question:

2. Describe carefully the theory underlying the Oral Law. What features of the Written Law made this theory necessary? What section in the Written Law made this theory possible?

Reading:

The Oral Law continued to grow rapidly. Each generation multiplied accretions to the expanding body of law, lore, and doctrine. At the end of the second century C.E., Rabbi Judah Ha-Nasi (the Patriarch) assembled and edited a compilation of Oral Law, known as Mishna, meaning "study." It gained immediate acceptance as the authoritative work in the field of interpreting and amplifying the contents of Scripture, including, as well, Rabbinic enactments which particular circumstances required and which did not enjoy the ultimate authority of laws derived from interpretations of the Bible. Nowhere in the work is Rabbi Judah Ha-Nasi specified as its redactor and compiler. He is, however, universally regarded as the scholar responsible for gathering into a single text the material he believed worthy of preservation. The Mishna has retained a position of authority second only to the Bible itself...

The Mishna, however, is not a code cataloguing laws and practices in dry and precise manner. For it was meant to be more than a guide for the rendering of accepted and authoritative decisions. It was meant, in the words of George Foot Moore, to be "an instrument for the study of Law, an apparatus of instruction." Hence, it embodies not alone decisions but also legal principles, not alone the view of the majority which was to be followed by subsequent sages, but also the minority opinion which, from a strictly practical view, had only academic value. Professor Ginzberg points out that of 523 chapters contained in the Mishna, only six are free from disagreement between the authorities. The text thus provides a basis for study, for an examination of premises and conclusions, and for a comparative study of the differing views which it included. The students were to be stimulated to follow the process of reasoning used by the masters whose views are recorded in the Mishna. It was not desired to make the Mishna a stop-gap to independent thought and analysis, but a stimulant to logical deduction, inference, and analysis. In summary, we may say that the reasons which prompted the gigantic work which the Rabbi undertook in the compilation of the Mishna were four-fold. First, the enormous growth of oral law scattered over so many diverse collections called for a single authoritative text. Second, the desire to provide some measure of uniformity in the interpretation of the law dictated the editing of the Mishna. Third, there was a necessity to provide an organized text to become the basis of instruction in the academies of higher Jewish learning. Finally, there was an apprehension that a recurrence of political disturbance or oppression might endanger the survival of the Oral Law, unless it was preserved in a single authoritative collection. A gap of one generation caused by social upheaval would prove fatal to the preservation and transmission of an oral law unless it were assembled and recorded...

Question:

3. For a long time there was strong opposition to writing down the Oral Law. In view of the functions which the Oral Law was supposed to serve, why was there this opposition to writing it down? (Hint: Explain why Adler says later, "Law, in a sense, freezes life at the instant of legislation.") What new factors prompted the compilation of the Mishna and its reduction to writing? Who did this? When?

Reading:

The word Mishna stems from a Hebrew root meaning "to learn" as a derivative of the primary meaning, "to repeat," "to rehearse." Learning is achieved by a tireless process of reiteration, re-examination, and recapitulation. When the term Mishna is used without any qualifications, it refers to the work edited by Rabbi Judah Ha-Nasi. It may also mean a single paragraph or section of that work, in contrast to "Mikra" which refers to a single verse in Scripture. The designation Mishna may likewise be applied to any of the collection of earlier teachers. Thus we may speak of the Mishna of Rabbi Akiba or the Mishna of Rabbi Meir. It means the content of the teaching contained in these collections as well as the method followed. For there is an important difference between the approach of the Mishna and that associated with the other type of Rabbinic literature known as Midrash. The latter attaches its elaborations and comments to a verse of Scripture. The verse is always cited and serves as the starting point for the extended meanings which the Oral Law wove about the specific Scriptural statements....The Mishna, however, becomes, so to speak, physically independent of the text of the Bible, though in spirit and content it remains, to be sure, bound to and based upon the Torah. A verse of the Bible may be cited as proof, but a Rabbinic law becomes a "Halacha" with an identity of its own, distinct from the verse. We have interpretation of the subject in the spirit of the Torah and with full acceptance of the supreme authority of the Torah, but not necessarily associated with a specific Scriptural verse or passage. The Mishna is not a running commentary. It is a distinct structure of law and lore, rising upon the foundation of Torah but operating within the orbit of its own rules of interpretation, inference, and deduction. While subordinate to Scripture in authority, it is a complementary legal code, with a measure of autonomy in its own right...

The separation of the Oral Law from a necessary and direct dependence upon the actual text of Scripture permitted its development as a separate and distinct entity. We have seen that the earliest teachers of the Oral Law were known as Soferim, Men of the Book. The sages of the Mishna are called Tannaim (singular Tanna), "repeaters," "students," and "teachers." The language of the Mishna is Hebrew, though linguistic elements from Aramaic, Greek, and Latin found their way into Mishnaic Hebrew, and thus testify to a significant interaction between the Jewish and other cultures. The style of the Mishna is compact and without ornamentation. There is an evident striving for clarity and conciseness. The Mishna escapes dryness and rarely deteriorates into unredeemed severity and legal dullness. For one thing, the drama of controversy is present almost throughout the Mishna. The clash of differing opinions and opposing interpretations enlivens even passages dealing with abstruse and technical subjects. For another, the Mishna does not hesitate to venture frequently on excursions into the more attractive fields of narrative, biographical account or reminiscences, homiletical exposition, and ethical and doctrinal discussion...

Question:

4. Distinguish between the methods of the Midrash literature and the Mishna. Then describe the style of the Mishna briefly. (We shall see concrete examples of Mishnayot and Midrashim in the next chapter.)

Reading:

The Mishna is divided into six main divisions called Orders. In Hebrew, these divisions are termed Shisha Sedarim, Six Orders. (The Talmud is therefore often called "Shass," a word composed of the first letter of the words Shisha Sedarim. In many synagogues of Eastern Europe there was, as there still is in some synagogues in America, a Chevra Shass, comprising a group of men who daily studied the text of the Talmud.) It was Rabbi Akiba who developed this arrangement in order to systematize the enormous material of the Oral Law. Each order includes a number of Massechtiyot, or tractates, or volumes. This Hebrew term is derived from a root meaning a weaving, and corresponds to the origin of our word "text" from the stem likewise signifying weaving, as in textile. There are in all 63 tractates. Each tractate is divided into chapters. Each chapter, called a "Perek," is further subdivided into sections called, in the Babylonian Talmud, a "Mishna." (In the Palestinian Talmud, which we shall discuss later, each section is called a "Halacha.") A brief enumeration of the contents of each of the six orders of the Mishna suggests the wide scope of its subject matter.

I. Zeraim (Seeds). The eleven tractates in this division deal with laws of benedictions and prayers, laws pertaining to agriculture and fruits of the field, the Sabbatical year, tithes, and offerings to the priests.

II. Mo'ed (Festivals). This division embraces twelve tractates devoted to the laws of Sabbath (the tractate "Sabbath" is the largest in the Mishna), the High Holy Days, Passover and the Paschal sacrifice, the Temple tax, the festival of Succoth, the Fast Days, Purim, the work that may be done and which is prohibited, the methods of observance, etc.

III. Nashim (Women). In the seven tractates of this order we have discussion centering on marriage, betrothal, divorce, levirate marriage, vows, the trial of the wife suspected of unfaithfulness, etc.

IV. Nezikin (Damages). This order of ten tractates deals with the phases of law that we would include under the terms civil and criminal law. We have here the laws of damages and compensation, property, trade, employer-employee relationships, real estate, inheritance, court procedures, testimony, evidence, punishment for criminal offenses, the administration of oaths, and regulations associated with the idols and pagan practices of neighboring peoples. Nezikin includes also the best known of

the tractates of the Talmud, that of Abot, the
Ethics of the Fathers. This famous volume, frequently incorporated in its entirety in the prayerbook, demonstrates the continuity of the Oral Law
with the Law of Moses, and cites ethical maxims by
many of the teachers of the Mishna.

- V. Kodashim (Sacred Things). The eleven tractates in this division largely treat of the laws related to the Temple and its sacrificial cult. Animal sacrifice, meal offerings, proper method of slaughtering the animals, the first-born of man and animal, pledges and the profanation of sacred things, Temple furnishings and practices, are the chief subjects dealt with in Kodashim.

- VI. Tohorot (Purifications). We have in the twelve tractates of this order a treatment of vessels that are rendered ritually impure, such impurity being caused by the contact with or proximity to a dead body. The order deals with the uncleanness of leprosy, methods of purification, the menstrual impurity of women, and with the impurity of those who are afflicted with unclean issue from their body.

Explicit Scriptural ordinances were not the only source
for the vast legislation that is to be found in the Mishna.
Practices long in vogue, oral traditions, inferences and
deductions from Biblical verses and regulations derived
by a unique system of interpretation, all became part of
the Oral Law, and all were regarded as invested with unquestioned authority...

Question:

5. Name and describe the Shisha Sedarim of the Mishna.

Question:

6. What sources were used to arrive at laws in the Mishna? Why were laws coming from extra-Biblical sources nevertheless regarded as authoritative?

Reading:

Kindred to the Mishna edited by Rabbi Judah Ha-Nasi is a work known as Tosefta. The term means "Supplement" and it includes sections of earlier collections of Oral Law as well as material that did not find its way into the authoritative work of Rabbi Judah. Subsequent additions, originating after the death of the editor of the Mishna, are likewise included in the Tosefta. Like the Mishna, the Tosefta is divided into tractates, though the organization of the subjects varies from that of the primary work. Isolated passages that became disassociated from the collection of which they were part, or somehow survived collections which had been lost and were not ingathered by the Mishna, are known as Baraitot, meaning "external to" or "outside of." They are sometimes cited by later authorities in the discussions which developed about the Mishna. Thus, while Rabbi Judah Ha-Nasi's text did not embrace all the available material, it is the supreme work of the Oral Law, exerting an incalculable influence on its subsequent development.

Question:

7. What is a Tosefta? What is the Tosefta? What is a "Baraita? How do they differ in authority from Mishnayot?

Reading:

We have seen that a significant portion of the Mishna was no longer applicable to existing conditions by the time its compilation had been completed. Yet the problem in law is not with its patently obsolete parts, but with its apparently operative sections. Law, in a sense, freezes life at the instant of legislation. But life goes on. New situations arise which are not provided for in the code if its literal meaning alone is invoked. New conditions and experiences bring about a change of view to which the earlier promulgation does not do justice. Hence, Judaism, once again, as in the case of the Mishna, had recourse to its proven and classic method of interpretation. But now it was the Mishna, not the Bible, which became the subject of interpretation and elaboration.

The Mishna was complementary to the Bible. Now an extension of the Mishna was developed. It is called the "Gemara," from an Aramaic root meaning "study" or "instruction." The Gemara is sometimes also called Talmud, although the term Talmud is more generally applied to the entire Oral Law embracing both Mishna and Gemara. The Mishna is several times more voluminous than the Scripture on which it is based. The Gemara which represents the extension of the meaning and application of the Mishna is, in turn, many times larger than the text from which it takes its departure...

The Mishna is concise and not given to lengthy discursive argumentation, though it does record the controversies between various schools and between individual teachers. The Mishna, however, is definitely intent upon brevity. The Gemara, on the other hand, may be described as a full-scale transcript of the give and take of the discussions in the academies. It is alive with debate and the clash of differing opinions. It bristles with challenge and argument. It is prolix and allusive. It reflects the freedom and latitude which oral discussion encourages. It does not hesitate to digress and wander afield when a term, a law, an incident, or a reference to a particular teacher lights up an association with, or stimulates the recollection of, something not related to the main line of the argument. The citation of a verse suggests another and not necessarily relevant interpretation or comment. As in all good conversation, much of the charm and interest derive from the admixture of the incidental, anecdotal, and even fanciful, with the solid core of consistent and informed exposition of a view. A large part of the Gemara is non-legal in character. The broadest definition of the term "law" could not possibly include the range and variety of material found in the Gemara. A wise teacher would interrupt a lengthy and difficult legal argument with a digression of a less taxing and more edifying nature. The sages declare that one should not disdain the parable, though unimportant in itself, since it can be a valuable aid in acquiring understanding of the words of the Torah. They characteristically offer a parable in defense of the parable. They say that it may be likened to a king who has lost a precious pearl and finds it by the light of a candle costing a trifle. Thus we find legend and history, contemporary science and folklore, Biblical exegesis and biography, homily and theology woven together in what, to one unfamiliar with the ways of the academies, would seem to be a curious medley of unorganized data drawn from a baffling number of unrelated categories. The Gemara does, however, return to the original subject, though the digression may spread over several pages. What the argument, by reason of this apparent looseness of method, may seem to lose in directness and cogency, the Talmud gains in breadth and vitality. To pursue the Talmudic treatment of a specific subject, you cannot turn to an index, look up the particular volume in which the subject is discussed, and relax in the assurance that you have exhausted your study. The same subject is dealt with in many places and in several of the sixty-three volumes of the Talmud. One particular tractate may contain the locus classicus of the particular law or decision. Yet, for thoroughness, one would have to examine the other volumes where, though this subject may be introduced only casually or as an excursus in an argument in another theme, the treatment may have serious import for the analysis of the concept, and cannot be ignored.

The free and wide-ranging manner of the Talmud does not detract from the legal and intellectual acumen and profundity of its treatment and analysis. It remains to this day one of the most incisive and penetrating legal systems ever to be formulated. Its apparent discursiveness and its hospitality to the extraneous and incidental enable it to mirror the life of the centuries during which it grew, in an infinitely more comprehensive way than it could have possibly done if it had hewn strictly to a rigid line of legal discussion and interpretation. It is the life of its time, and not only the law that we find in its pages. It is thus not simply a fundamental text for the study of the development of Jewish law, nor only an indispensable source of material for the historian, nor exclusively an invaluable guide in tracing the evolution of Jewish religious concepts and practices. It is all these and more. It is a profoundly significant human document, revealing the variety of universal aspirations, needs, and responses of men, as suggested by this literature, created by a specific society during approximately a half-millenium. The Talmud presents us with no still-life portrait, but with a stream of life, active, restless, vital, within its banks.

Two versions of the Gemara exist -- the Palestinian, also known as the Jerusalem Talmud, and the Babylonian Talmud. Since many of the sages of Babylonia studied in Palestinian academies, and since there were close relations between the two communities, it is not unusual to find the same teachers cited in both versions. Both Talmuds are, of course, based on the same Mishna and differ only in the Gemara. Of the two, the Babylonian is the larger and more fuller in its treatment. It is generally regarded as the more authoritative and has been more widely studied in the academies to this day...

The two academies of Pumbeditha and Sura were the most notable academies, although lesser schools also existed. Here students engaged in intensive study. The interpretations and discussions served to clarify and amplify the text of the Mishna and keep it viable as the basis of legal and religious decisions and enactments. The fifth century witnessed an outbreak of restrictive measures and legislation directed against Jews. The kings, determined to make Zoroastrianism not alone the state religion but also the religion of all of the inhabitants of the empire, pursued a vigorous policy of repression. There took place enforced conversion of Jewish children, the burning of synagogues, and the prohibition of fundamental Jewish observances. Many Jews sought refuge in other lands. The darkening clouds dictated the wisdom of collecting, organizing, and editing the vast material which had been accumulating through several centuries of study and discussion. The pioneer in this herculean task, the scope of which only the most scholarly could estimate, was Rabbi Ashi, who headed the academy of Sura for more than a half-century (375-427 C.E.) His recognized many-branched learning, his spotless character and saintly life, and the prestige he enjoyed superbly qualified him for this massive responsibility. He devoted more than fifty years to the work of assembling and collecting the material. His successors continued the task he had so devotedly undertaken. The final work of editorial selection and revision was done by Rabina, who died in 500 C.E. With Rabina, the Talmudic period comes to a close.

Question:

8. Distinguish between the styles and languages of the Mishna and Gemara.

Question:

9. What is the Talmud? How many are there? Which is more authoritative? Try to guess why. Who are the two men generally regarded as responsible for the compilation of the Babylonian Talmud? When was that completed?

Reading: This Is My God by Herman Wouk

Christianity and Islam rose in the ruins of Rome, and their wars scattered the Jews like leaves. There would be now invasions, now peace; now kind rulers, now tyrants; now tolerance for the Jews, now conversion or death; now a spell of safety, now panic, pillage, and a new mass flight or expulsion. Without the Talmud to give them identity, discipline, and force, it seems hard to believe that the Jews would have gotten through the vast long ordeal.

This disorderly era created two new strata of jurists.

The Reasoners -- the Hebrew term is Savora'im -- were the final editors of the Talmud. They put in order what the Commenters had left to them, looking to the text of the Talmud as the source, rather than to the debates of the schools. The reliability of oral tradition was giving way in the anarchy of the times. Luckily, the Talmud was in hand. There could not be a more authentic Hebrew jurisprudence, descended from Moses to the sinking academies of Babylon, and there preserved in writing. All the care of the Savora'im was to save this legacy.

The Gaonim were university presidents, heads of the two major Babylonian academies. The Jews have never had a papacy, but the nearest thing in moral force in our history was the Gaonate, which lasted from the close of the Talmud to about the year 1000. The decisions of the Gaonim, clarifying and spelling out the Talmud law, shaped the life of the Jewish settlements all through Europe and Asia. The Gaonate came to an end with the disasters that overwhelmed the community in Babylon. After nearly three thousand years, the religion of Abraham at last left its home in the Middle East, not to return until our own lifetimes. The mastery of our learning, with final legal authority, passed westward to Spain and France...

Question:

10. How did the work of the Savora'im differ from that of the Gaonim? When and where did they live?

Reading:

We have come -- in Jewish time -- to the recent past.

It may seem stretching it a bit to include in modern times a period that goes back six hundred years before Shakespeare, five hundred before the discovery of America, two or three hundred before the language in which I am writing this book even existed. But let us see. The United States is 183 years old. Would it be reasonable to call the years since 1914 the recent past? I think so. Applying the same proportions, Jewish history breaks into the recent past around the year 1000, with the coming on stage of the legal lights known as the First Ones -- in Hebrew, the Rishonim.

On the bookshelves opposite my desk stands the great code of Moses ben Maimon of Cordova; five thick volumes bound in dark red, ranged beside the Talmud, as tall if not as broad -- his Strong Hand, or Mishna Torah (Law Review), written toward the end of the twelfth century.

In his work we have left the Orient. We have left the Holy Land and the lively debates of an old people still on their own soil or in neighboring Babylon, turning over memories of their forebears' ways and laws, living out the last flares of nationhood in the manners, speech, and spirit of Semitic countries. We are in Europe. The rational tone, the inquiry after abstract principle, are Greek. The method, the orderly structure, are Roman. Here the two ancient cultures which seemed Judaism's arch-foes, yet, which combined with the Hebrew spirit, made the modern world, flow into Jewish law.

Maimonides was not the first of the First Ones -- their labors had begun two hundred years before him -- but his was the work in which this great change visibly took place. Alfasi of Morocco had prepared a daringly edited Talmud hewing to the law, cutting out half the abstract discussion and all the tales and old science. Rashi had already written his master commentaries. Digests and codes of the common law were appearing. The aim in all these First Ones was the same: to set in order the heaped-up Jewish tradition, by the critical standards of Western intelligence. Maimonides did the job definitively. In him Europe does not conquer Judea, but by altering the measuring rods of the mind, it enters our tradition once for all.

The Rambam opens his effort with a Book of Knowledge, a swift broad look at medieval science. His first pages offer a logical sketch of the nature of God; and we see at once that here is a Talmudist who has mastered Aristotle as well as Scripture. His astronomy is from Ptolemy, and his medicine mainly from Galen and Hippocrates, with some of his own empiric wisdom added. The crucial point to note is the way he begins, the frame in which he finds it necessary to set down his code. The Talmud opened by asking when one recited the Sh'ma in the evening.

Through fourteen books the Rambam rears his structure; a new Talmud put together out of the old; symmetrical, orderly, accessible to the eye. With a flick of pages, the reader can find the answer to any question of law or custom in Judaism. To do this before the Rambam meant a wearying hunt through the forested folios of the Talmud (if one could read the Talmud) and another long search of the Gaonate books to determine the last word in practice. Maimonides did the immense task on every single point of the written and oral law.

The Case Against Maimonides

The Mishna Torah swept the Jewish world the way Rabbi Judah's Mishna had, a millenium earlier. It also stirred up a storm of protest among scholars. An upstart had laid violent hands on the Talmud. He had presumed to decide hard points of doctrine and practice which had left the greatest Gaonim at odds. He had been brazen enough to lay down the law of Judaism without citing his authorities, asking the house of Israel in his boundless conceit to rely on his judgment for accuracy and finality. He had offered himself as the sole conscience and counsellor of a people. He had introduced the ideas and the methods of the idolaters into the sacred precincts of Jewish law. And so on. Some of the most eminent men of his time raised these cries.

What they said was true enough, in a way. All **men** and all writings have their imperfections. Calumny is at its best in poisoned exaggerations of real weaknesses and silence on merits. Maimonides later admitted his regret at not having cited his sources, point by point. His aim had been to reduce controversy by cutting out minority opinions and divisive arguments. He must have assumed that the Mishna Torah would justify itself by its completeness and clarity. Calm reliance on his own strength of mind, absolute confidence in powers equal to the huge task, pervade the pages of the Rambam.

The enemies of Maimonides succeeded in denying him the place he sought in Judaism. Perhaps it would be more accurate to say that his own peculiar distinctions and limits -- turned against him with inflamed energy by his foes -- brought him down. His stated purpose was to give the Jews a codified Talmud, a ready reference book of Hebrew law. His code never quite achieved that place. By a recurring irony of Jewish history, a disciple, not the master, entered the promised land.

Question:

11. How does the Mishna Torah differ from the Talmud? Why is it false to say that it is strictly a book of laws? What forms of Greek influence appear in the Mishna Torah? (Remember the Greek idea of ordering exclusively by subject.) What are the problems with the Mishna Torah?

Reading:

Nobody could have guessed in advance, I think, that this code, of all codes, would be the one to carry the lightnings of Sinai into the twentieth century. To this day, five hundred years after Joseph Caro wrote it, there is no rival in sight. It is the Blackstone of Jewish law.

There it stands, opposite my desk, beside the Rambam, four sections in eight tall volumes -- the Shulkhan Arukh, the Ready Table.

Caro, born some two and a half centuries after the Rambam, was one of his humble armor-bearers; his commentary generally defends Maimonides from the barbs of his enemies. He bore armor, too, for another great code-maker, the Tur, whose popular law digest was the answer of strict tradition to the modernism of the Mishna Torah. Caro's commentary on the Tur's code, the work of a lifetime, was a gigantic display of Jewish legal learning; it is considered by many the most impressive in our literature. Called The House of Joseph, it is much larger than the Tur code itself.

In his old age Caro decided that a brief extract from The House of Joseph might be useful as a reference manual for laymen. He compiled a book which, he said, was so short, simple, and clear that the average layman could run through it once a month and so keep the main heads of Jewish practice in his mind. This was the Shulkhan Arukh -- the work which today occupies every serious Jewish scholar from perhaps his fifteenth year to the grave; which is the backbone of all rabbinic training; which, with its commentaries and the later court decisions, constitutes present-day Jewish law; which the reader is usually appealing to when he consults a rabbi for a ruling.
The unpretentiousness of the Shulkhan Arukh is striking. Where Maimonides opens his code with answers to the most terrible questions of theology, Caro reverts to the old tone of the Talmud and starts by telling what the pious Jew does when he gets up in the morning. So he goes on, point by point, largely following his two masters, Rambam and Tur, but leaving out any philosophizing that does not touch action. Often he uses the language of his masters, word for word, and he takes his structure from the Tur. The Ready Table is no triumph of style like the Mishna Torah. It is curt, choppy, cut to the bone, dry; but plain and understandable as any writing can be, and charged with the authority of total grasp...

My grandfather's personal law library, when he died, ran to some four hundred volumes. I am told by experts that it is a jewel collection of classics. His prized rarities were the decisions and opinions of the most recent stratum of Hebrew jurists, the Later Ones, or Akharonim.

These authorities of the seventeenth to the twentieth century -- men like the Vilna Gaon, Haym Volozin, Akiba Eger, Hazon Ish, Hafetz Haym, and a score of other luminaries -- wrote many of the commentaries which are banked in the great folios of the Shulkhan Arukh. They also published a quantity of important law in separate volumes. These works of the Later Ones usually came out in small editions and soon vanished from the market, in the central law libraries in the yeshivas, or into collections like my grandfather's. It is in these books that a rabbi confronted with a decision today is likely to find the law. These works of the Later Ones presuppose, of course, and stand on, the major codes and the Talmud. But their instances come down to the present time and are diverse enough to touch most of the things that happen in Jewish life.

With the fall of the Jewish State in the year 70, the Mosaic civil and criminal law, by the edict of its own jurists, gave place to the civil and criminal laws of lands where the Jews lived. The law in these lands has for the Jews, under Talmud enactment, the full force of religious law, except when it challenges their right to worship God in their own way. The laws of Moses on the service of God remain binding. There are no sanctions to force compliance. The power of the law of Moses is today, and for many centuries has been, wholly moral; and in this, too, the legislation is unique.

That power, such as it is, has kept in life and identity the people known as the Jews.

Question:

12. Describe the style of the Shulkhan Arukh. How does it differ from the style of the Mishna Torah?

Question:

13. In lands outside of Israel, in what cases must the Jews obey the law of the land? Jewish law? Discuss the problems and advantages with enforcement by moral sanction only. <u>What extra responsibilities does the lack of any but a moral sanction place upon the modern Jew?</u>

Question:

14. Review question. Check to see that you recall some of the chief terms, names, and events in the development of Jewish law by identifying the following, as briefly, but as specifically, as you can:

    a. Ezra
    b. Soferim
    c. Mishna
    d. Rabbi Judah Ha-Nasi
    e. Mikra
    f. Process of Midrash and Rabbinic literature, known as Midrash
    g. Shisha Sedarim (name them, too)
    h. Massechet
    i. Perek
    j. Baraita
    k. Tosefta
    l. Gemora
    m. Talmud
    n. Pumbeditha and Sura
    o. Rabina and Rav Ashi
    p. Savoraim
    q. Gaonim
    r. Rishonim
    s. Moses ben Maimon
    t. Mishna Torah
    u. Rambam
    v. Tur
    w. Joseph Caro
    x. Shulkhan Arukh
    y. The House of Joseph
    z. Akhronim (name some)

Note: In preparation for the next chapter, note one other fact that has not been covered in this chapter. There are two types of Midrash: <u>Midrash Halacha</u> (interpretations of the legal sections of the Bible), and <u>Midrash Aggada</u> (interpretations based on Biblical verses which are not laws). Further, there are three books of <u>Midrash Halacha</u> which have reached us virtually in full: the <u>Mekhilta</u> (interpretations based on the laws in Exodus), the <u>Sifra</u> (interpretations of the laws of Leviticus), and the <u>Sifre</u> (interpretations of the laws in Numbers and Deuteronomy). We shall be studying selections from the <u>Mekhilta</u>.

Chapter 16

Illustrations of the Major Stages of Development in Jewish Law

A. The Bible and Midrash Halacha

Reading: Exodus 12:14-17

This day shall be to you one of remembrance: you shall celebrate it as a festival to the Lord throughout the generations; you shall celebrate it as an institution for all time. Seven days you shall eat unleavened bread; on the very first day you shall remove leaven from your houses, for whoever eats leavened bread from the first day to the seventh day, that person shall be cut off from Israel.

On the first day you shall hold a sacred convocation, and on the seventh day a sacred convocation; no work at all shall be done on them; only what every person is to eat, that alone may be prepared for you. You shall observe the (Feast of) Unleavened Bread, for on this very day I brought your ranks out of the land of Egypt; you shall observe this day throughout the generations as an institution for all time.

Question:

1. This Biblical quotation comes from the description of the Exodus from Egypt, in which the institution of Passover is first mentioned. On the basis of your reading of the Biblical passage alone, who is forbidden to do work on Passover? Jews only? May non-Jews do work for themselves on Passover? For Jews? Is the answer clear? Why, or why not?

Question:

2. Is there any obvious connection between this passage in regard to Passover and any of the laws of Shabbat?

Reading: Mekhilta Bo (Masechta D'Pischa), chapter 9

No Manner of Work Shall Be Done in Them. This means, neither you nor your fellow-Jew shall do any work, nor shall a non-Jew do your work. So you interpret it. But perhaps it means, rather: Neither you nor your fellow-Jew shall do any work, and the non-Jew shall not do even his own work? But Scripture says: "Six days shall work be done but on the seventh day is a Sabbath of solemn rest, a holy convocation; ye shall do no manner of work" (Lev. 23:3). Thus you learn that "no manner of work shall be done in them" means, neither you nor your fellow-Jew shall do any work, but a non-Jew may do his own work -- these are the words of R. Josiah.

R. Jonathan says, there is no need of this proof. Has it not already been said: "Remember the Sabbath day, to keep it holy. Six days shall thou labor, and do all thy work; but the seventh is a Sabbath unto the Lord thy God" (Ex. 20:10). Now, by using the method of *Kal vahomer* it can be reasoned: If on the Sabbath, in regard to which the law is more rigorous, you are not warned against the non-Jew's work as you are against your own work, it is but logical to assume that on holidays, in regard to which the law is less rigorous, you surely are not warned against the non-Jew's work as you are against your own work.

Question:

3. In question 1, we mentioned the problem of deciding who is forbidden to work on Passover if we can use only Exodus 12:16 as evidence. What extra piece of evidence does R. Josiah in the Mekhilta introduce? How is that related to our problem in regard to Passover? (Hint: What word or concept is used in both laws?) In our sample cases from American law, where did the Supreme Court use the same technique, i.e., citing other laws or court decisions which differ widely in context from our present case, but which the Court now uses as relevant precedents? Why does the Court (either Jewish or American) use such far-fetched sources? That is, if it has no clearcut precedent, why does it not simply state its new law rather than bother with trying to find some basis for its decision in the implications of previous but unrelated cases? (Hint: why have precedents at all?)

Question:

4. R. Josiah uses the verse in regard to Shabbat to solve his problem in regard to Passover. What is his ruling? (Hint: During the six days of the week, you are to do work, but the Torah does not prohibit you from hiring a Jew or Gentile to help you do it. Thus, it appears from the juxtaposition of the requirement to "rest" next to the requirement to work, in Leviticus 23, that the "rest" required on Shabbat should include yourself, other Jews, and Gentiles also. That is, we learn certain details about the law of "resting" on Shabbat from the context in which the law appears: just as your "work" may be done by yourself, another Jew, or a Gentile, so too your "rest" must include yourself and your employees, be they Jew or Gentile. Now, then, having learned this in regard to Shabbat, R. Josiah applies it to Passover and decides that...)Once R. Josiah has completed his exposition, has he made a ruling in regard to Passover only (his original problem) or in regard to Shabbat too?

Question:

5. R. Jonathan agrees with R. Josiah's ruling, but offers a different way of arriving at it. R. Josiah learned about the laws of Shabbat from their context and then applied them, by analogy of word or concept, to Passover. Instead, R. Jonathan uses a form of reasoning known as Kal V'chomer: if we would expect a certain quality to be in a set of objects A more than we would expect it to be in another set of objects B, then, if we discover that that quality in fact is in B, we reason that it must be in A too. For example, in your class it may be the case that a certain boy, Allen, is more intelligent than another boy, Bob, and therefore, if Bob got the answer to a certain question, you would expect Allen to get it too. In that example, A = Allen, B = Bob, and the "quality" is intelligence. Now, then, try to state R. Jonathan's reasoning in regard to Shabbat and Passover in your own words. As we noted in the beginning, R. Jonathan agrees with R. Josiah's ruling. What does that remind you of in regard to Supreme Court decisions? (Hint: Consider the phenomenon of concurring opinions.)

Reading: Exodus 20:8-11; 23:12; *Mekhilta Mishpatim* (Masechta D'Kaspa), chap. 20

Exodus 20:8-11:

Remember the Sabbath day and keep it holy. Six days you shall labor and do all your work, but the seventh day is a Sabbath of the Lord your God: you shall not do any work -- you, your son or daughter, your male or female slave, or your cattle, or the stranger who is within your settlements. For in six days the Lord made heaven and earth and sea, and all that is in them, and He rested on the seventh day; therefore the Lord blessed the Sabbath day and hallowed it.

Exodus 23:12:

"Six days you shall do your work, but on the seventh day you shall cease from labor, in order that your ox and your ass may rest, and that your bondsman and the stranger may be refreshed."

Mekhilta Mishpatim:

And That Your Bondsman .. ..May Be Refreshed. This refers to an uncircumcised slave. You say it refers to the uncircumcised slave. Perhaps, however, it only refers to a son of the Covenant? When it says: "Nor thy man-servant nor thy maid-servant" (Ex. 20:10), behold, the Son of the Covenant is there spoken of. Hence, what does Scripture mean by saying here "And the son of thy handmaid...may be refreshed?" It refers to the uncircumcised slave.

Question:

6. The Mekhilta here assumes that no two verses in the Torah say the same thing, that there is nothing superfluous in the Torah, and therefore, if two verses appear to say the same thing, it must show how they differ. Why does the Mekhilta (and virtually all subsequent Jewish law) assume that? Does secular (e.g., American) law assume that? On the basis of this selection and any other Jewish law which you might know, do you think that this assumption has any practical outcome, or is it only a method of interpretation that is used to derive laws that would have been

derived in some other way, anyway, if we did not make the assumption? That is, does the assumption actually lead to new laws or only to new derivations of laws? (Hint: Be careful! The answer is not at all clear. Refer back to this question when you have completed this leaflet and have thus been exposed to a little more Jewish law.)

Reading: Exodus 31:12-17; Mekhilta Ki Tissa (Masechta D'Shabta).

Exodus 31:12-17:

And the Lord spoke to Moses, saying: Speak to the Israelite people and say: Nevertheless, you must keep My Sabbaths, for this is a sign between Me and you throughout the generations, that you may know that I the Lord have consecrated you. You shall keep the Sabbath, for it is holy for you. He who profanes it shall be put to death; whoever does work on it, that person shall be cut off from among his kin. Six days may work be done, but on the seventh day there shall be a Sabbath of complete rest, holy to the Lord; whoever does work on the Sabbath day shall be put to death. The Israelite people shall keep the Sabbath, observing the Sabbath throughout the generations as a covenant for all time; it shall be a sign for all time between Me and the people of Israel. For in six days the Lord made heaven and earth, and on the seventh day He ceased from work and was refreshed.

Mekhilta Ki Tissa:

"For this is a sign between Me and you." And not between Me and the other nations of the world. "Between Me and the people of Israel." And not between Me and the other nations of the world.

Question:

7. The first selection from the Mekhilta which we read said that a Jew may not ask a Gentile to do his (the Jew's) work for him. What is the law that results from the last two selections? That is, what may a Gentile do on Shabbat, according to Jewish law? You will see how this takes on important consequences as the law develops.

Question:

8. Now that you have read three selections from Midrash Halacha, let us try to characterize it. How does each section in it begin? What is constantly referred to? What are some of the methods used in the derivation of its laws? Do conflicting opinions appear? Now recall the previous chapter: Who formulated these laws? When did they live? What does "Midrash Halacha" mean? What are the names of the three books of Midrash Halacha, and what book(s) of the Bible does each cover? Why is there no Midrash Halacha to Genesis and Exodus, chapters 1-11?

B. The Talmud: The Mishna and the Gemara

Reading: Mishna Shabbat 17b-18a

Beth Shammai Rule: One must not sell to a Gentile, or help him to load (an ass), or lift up (an article) upon him unless he can reach a near place; but Beth Hillel permit it. Beth Shammai maintain: Hides must not be given to a tanner, nor garments to a Gentile fuller, unless they can be done while it is yet day; but in all these (cases) Beth Hillel permit (them) (18a) before sunset.

Question:

9. In just reading this Mishna, what questions do you have concerning it? We shall not be quoting the entire Gemara on this Mishna, but see how many of your questions are the same questions raised by the section we quote. What kinds of questions are not asked?

Question:

10. Who made this law? Do they justify it by reference to the more basic Torah law? Where, then, do they get their authority? (Hint: See Deuteronomy 17:8ff.)

Reading: Gemara Shabbat 18b-19a

Beth Shammai Maintain: One Must Not Sell (etc.) Our Rabbis taught: Beth Shammai maintain: A man must not sell an article to a Gentile, nor lend (it) to him nor loan him (money) nor make him a gift (on the eve of Sabbath) unless he can reach his house (before sunset); while Beth Hillel rule: (unless) he can reach the house nearest the (city) wall. (1) R. Akiba said: (Unless) he can depart from the door of his (the Jew's) house (before the Sabbath). Said R. Jose, son of R. Judah: The words of R. Akiba are the very words of Beth Hillel. (2) R. Akiba comes only to explain the words of Beth Hillel. (3)

Our Rabbis taught: Beth Shammai maintain: A man must not sell his leaven to a Gentile, unless he knows that it will be consumed before Passover: this is Beth Shammai's view. But Beth Hillel say: As long as he (the Jew) may eat it, he may sell it...

Our Rabbis taught: Food may be placed before a dog in a courtyard, (and) if it takes it and goes out, one has no duty toward it. (4) Similarly, food may be placed before a Gentile in a courtyard, (and) if he takes it and goes out, one has no duty toward him. What is the purpose of this further (dictum)? (Surely) it is the same (as the first), you might argue. The one is incumbent upon him, whereas the other is not. (5) Therefore we are informed (otherwise). (6)

Notes on this section:

(1) If the Gentile lives in another town, it is sufficient if he can take it to the nearest house there, even if he cannot reach his own before the Sabbath. (2) Their views are identical. (3) i.e., he states Beth Hillel's ruling, not an independent one, and thus differs from the first Tanna's interpretation of Beth Hillel's attitude. (4) To restrain it from carrying it out into the street. (5) He has a duty towards his animals which he does not owe to a stranger, and therefore I might think that in the latter case food must not be given, since it may be carried out. (6) That even so, food may be placed before a Gentile. Because, though one has no legal obligation, he has the duty of charity towards him, just as towards a Jew, as stated in Git. 61ª (Tosaf).

Question:

11. Read through the first two paragraphs of the selection. Try to characterize the difference between the position held by Beth Shammai and that held by Beth Hillel. Prove your general characterization of their positions by showing how each of the specific rulings mentioned in the text follows logically from the general rule which you have formulated.

Question:

12. Beth Hillel are originally quoted as saying one thing, and then R. Akiba quotes them as saying something else. Why did such confusion arise?

Question:

13. The words "our Rabbis taught" in each of the three cases here introduce a Baraitha. Where does a Baraitha come from? What purpose does it serve? Is its style more like that of the Midrash Halacha or of the Mishna?

Question:

14. Note the last Baraitha carefully. Taking an object from the private domain of one individual to the public domain is one of the 39 acts which the Jew is prohibited from doing, according to the Rabbis' interpretation of the Torah (i.e., it has the status of a Pentateuchal law). Is a Gentile allowed to transfer an object in that way on Shabbat? (Hint: Consider the last two selections of Midrash Halacha above). What is the law, then, if you invite a Gentile over for dinner on Shabbat and he takes some of the dessert home with him? Must you ask him not to do so because of the laws of Shabbat? (Hint: Consider the Baraitha). May you urge him to take some food with him? May you ask him to deliver some food for you to someone else's home? May you allow him to come in and take his own property out of your house on Shabbat? (Be careful! When does it cease to be the Gentile's own work for himself, and therefore permitted, and when does it begin to be a case of the Gentile doing your work on Shabbat, which is prohibited, as according to the first selection from the

Mekhilta above? These questions will be asked by the later codifiers of the law, and they will each have to reckon with this Baraitha.)

Reading: Shabbat 121a, Mishna, and part of the Gemara

Mishna: If a Gentile comes to extinguish, we do not say to him: "Extinguish it" or "Do not extinguish," because his resting is not our obligation. But if a minor comes to extinguish, we must not permit him, because his resting is our obligation.

Gemara: Our Rabbis taught: It once happened that a fire broke out in the courtyard of Joseph b. Simai in Shihin, and the men of the garrison at Sepphoris (1) came to extinguish it because he was a steward of the king. (2) But he did not permit them, in honour of the Sabbath, and a miracle happened on his behalf; rain descended and extinguished (it). In the evening he sent two sela to each of them, and fifty to their captain. But when the Sages heard of it they said: He did not need this, for we learnt: If a Gentile comes to extinguish, we do not say to him, "extinguish" or "do not extinguish."

But if a minor comes to extinguish, we do not permit him, because his resting is our obligation. You may infer from this (that) if a minor eats nebeloth (3), it is the duty of Beth din to restrain him? (4) Said R. Johanan: This refers to a minor acting at his father's desire. (5) Then, by analogy, in respect to the Gentile, he (too) acts at the Jew's desire: is this permitted? -- A Gentile acts at his own desire. (6)

Notes on this section:

(1) The Acropolis mentioned in Josephus, Vita 67. (2) Agrippa II, v. Klein, S. Beitrage p. 66, n. 1. and Graetz MGW, 1881, p.484. (3) V. Glos.: i.e., any forbidden food. (4) Lit., "to keep him away" -- in Yeb. 114a this is in doubt. (5) But where he acts entirely of his own accord it may not be so. (6) Though he knows that the Jew too desires it, he may nevertheless act on his own accord. But a minor is more likely to be directly influenced by what he understands to be his father's wish.

Question:

15. What is the general principle enunciated in the first clause of the Mishna in regard to a Gentile doing work on the Shabbat? From your knowledge of the Mekhilta readings above, what verse in the Torah is the -- or, at least, a -- basis for this ruling? Does the Mishna ever mention it? Does the Gemara? Note that, in regard to more controversial laws, the Gemara often refers back to the way in which the law is derived from the Torah. Why is this important? Why, then, do you think that R. Yehuda Hanasi, in editing the Mishna, left the derivations out? (Hint: What were the historical circumstances under which he edited the Mishna? Given those circumstances, do you think that he would be more interested in preserving the laws, or the ways in which the laws were derived? Which form, then, would suit his purposes better -- that of the Midrash Halacha or that of the Mishna?) Summarize, then, the crucial difference in style between the Midrash Halacha and the Mishna.

Question:

16. What is the difference in law, as worked out by Mishna and Gemara, between what you can have a Gentile do for you on Shabbat and what you can have a Jewish child do for you? Why is this differentiation made? Note how the next Mishna which we shall now quote further limits what you can have a Gentile do for you on Shabbat.

Reading: Shabbat 122a-b, Mishna and Gemara

Mishna: If a Gentile lights a lamp, an Israelite may make use of its light; but if (he does it) for the sake of the Israelite, it is forbidden. If he draws water (1) to give his own animal to drink, an Israelite may water (his) after him; but if (he draws it) for the Israelite's sake, it is forbidden. If a Gentile makes a stairway to descend by it (2) an Israelite may descend after him; but if, on the Israelite's account, it is forbidden. It once happened that R. Gamaliel and the elders were traveling in a ship, when a Gentile made a stairway for going down, and R. Gamaliel and the elders descended by it.

Gemara: Now these are (all) necessary. For if we were informed (about) a lamp, that is because a lamp for one is a lamp for a hundred; but as for water (I might say), let us forbid it (3) lest he come to increase (the quantity drawn) on the Israelite's account. (4) What is the need of (the ruling about) a stairway? (5) -- He tells us the story of R. Gamaliel and the elders.

Our Rabbis taught: If a Gentile gathers herbs (6) an Israelite may feed (his cattle therewith) after him, but if (he gathers) on the Israelite's account, it is forbidden. If he draws water to give his cattle to drink, an Israelite may water (his) after him, but if on the Israelite's account, it is forbidden. When is that? If he does not know him; but if he knows him it is forbidden. But that is not so? For R. Huna said in R. Hanina's name: A man may stand his cattle on grass on the Sabbath (7) but not on mukzeh (8) on the Sabbath! (9) -- It means that he stands in front of it (the animal) (10) and so it goes (there) and eats.

The Master said: "When is that? If he does not know him; but if he knows him it is forbidden." But R. Gamaliel (is a case where) he knew him? (11) -- Said Abayae: It was not (made) in his presence. (12) Raba said: You may even say that it was in his presence: "A lamp for one is a lamp for a hundred." (13) An objection is raised: R. Gamaliel said to them, "Since he did not make it in our presence, let us go down by it?" -- Say: "Since he made it, let us go down by it."

Come and hear: If a city inhabited by Israelites and Gentiles contains baths where there is bathing on the Sabbath, if the majority are Gentiles, one (an Israelite) may bathe therein immediately; (14) if the majority are Israelites, one must wait until hot water could be heated. (15) -- There, when they heat, they do so with a view to the majority. (16)

Come and hear: If a lamp is burning at a banqueting party (17), if the majority are Gentiles, one may make use of its light; if the majority are Israelites, it is forbidden; if half and half, it is forbidden. (18) -- There too, when they light it (122b) they do so with a view to the majority.

Samuel visited the house of Abin of Toran. (19) A Gentile came and lit a lamp, (whereupon) Samuel turned his face away. (20) On seeing that he (the Gentile) had brought a document and was reading it, he observed: "He has lit it for himself"; (so) he (too) (Samuel) turned his face to the lamp.

Notes on this section:

(1) From a pit in the street. (2) Rashi: a gangway from a large ship to dry land. (3) Even when the Gentile draws it for his own use. (4) Whilst ostensibly drawing it for himself. (5) That is analogous to a lamp -- the same stairway suffices for many as for one. (6) As animal fodder. (7) i.e., on grass attached to the soil, and we do not fear that he may thereby come to cut grass for his animal. (8) Fodder stored away for later use; this may not be handled on the Sabbath as mukzeh (v. Glos.); hence its designation. (9) Lest he take it and feed the animal. But grass cut on the Sabbath is also mukzeh and may not be handled, since it was not fit for handling as detached before the Sabbath. (10) Barring its way to elsewhere and so making it go on to the detached grass; but he does not actually lead the animal himself; then it is permitted. (11) Since he traveled with R. Gamaliel in the boat. (12) Then the Gentile certainly did not make it for him. (13) He needed the gangway for himself, and there is no extra work even if he had R. Gamaliel in mind. But one may cut more grass on the Jew's account. (14) After the Sabbath, because it was heated primarily for Gentiles. (15) After the Sabbath, so as not to benefit from the heating of the water on the Sabbath. Now, the water had to be heated for the Gentiles, in any case, and there is no real difference between heating for one or for many; further, it was not heated in the Jews' presence, yet one must not benefit from it. This contradicts both Abayae and Raba. (16) Hence it is regarded as specifically for Jews. (17) Having been lit on the Sabbath. (18) This contradicts Raba. (19) MS. M. To Abitoran. (20) So as not to benefit from it.

Question:

17. What is the point of bringing in the episode with R. Gamliel, given that it only is an instance of the more general

law immediately preceding it? Does that remind you of anything in the Congressional Record? (Hint: Do you remember when and why the names of former Presidents were introduced?) Note that the Gemara thinks that the story of R. Gamaliel is more important than the general ruling; that, in fact, if it were not for the story, the general ruling would have been considered redundant and would have been left out. Do you now understand why?

Question:

18. Note that the Gemara assumes that no clause in the Mishna can be merely redundant. What does that remind you of in regard to Midrash Halacha? (Hint: Review question 6.) Why does the Gemara assume that? In your own words, explain how the Gemara here deals with the apparent redundancy in the Mishna's four clauses (in regard to the lamp, the water, the stairway, and R. Gamaliel).

Question:

19. This Mishna adds an important qualification to what you can have a Gentile do for you on Shabbat. What is it? How does the Baraitha quoted in the Gemara further define this qualification? Recalling the Mekhilta selections, explain what the basis of this qualification is in the Torah.

Question:

20. What is the problem in regard to the case of R. Gamaliel? How is it solved by Abayae? By Raba? What, then, is the final law in regard to what you can have a Gentile do for you on Shabbat? Show how this law is illustrated and defined more closely in the last three paragraphs of the selection of Gemara here. (Incidentally, the words "Come and hear" introduce a Baraitha. In what other way have you seen a Baraitha introduced? Hint: See question 13.)

C. The Mishna Torah by Moses Maimonides (Rambam)

Reading: Hilchot Shabbat, 6:1-4; 7-8; 19 (second line); 21

Chapter VI

1. It is forbidden to tell a heathen to do any work for one's own benefit on the Sabbath, notwithstanding that a heathen is not commanded to observe the Sabbath. It is indeed forbidden to do so even if the heathen is told before the Sabbath, and even if the work will not be put to use until after the Sabbath. This prohibition was enacted by the Scribes in order to prevent Israelites from regarding Sabbath observance as a trivial matter and being thus led to perform prohibited work themselves.

2. If a heathen does work on the Sabbath on his own initiative, the rule is as follows: If he does the work for an Israelite, no benefit may be derived from it until after the Sabbath and until sufficient time has elapsed for the work to have been done after the Sabbath; always provided that the work was not done so publicly that everyone was aware that it was done for a certain Israelite on the Sabbath. If, however, the heathen has done the work for himself, it is permissible for an Israelite to benefit from it on the Sabbath.

3. For example, if a heathen lights a lamp, an Israelite may make use of its light; but if the lamp was lit for an Israelite, its use is forbidden. If a heathen makes a gangway to disembark from a boat on the Sabbath, an Israelite may use it after him; but if the heathen has made the gangway for the Israelite, the latter may not use it. If a heathen fills a drinking trough to water his animals on the Sabbath, an Israelite may water his own animals afterward; but if the water was drawn for the Israelite, he may not use it. If a heathen gathers herbage to feed his animals, an Israelite may feed his own animals with it afterward -- provided that the heathen is not acquainted with the Israelite, for otherwise he may do additional work for the Israelite's sake, and thus work for the benefit of the latter. Similarly, in any case in which it is possible that a heathen might increase the amount of work done, an Israelite may not benefit from that heathen's work, unless the heathen does not know him.

4. In cases where it is impossible to increase or decrease the amount of work done, as in lighting a lamp or making a gangway, an Israelite may benefit from the work after the heathen has done it, even if they are acquainted with each other, seeing that the work was done for the heathen's own benefit.

If a lamp is burning on the Sabbath at an assembly, the rule is as follows: If most of those present are Israelites, they may not make use of the light, since whoever lit the lamp did so with the majority in mind. If the majority are heathens, the light of the lamp may be used by Israelites. If half are Israelites and half heathens, the light may not be used.

If a fire breaks out on the Sabbath and a heathen comes forward to put it out, one should not say to him, "Extinguish it," or "Do not extinguish it," for a heathen's abstention from work on the Sabbath is not an Israelite's responsibility. The same rule applies in all similar cases...

7. If a town inhabited by both Israelites and heathens has a bathhouse open for use on the Sabbath, the rule is as follows: If the heathens are in the majority, an Israelite may bathe therein immediately after the termination of the Sabbath. If Israelites are in the majority, there must be a delay for as long as it takes to heat the water, since the water will have been heated for the majority. If half are Israelites and half heathens, there must likewise be a delay for as long as it takes to heat the water. The same rule applies in all similar cases.

8. An Israelite who requests a heathen to do certain prohibited work for him on the Sabbath, although he has transgressed and incurred a disciplinary flogging, may benefit from that work on the following evening, providing that he waits for as long as it took to do it. The only reason that the Sages insisted in every case on a delay for as long as it took to do the work, is as follows: If benefit from prohibited work were permissible immediately after the Sabbath, one might be tempted to tell a heathen to do it in order to have it

ready to hand at that very time. On the other hand, once benefit from the work is prohibited until after as long a delay as it would take to do it, one would be unlikely to ask a heathen to do the work for him on the Sabbath. For he would gain nothing by it, since he must wait anyway in the evening for as long as it would take to do the particular work that was done for him on the Sabbath...

19. Even if the remuneration is fixed in advance, an Israelite should not give to a heathen craftsman on a Friday any materials with which to make articles, unless there is enough time for the heathen to leave the Israelite's house with them before dusk. Similarly, an Israelite should not sell or lend articles to a heathen, or grant him a loan, or give him an article in pledge or as a gift, unless there is enough time for the heathen to take the article out of the door of the Israelite's house before the arrival of the Sabbath. For as long as the heathen remains in the Israelite's house, no one outside would know when the article was given to him, and if the heathen should then leave the Israelite's house on the Sabbath holding the Israelite's article, it would seem as if the latter had granted the heathen the loan, or had given him the pledge, or had fixed the craftsman's fee, or had sold him the article, on the Sabbath...

21. If a heathen carries articles of his own into an Israelite's house on the Sabbath, this is permissible. It is permissible even if the Israelite tells him to put the articles down in a specified corner of the house. Furthermore, one may invite a heathen to one's home on the Sabbath and place food before him to eat, and one need not interfere if he takes the food out of the house, since an Israelite has no responsibility for a heathen's observance of Sabbath rest.

One may likewise put down food in a courtyard for a dog, and need not interfere if the dog takes the food out of the courtyard.

Question:

21. Read through the above selection from the Mishna Torah. How does it differ in style from Midrash Halacha? From the Mishna? From the Gemara? In his introduction to the Mishna Torah, Maimonides notes that in his time there were many troubles, and as a result, nobody had time to learn the Tannaitic and Amoraic sources thoroughly. He, therefore, in writing his work, hoped "to bring together from these many sources all the conclusions in regard to the prohibited and the permitted, the impure and the pure, together with the rest of the laws of the Torah, all in clear, concise language, until the entire Oral Law would be set before everybody without difficulty or objection, so that one man should not say one thing and another something else...so that a man would not need any other book in the world in regard to Jewish law, but rather, this book would include the entire Oral Law, with the changes, customs, and decrees that were enacted from the days of Moses, our Teacher, through the conclusion of the Gemara, and the many explanations which the Geonim offered in all their works after the Gemara. Therefore, I named this book the Mishna Torah -- literally, "second to the Torah" -- for a man should read the Written Torah first, and afterwards read this book, so that he would know the entire Oral Law and would not need to read any book other than these." Explain how his style -- and especially its differences from the styles of previous works in Jewish law -- helps him to achieve his purpose. What dangers are there in such a purpose and such a style? (Hint: Does he quote his sources? Why, then, should anyone who has done some reading in Jewish law himself necessarily obey Rambam? Furthermore, even if he did quote his sources, does he mention contrary opinions? Why, then, is Rambam's interpretation of Jewish sources, and the laws that derive from them, necessarily the correct one? And what happened to the freedom and fun of argument and counter-argument that we saw and cherished in the Talmud?) Do you think that it is worth risking these dangers in order to accomplish the advantages which Rambam aims to achieve?

Question:

22. Go through each of the clauses of the selection and try to identify the source (in either Midrash Halacha, Mishna, or Gemara) of Rambam's ruling and examples. Do you see now how he has put together sources from many different places in order to present the laws in an organized fashion?

Question:

23. Point out several instances where Rambam spells out the principles involved in specific cases where the Talmud just gave the ruling in the specific case. For what purposes is this helpful? In three places in our selection Rambam also suggests the motivation behind a law. Why is this helpful?

Question:

24. Where does Rambam decide according to one of two or more opinions that appear in the Talmud? What is the basis of his selection here? Do you think that the selection is always as clear-cut? Why, or why not?

Question:

25. In this selection, does Rambam ever differ with an undisputed conclusion in the Talmud? Your answer will be important, as we now turn to the second of the two most important Jewish law codes, the Shulkhan Arukh.

D. Shulkhan Arukh by Joseph Karo

Reading: Shulkhan Arukh, Hilchot Shabbat, #246:2; #325: 1-2,4,10,11,12.

246:2: It is forbidden to lend any object to a Gentile during Shabbat, and even on the eve of the Sabbath if it is close to sunset -- that is, as long as there is not time to take it out of the lender's house before sunset -- because anyone who sees (the borrower take it out of the Jew's home after sunset) would think that the Jew commanded him to take it out.

325:1: It is permissible to invite a Gentile on Shabbat, and it is permissible to place food before him in the courtyard so that he may eat it, and if (instead) he took it out (of the courtyard), we need not try to stop him. This permission, however, applies only when the Gentile is in the courtyard, but if he is standing outside the courtyard and reaches inside it, so that we know that he will take the food outside (it is forbidden to give him food). And similarly, we may not give him other types of objects which normally are taken out of the courtyard, even if he is standing inside the courtyard and even if the objects belong to him (the Gentile), because anyone who sees (the Gentile take it out of the Jew's courtyard) does not know that the objects belong to the Gentile.

325:2: Where we must take account of preserving peace (and good will for the Jewish community, e.g., if a Gentile is sick and sent a messenger to the Jew to ask for food), or where the Gentile is strong, we may give him (an object other than food on Shabbat) or send it to him through a Gentile messenger.

325:4: In regard to bread which a Gentile baked for himself on Shabbat, some authorities prohibit it and some permit it; and so, at a time of emergency, or for the sake of fulfilling a commandment like that of making a meal in honor of a circumcision, or for the sake of reciting the blessing Hamotzi (i.e., "Blessed art Thou, O Lord our God, King of the Universe, Who brings forth bread from the earth"), we may rely on those who permit such bread.

325:10: If a Gentile drew water for his cow from a pit, which is in private domain, and transferred it to the public domain, a Jew may use that water to water his own cow too, provided that the Gentile does not know him, so that we need not be afraid that the Gentile will purposely draw more water for the sake of the Jew. But if the Gentile drew the water for the sake of watering a Jew's cow, it is forbidden for Jews to use that water in any way, and it is even forbidden for any other Jew to use it...

325:11: ...And similarly, wherever there is room for the doubt that the Gentile may have intentionally done more work in order to help the Jew (no Jew may benefit from such work). But where there is no room for that doubt, as, for example, when the Gentile lit a candle for himself or made a ramp on which to descend (from a ship), it is permitted for a Jew to benefit from the Gentile's work, even if the Gentile knows him, because one light and one ramp are sufficient for everyone.

325:12: If the Gentile specifically says that he is doing the work for the Jew, or even if he does not say so but his acts prove that he is doing the work for the Jew, as, for example, if he lit a candle in the Jew's house and then left, it is forbidden for the Jew to benefit from such work, even if the Gentile does not know the Jew.

Question:

26. Read through the entire selection and compare its style with Midrash Halacha, the Mishna, the Gemara, and especially the Mishna Torah. Does the Shulkhan Arukh have the same clear organization that the Mishna Torah does -- i.e., topics arranged in logical order and explicated by generalizations, followed by specific examples? If you were searching for the laws on any given subject, could you look at the chapter in the Shulkhan Arukh that seemed to be relevant and be reasonably sure that you had read all of the important material in the Shulkhan Arukh on that subject? (Hint: Note where our selections come from.) Could you do that with Rambam's code? Are disagreements expressed? Where?

Question:

27. In regard to what laws does the Shulkhan Arukh differ from the Talmud and Mishna Torah in our selection? Why do you think that it does so? (The answer is not obvious. One rather plausible suggestion is that it differs for social reasons, i.e., the rabbis in Karo's time were concerned about assimilation, and thus limited the ways in which Jews could mix socially with Gentiles as much as possible. If that is true, what does that tell you about the relationship which the Mishna Torah and the Shulkhan Arukh have to the Talmud? That is, which of them more nearly reflects the Talmud, and which is heavily influenced by post-Talmudic changes in Jewish laws and customs that developed among the people?)

Question:

28. If the Shulkhan Arukh is not as clearly organized as the Mishna Torah, and if it sometimes differs radically from the Talmud, why is it considered the most authoritative work in Jewish law? (Hint: Review the Karo-Isserles history and the last comment in question 27.) What are the implications of this in regard to our ability to change Jewish law in our own day? As you might have guessed, the answers that people give to this last question -- about how much and in what way we can change Jewish law -- differ widely, and we shall now turn in our next three chapters to the answers given by Orthodox, Reform, and Conservative Judaism.

UNIT VI

MODERN APPROACHES TO JEWISH LAW

Chapter 17

The Orthodox Response to Jewish Law

We need to have the Law in order to achieve our goals. That is what we established in our third unit, and all three branches of modern Judaism agree with that point (as opposed to Christianity). However, the extent to which we in the twentieth century can change traditional Jewish law, developed along the lines that we discussed in the last unit, is a matter of deep disagreement, stemming from three totally different concepts of what our relationship is to that body of law. In this chapter we shall discuss the view of Orthodox Judaism, and we shall continue in the succeeding chapters with the Reform and, then, Conservative approaches, thus following the chronological order of their development.

Warning: Don't think from the outset that just because Orthodox Judaism is orthodox, it must lack all rhyme or reason. Remember that rational men judge positions <u>after</u> they know <u>both</u> the strong and weak points.

> Reading: *Judaism Eternal* by Samson Raphael Hirsch
>
> To reform Judaism according to the needs of time -- this, according to our critics, is the task of our time, as it has been the task of all times. It was this which occupied the great teachers of every age, and it is only we backward obscurantists who obstinately refuse to listen to such wisdom and act on it.
>
> Let us see. To bring Judaism up to date, to adapt it to the needs of the time, to harmonize it with the views generally prevalent at any given period and with the conditions and needs of any given time -- this would be the object. If we alter our Judaism so as to bring it into line with

the views prevailing in our time among our non-Jewish brethren, if we remove everything which it is inconvenient and burdensome to carry out in the conditions of our time, or the practice of which could cause us to be misunderstood and misjudged by our fellow-citizens, then, is it not so, we have taken to heart and acted on modern wisdom...

What would have become of Judaism if our ancestors had considered it as their task to bring Judaism at every period up to date, i.e., to bring it into consonance with the views and conditions prevailing in their environment at any given time? What would have happened if they had done so, if they had taken, in Egypt, the wisdom of the priests of Merce; among the Babylonians, the mysteries of Mylitta; among the Persians, the magic of Zoroaster; among the Greeks, the Elusinian mysteries of the Olympian mythology; of the philosophic system in favor at any time in Alexandria and Rome, the syncretism of all possible beliefs and views; among the Celts, the wisdom of the Druids; and, in the middle ages, cloisters and monks, as their standard for reforming Judaism? What is to happen today if, in obedience to this modern teaching, the Jews in all climes and all countries are to reform their Judaism in such a way as to adapt it to the views and customs of their fellow-countrymen? In heaven's name, what kind of monstrosity would it be which passed as Judaism? Views, customs, needs, vary from land to land, from decade to decade. But where is there a religion which was doomed to wander through all lands and all times like Judaism -- and we are told to bring it everywhere up to date!

But, above all, what kind of thing would Judaism be if we dared to bring it up to date? If the Jew were permitted to bring his Judaism up to date at any time, he would no longer need it anywhere; it would not be worthwhile anywhere to speak any longer of Judaism. We should then seize Judaism and cast it out among other misbegotten products of delusion and superstition, and hear no more of Judaism and the Jewish religion.

If the Bible is to be for me the word of God, and Judaism and Jewish Law the revealed will of God, is it possible for me to ask my belly, my sensual enjoyment and comfort, my temporary advantage, whether it is also sweet or easy, or profitable or agreeable? Is it possible for me to take religion, my religion, which has been given to me by God as a standard with which to measure myself, my generation, and all my action and inaction, and trim it to fit the meanness, the sensuality, the petty-mindedness of my own desires, at any particular time? Can I falsify the Divine measuring-rod to suit my own passing needs, and then boastfully exclaim: "Look, here is Judaism thoroughly sifted and brought up to date, here is the word of God Almighty cut down to the measure of my own weakness. See how well in step with it we are, both I and my generation!"

From the very beginning, God placed Judaism, and with it its adherents, in opposition to the age. For thousands of years Judaism was the only protest against a completely pagan world. And if this opposition diminished from century to century, this was not because Judaism altered itself to suit the non-Jewish conditions at any given time, but because more and more seeds of the Jewish spirit, sparks from the Jewish word of God, found a lodgment in the bosom of the non-Jewish world, and more and more the Jewish word of God fulfilled its silent mission on earth.

In point of fact it was not "orthodox" Jews who introduced the word "orthodoxy" into Jewish discussions. It was the modern "progressive" Jews who first applied this name to "old," "backward" Jews, as a derogatory term. This name was first resented by "old" Jews. And rightly so. "Orthodox" Judaism does not know any varieties of Judaism. It conceives Judaism as one and indivisible. It does not know a Mosaic, Prophetic, and Rabbinic Judaism, nor Orthodox and Liberal Judaism. It only knows Judaism and non-Judaism. It does not know Orthodox and Liberal Jews. It does indeed know conscientious and indifferent Jews, good Jews, bad Jews, or baptised Jews; all, nevertheless, Jews with a mission which they cannot cast off. They are only distinguished according as they fulfill or reject their mission.

Question:

1. Hirsch brings two arguments against changing Judaism to suit it to the times: (a) Such a policy, if carried out consistently, would mean the assimilation and death of Judaism and whatever good it is trying to achieve; and (b) even if Judaism would survive, such a policy would make

Judaism worthless, since it would then simply condone whatever one wanted to do. Use concrete examples in explaining both of these claims carefully. Do you agree? Explain why or why not.

Question:

2. In accordance with the points (a) and (b) of question 1, what does Orthodox Judaism think of other forms of Judaism? (Hint: Rackman calls Orthodox Judaism "authentic" Judaism, and consider the last paragraph in the Hirsch reading above.)

Reading:

The subordination of religion to any other factor means the denial of religion: for if the Torah is to you the law of God, how dare you place another law above it and go along with God and His Law only as long as you thereby "progress" in other respects at the same time? You must admit it: it is only because "religion" does not mean to you the word of God, because in your heart you deny Divine Revelation, because you believe not in Revelation given to man but in Revelation emanating *from* man, that you can give man the right to lay down conditions to religion.

"Religion Allied to Progress" -- Do you know, dear reader, what that means? Virtue allied to sensual enjoyment, rectitude allied to advancement, uprightness allied to success. It means a religion and a morality which can be preached also in the haunts of vice and iniquity. It means sacrificing religion and morality to every man's momentary whim. It allows every man to fix his own goal and progress in any direction he pleases, and to accept from religion only that part which does not hinder his "progress" or even assists it. It is the cardinal sin which Moses of old described as "a casual walking with God." (Leviticus 26:21f)

"The children of Israel shall keep the Sabbath throughout all their generations for an everlasting covenant..." "The seventh day is a Sabbath unto the Lord thy God, thou shalt not do any manner of work." "Ye shall not light a fire on the Sabbath day" -- thus speaks the book of religion.

But "progress" says: "If we were to observe the Sabbath we should have to forego many a profession, many a branch of trade or industry. Civilization with its improved means of communication and transport cannot tolerate one whole day's rest in seven (the smouldering tobacco leaf is also part of civilization!) Civilization requires it and progress commands; the Sabbath is overthrown and progress is victorious and the servant of religion stamps as holy a Sabbath celebrated without Sabbath rest, inaugurates the desecrated Sabbath with the sounds of the organ, and allows that which religion has enjoined as an everlasting covenant to be crushed beneath the elephantine march of progress."

Read through the pages of the Torah and see if there is any part of the Divine commandments and prohibitions beyond which your religion allied to progress does not intend to progress. The laws of chastity, you think? You excuse your children the Fourth Commandment in the name of progress: they will excuse _themselves_ the Fifth and Seventh Commandments, in the name of what _they_ call progress. And why should they not? How can they fail to notice that you are not -- cannot be -- really in earnest about the Divine origin and sanctity of this whole law which you abrogate at will? Does not the same God speak to _them_ as speaks to you? And why should they not follow their own judgment and inclination, seeing that you follow yours? Do they not but follow your precept and example, if they observe only that part of the Jewish religion -- even of that which you enjoin upon them -- which does not hinder them in their progress towards their goal?

3. -- Our Principle

Now what is it that we want? Are the only alternatives either to abandon religion or to renounce all progress with all the glorious gifts which civilization and education offer mankind? Is the Jewish religion really of such a nature that its faithful adherents must be the enemies of civilization and progress?

We declare before heaven and earth that if our religion demanded that we should renounce what is called civilization and progress we would obey unquestioningly, because our religion is for us truly religion, the word of God before which every other consideration has to give way. We declare, equally, that we would prefer to be branded as fools and do without all the honor and glory that civilization and progress might confer on us rather than be guilty of the conceited mock-wisdom which the spokesman of a religion allied to progress here displays.

For behold whither a religion allied to progress leads! Behold how void it is of piety and humanity and into what blunders the conceited, Torah-criticizing spirit leads. Here you have a protagonist of this religion of progress. See how he dances on the graves of your forefathers, how he drags out their corpses from their graves, laughs in their faces, and exclaims to you: "Your fathers were crude and uncivilized; they deserve the contempt in which they were held. Follow me, so that you may become civilized and deserve respect!"

Such is the craziness which grows on the tree of knowledge of this "religion allied to progress!"

If our choice were only between such craziness and simple ignorance, again we say we would remain ignorant all our lifelong rather than be thus Godlessly educated, even for one moment.

There is, however, no such dilemma. Judaism never remained aloof from true civilization and progress; in almost every era its adherents were fully abreast of contemporary learning, and very often excelled their contemporaries. If, in recent centuries, German Jews remained more or less aloof from European civilization, the fault lay not in their religion, but in the tyranny which confined them by force within the walls of their ghettoes and denied them intercourse with the outside world. And, thank Goodness, even now our sons and daughters can compare favorably in culture and moral worth with the children of those families who have forsaken the religion of their forefathers for the sake of imagined progress. They need not shun the light of publicity or the critical eye of their contemporaries. They have lost nothing in culture or refinement, even though they do not smoke their cigars on the Sabbath, even though they do not seek the pleasures of the table in goods forbidden by God, even though they do not desecrate the Sabbath for the sake of profit and enjoyment.

Indeed, we are shortsighted enough to believe that the Jew who remains steadfast amidst the scoffing and the enticements of the easy-going world around him, who remains strong enough to sacrifice to God's will profit, inclination and the respect and applause of his fellows, displays far greater moral strength, and thus a higher degree of real culture, than the frivolous "modern Jew" whose principles melt away before the first contemptuous glance or at the slightest prospect of profit, and who is unfaithful to the word of God and the teachings of his fathers in order to satisfy the whim of the moment.

Judaism is the religion which does not say, "There is no salvation outside of me." Judaism which is disparaged on account of its alleged particularism is precisely the religion which teaches the precious goal. Of all men, it is the Rabbis, so loudly decried on account of their particularism, who, pointing to the predictions in the mouth of the prophets and singers of a glorious new day for humanity, emphasize that there is no mention in them of priests, Levites, and Israelites, but that only the just, honest, and upright are spoken of; and so the just, honest, and upright of all peoples are included in the noblest blessings.

Thus it is just the most isolated Jew who bears in his breast the most universal thoughts and sentiments.

With serene glance he wanders through the world and down the ages, and joyfully welcomes every apparition in which, wherever and however it may be, he sees the seeds of a pure worship of God and of the ennoblement of man, the recognition of God and of the divine destiny of man cultivated and preserved in non-Jewish circles. And though he knows that until that morning comes he will nowhere find full and eternal salvation established on earth, yet he rejoices to see anywhere the sum total of truth and goodness increased on earth, he sees in every sunrise the beams of the morning which will one day dawn cloudlessly over mankind.

Hence the Jew will not frown upon any art, any science, any
culture provided only that it is found to be true and edifying and really to promote the welfare of mankind. He
has to taste everything by the unimpeachable touchstone of
his divine law; whatever does not stand this test does not
exist. But the more firmly he takes his stand on the rock
of his Judaism, the more fully he is penetrated with the
consciousness of his own Judaism, the more ready will he be
to accept and gratefully appropriate whatever is true and
good in other sources according to Jewish standards; in
whatever mind it originated, from whosoever mouth it issued,
he will always be ready, as the Sages say, to receive the
truth from him who spoke it. Nowhere will he ever sacrifice a single thread of his Judaism or trim his Judaism to
the needs of the time. Wherever the age offers him anything which is consonant with his Judaism he will willingly
adopt it. He will in every period regard it as his duty to
pay due appreciation to the age and its conditions from the
standpoint of his Judaism, and to make use of the new means
provided by any period in order that, in the conditions of
that period, he may be able to make the old Jewish spirit
expand in new beauty and may perform his duty to it with
ever renewed vigor and loyalty.

Question:

3. What, according to Hirsch, is the attitude of Orthodox Judaism to secular culture? That is, (a) under what conditions
would Orthodox Jews reject it? Why would they reject it
then? (Note the answer carefully; it has more force than
is at first apparent.) (b) Under what conditions would
Orthodox Jews use secular culture? To what purpose would
they use it then? Why would they use it at all? (c) According to Hirsch, is such a limited use of secular culture
harmful to Orthodox Jews? Why, or why not? (Hint: Are
secular "civilization" and "progress" necessarily "good"?)
(d) In what points would you <u>agree</u> with Hirsch? (Answer
this question carefully and fairly.) Why do you disagree
where you do disagree? (Note: Not all Jews who claim to be
Orthodox agree with Hirsch.)

Reading:

There is perhaps not another word in our language which, to
the same degree as "ceremony," connotes, at the same time,

solemnity of form and hollowness of content. Not to join in a ceremony, or to infringe one, is never a crime but, at most, an offense against decency. Yet, people have dared to apply this most hollow, vague, and nebulous of words to "law," to this finest, most earnest, and inviolable standard of human action, to the law of God, the all-powerful, all-wise, all-good, and just Lord and Father of men! I say, the laws of God; for if this also were just a ceremony, if the term "Divine Laws" were applied only out of decency, out of consideration for sensitive persons, or in order to preserve appearances, it would no longer be worth discussing.

Certain laws of Judaism, then, whose Divine origin was not denied, were yet called "ceremonial law"; and the laws having been called thus, people having become accustomed to think of them as ceremonial law, the logical outcome was the doctrine that with ceremonial laws one does not have to stand on ceremony! Ceremonies are tolerated so long as they are considered respectable; but to offend against a ceremony is no crime. For the sake of ceremonies it is not necessary to make sacrifices, to forego any advantage, enjoyment, or convenience. To make for its sake any sacrifice, however small, would be stupidity. This was so self-evident a proposition that there was no need to preach it. Once the term "ceremonial law" had been brought into use, everyone felt justified in granting himself a dispensation from it at will.

Even if these laws were ceremonies, but God -- your God -- demanded their performance by you, all your wisdom and the sum total of all mortal wisdom could never absolve you from observing them most conscientiously. But this argument which, I should imagine, appeals to ordinary common sense, has been prudently suppressed, or else parried by paying God the "compliment" of arguing that, surely, He is sensible enough -- like us -- not to be too serious about ceremonies!

The most diverse laws were called ceremonial laws, and this process was carried to ridiculous lengths.

The Sabbaths and Festivals, circumcision, the dietary laws, and the laws of chastity, and so on, in short, all those laws that stand in the way of physical desires and social intercourse with non-Jewish people -- in a word, all those laws which it is felt burdensome to perform, were put in a large folder marked "ceremonial laws," and, thus labeled, relegated to the archives. The only laws which escaped this clearing mania were those which concern chiefly the moral behavior of man towards his fellows, and which were, in contradistinction, called "moral laws."

Let us, then, consult the source, the Book of Law itself, to see whether, in the first place, it is possible that these laws which have been dubbed "ceremonial laws" could really be nothing but meaningless ceremonies and trappings; so much so, that they could -- as has been done in a well-known modern textbook of the "Mosaic religion" -- be consigned to an appendix.

Who dare to say the Rabbis were, that God Himself was, unaware of the sensual nature of man, the march of time, the tribulations of the people, and the pride of human intelligence; that they had not foreseen how obnoxious these laws would be to physical desires, to social intercourse with non-Jew and to shallow common sense, and that to all these opposing influences God has exposed His Law, the expression of His sacred, eternal and solemn will, unprotected? We should be fools to suppose that the sensual nature of man was ever more modest, that social intercourse with non-Jews was ever smoother, or the task of being a Jew any easier and less fraught with sacrifice. "Perform ye My _Mishpatim_ (legal ordinances) and keep ye My _Chukkim_ (laws), I am the Lord your God."

Mishpatim were explained by the _Siphra_ more than 1500 years ago as those laws of the Torah which, were they not contained in the Torah, would have been prescribed by human intelligence, such as legislation concerning theft, idolatry, blasphemy, or murder. _Chukkim_ are those laws which are decried as unreasonable by man's sensual nature and by the non-Jewish world, such as the prohibition of pork, _Shaatnez_, _Chalitzah_, the purification of the leper, or the scapegoat used for the Day of Atonement. Because these laws are contested by man's sensual nature and the non-Jewish world, the admonition "I, God," is added -- I, God, have ordained these laws and thou hast no right to contest them.

Here you have the sum total of "modern" wisdom: Mishpatim and Chukkim! Judaism contains two types of laws. First -- Mishpatim -- those laws which our own intelligence enjoins upon us; these are the laws which still find favor at the bar of modern criticism. But these laws are not Judaism in its entirety. Judaism also contains Chukkim -- laws which we would not lay down if they had not been ordained, and which, having been ordained, have ever been obnoxious to man's physical desires and the non-Jewish world. These are nowadays called "ceremonial laws." Both <u>together</u> make up Judaism. You are a Jew only if you perform <u>both</u> with equal earnestness, with equal conscientiousness. Read the Divine Law, let your children read it. Point out to them the strictness with which God demands the performance not only of the Mishpatim but also of the Chukkim, the "ceremonial laws"! Show them how the Torah foretells degeneration, destruction, and downfall, as the result of the violation of these laws, and promises sanctification and well-being as the effect of their observance. Indeed, for the very reason that Chukkim have to contend with physical desires and with misunderstandings of the non-Jewish world, Holy Writ emphasizes them much more strongly, and frequently, and in greater detail. Apart from murder and incest, it rarely, if at all, speaks of "moral laws" in the solemn terms which we quoted above as being applied to circumcision, the Sabbath, and dietary laws. And, as if wishing to counter in advance the illusion that only the moral laws are eternal, while the ceremonial laws are subject to change either in time or from country to country, it uses, more particularly in connection with "ceremonial laws," the proviso "for all generations" "an eternal law," "wherever ye may dwell."

In the face of these awe-inspiring facts, this entire illusion must surely dissolve into thin air. We shall surely not continue to believe that this distinction between one word of God and another is admissible in the Jewish faith; to think that we may still call ourselves Jews even if we break without scruple the ceremonial laws of Judaism, or indeed, lift the scroll of the Law on high and pronounce, "This is the Torah which God gave unto us," while denying three-fifths of its contents as being ceremonial laws. There is no room for the use among Jewish-minded Jews of the term "ceremonial law," the intention of which originally was, perhaps, innocent, but which has, in the course of time, become the cause of dire and lamentable confusion.

Question:

4. What is the conclusion to which one comes when he classifies the laws of the Bible as either ethical or ceremonial? How does Hirsch try to show that this is an erroneous conclusion?

Reading: "Can We Moderns Keep the Sabbath?" by Emanuel Rackman, Commentary, Vol. 18, No. 3, Sept. 1954.

The Sabbath, that day of peace, now wages a war for survival. In an advanced technological society, her regulations are considered "dated"; one constantly hears it said, for instance, that a prohibition against riding could not possibly have included the automobile, and laws with respect to fire could not possibly apply to electricity. Furthermore, we are told that the traditional conception of Sabbath rest should be broadened to include newer forms of leisure activity: creative art is urged upon us as a Sabbath goal pretty much equivalent to the older goals of prayer and study. Finally, it is said that even a Jewish state cannot function without flouting the Sabbath: the essential services of modern life must be maintained day and night. How, then, can the Sabbath survive?...

The Bible had indicated that the Sabbath was not to be desecrated, even for the construction of God's sanctuary. The Oral Law inferred from this that nothing could be done on the seventh day to speed up the rearing of the Temple or the furnishing of its interior. Here, therefore, was a clue to the meaning of the prohibition against work. Work was any activity connected with the construction of the Temple. Upon analysis, thirty-nine categories were discovered, and these thirty-nine, in essence, turned out to be any taking from nature, or any creation from, or improvement upon, matter...

That is why one cannot help but be amused by some of the Law's reformers who, on the premise that the Sabbath is to promote rest and relaxation, conclude that creative art is an excellent form of Sabbath relaxation. To create is certainly permitted -- but never to create out of matter. Let the Sabbath observer create ideas, or cultivate sentiments, or even discover God and His will. But as for things material, only their consumption is permitted on the Sabbath, not their exploitation or manipulation.

This analysis of the Law has further significance. Often in human history we have had protests against civilization and its compulsions, and Jewish culture, too, has had its impulse to go "back to nature." The festival of Tabernacles is one expression of this impulse. And so was the Sabbath. "Back to nature" meant a static, as distinguished from a dynamic, existence -- living with nature rather than the pushing of nature. That is why the Law prohibited the use on the Sabbath of that which was dynamic in nature -- even animals and still growing vegetation. Moreover, just as one may not create instruments, one may not even use instruments already created if they have a dynamic character. Dishes for the serving of food were static -- they could be used. Millstones, however, were to come to a halt before the Sabbath day. And it is this hostility to the dynamic that is the very antithesis of the mood of our lives in a technological age. That is why the original rules are so desperately needed now. A day to go "back to nature" once a week is more important now for peace of mind and human dignity than it ever was. Living with nature, however, means not living in primitive simplicity, but rather, in accord with man's guiding principle -- God's will and reason. Man needs at least the one day to ask what are the ends for which he lives.

The automobile, for example, makes the prohibition against riding not obsolete, but all the more compelling, for the automobile only increases the dynamism of travel. The deeper significance of spending one day within a limited area is that man shall find meaning to his existence where he is -- not where he can escape to. Similarly, the prohibition against fire was not a prohibition with respect to its use, but rather, with respect to its creation and its creative power; electrically propelled motors come no less within the scope of the prohibition.

Using the terminology of means and ends, it can be said that the six days of toil are concerned with the means of life and Sabbath with its ends. The six days of toil represent the temporal and transitory -- the Sabbath represents the eternal and the enduring. That is why the

Hebrew language has no names for the days of the week -- they are all the first day, or the second day, or the third day, to "the Sabbath" -- the Sabbath is the goal toward which time itself moves...

The Rabbis, of course, found it necessary to make many additional rules, safeguards, around the Sabbath. In the main, these are the rules against which moderns are most rebellious. As a matter of fact, moderns frequently visualize the Rabbis as misanthropes whose sole purpose was to make our lives as miserable as possible. There have been others in the past who could not understand the Sabbath. Sadducees and Karaites regarded the prohibition against fire as a prohibition against its use, instead of a prohibition against its creation and the use of its potential for still further creation. In darkness they sanctified the Sabbath. Many even outlawed food and sexual intercourse for the day. For them, misery was the keynote of the Sabbath.

The point of view of the Rabbis, however, stands in bold contrast -- in fact, as a protest against these tendencies. The Rabbis prescribed the lighting of candles, and made the Sabbath lights in the home one of the most significant features of the day. And they made eating and cohabitation on the Sabbath not only permitted functions, but virtually mandatory ones. The Sabbath was not to frustrate man, but to help him fulfill himself.

In that large volume of the Talmud which deals with the Sabbath, one whole chapter is devoted to Sabbath lights and the use of oils that will not only burn well but also without unpleasant odors. The principal passages of this chapter are recited every Sabbath eve by most Jews as an established part of the service. And, lest there be Jews who think that eating on the Sabbath is not permitted, the Talmud prescribed not only the minimum number of meals for the day, but also elaborate techniques for keeping the food warm, despite the general prohibition against cooking and the making of fire. That husband and wife should have sexual intercourse on the Sabbath became standard; but there is also a full discussion of how women may make themselves most attractive with perfume and jewelry, despite the prohibition against the carrying of weights and the preparation of drugs. There was even a relaxation of some of the rules pertaining to the woman's ritualistic immersion after her menstrual period, in order that there might be no postponement of cohabitation on the holy Sabbath.

Further to prevent the many Sabbath prohibitions from becoming a barrier to the fulfillment of the Law's ideal, the Law emphasized two positive conceptions -- Qibud and Oneg -- the honor and joy of the Sabbath. The Sabbath was honored by festive dress and enjoyed with festive meals; it was welcomed with song and candlelight; its departure was toasted with wine and incense. On the other hand, just as concern with the minutiae of Passover observance caused Jews to become more impressed with the love of freedom, so the Sabbath's restrictions made for greater preoccupation with Sabbath goals.

Thus the Rabbis never lost sight of the Sabbath's affirmative aspects, which they expanded in every age. But they also had to expand the Sabbath prohibitions to meet changing conditions. The basic categories of prohibited work were established in times when hunting, fishing, cattle-raising, and farming were the principal occupations of man. In these endeavors there always was a direct taking and creating from nature. True, the Rabbis had to taboo many activities which resembled, or might induce, the basic activity prohibited by the Bible, in order to spread the knowledge of the Law and insure obedience to it. Yet, what of new enterprises -- such as trading, which involved only the transfer of ownership with no changes whatever in the nature of the things traded? And what of business planning? And partners' discussions among themselves? And the use of money itself? Relying upon a verse in Isaiah (58:13), the Rabbis expanded the Sabbath's prohibitions to include commerce of any kind, and the prohibition stands despite the fact that many retail storekeepers profess that they are Orthodox Jews. In fact, the Rabbis so expanded the prohibitions that they are adequate for an industrial age as well as a commercial one. Thus, without even considering the propriety of using electricity on the Sabbath, the viewing of television was prohibited a few years ago, in a responsum published by Yeshiva University's "Talpioth," because the vulgarity and the commercialism of the programs were not consonant with the mood of the Sabbath. Similarly, one can expect additional new prohibitions; our machine age needs, more than ever, the reminder that man himself is more than machine.

Question:

5. Rackman applies the principles of the Orthodox legal philosophy to concrete questions on the Shabbat. Give his position on each of the following issues relating to the Shabbat.

   a) Using creative art as a form of Sabbath rest

   b) Use of the automobile

   c) Use of electricity

   d) Cohabitation (i.e., sexual intercourse between husband and wife)

   e) Eating

   f) Operating a business establishment

   g) Television

Question:

6. What reason does Rackman give for the proliferation of prohibitions by the Rabbis?

Question:

7. What problems do you find with the Orthodox approach? What strengths?

Chapter 18

The Reform Approach to Jewish Law

We now turn to the second modern reaction to Jewish Law, the viewpoint of Reform Judaism.

(A) THE EARLY REFORM MOVEMENT

Reading: *The Rise of Reform Judaism* by W. Gunther Plaut

J. W. Schorr

The holy Torah, as given to us by Moses, lies before us. Who dares criticize it or doubt its veracity? Who would deny its divinity? Who cannot see that it is imbued with the divine spirit? The purity of its language, the clarity and grandeur of its teachings, the portrayals which leave far behind anything other old nations have to show forth in their myths, must convince even the most ordinary mind that God's spirit is revealed therein! Looking at the sources of the so-called oral teachings which are accessible to us and which are meant to constitute a supplement to the Mosaic law, an expert who examines them without prejudice will have to realize at once that their expression and wording is merely the work of earthborn humans, and therefore subject to error. Nevertheless, it stands there as an authority, surrounding the pure Torah like an iron wall to keep away the beam of light. However, instead of serving as a defense and bulwark, the Torah wastes away inwardly because no criticism has been permitted.

In stating this I presume by no means to rebuke the sages of ancient times, much less reject their teaching or even join the Karaites. Not at all! On the contrary, I am an adherent of tradition, and I honor its representatives. Indeed, I believe that they have developed these conclusions from the Torah with true piety and the purest intention. Also, through their assuidity and faithful care amidst the manifold persecutions and sufferings and among strange religions, they have energetically preserved our holy religion; without it, our religion might perhaps have vanished completely. But I maintain with the deepest conviction that the yoke which, for the prevention of error, they have imposed on our co-religionists, is, in our time, oppressive and can easily lead to the point where one might rather cast it off completely and withdraw altogether from any positive religion. Thus, what they wanted to prevent might, instead, be furthered by the very means they employed. Hence, in order to ward off in time the hovering danger of spreading irreligiousness, all present-day scholars and teachers of the people have the holy duty to fix their eyes sharply on their task and to examine carefully what our wise men thought proper to ordain in their time; and only after having gained this insight will they be able to judge our own times and abolish anything that is not in conformity with it, and instead, take measures corresponding to the new circumstances...

1. Mishna and Talmud were originally not conceived as law books for all times; rather, they represent late written collections of various decisions.

2. The ancient sages wished by no means to prevent posterity from modifying, adding to, or taking away from their decisions, in accordance with new times and circumstances.

3. They intentionally set down the most differing views, specifically also individual opinions and maxims, so that there might be a choice of assenting to one or the other opinion, according to the circumstances.

Michael Creizenach

The intention of the law was that the Israelite ritual system should never sink into the state of an old, amorphous mass of stone, but rather, that it preserve itself with everlasting vitality and that it develop continually according to the needs, circumstances, and educational levels of succeeding generations. This was actually brought about by the prophets, the Sanhedrin, and the Talmudists. Likewise, the Talmudists were far from expecting the slavish obedience we give them in ritual matters. They took all measures which they imagined were necessary for the preservation of religion in their days, leaving it up to later generations to proceed in a similar way. But they were unable to foresee that the precepts regarding the organization of the Synod might later on no longer apply. It is also not true that they used their religious authority mainly to impose burdensome strictures on the people; on the contrary, wherever they deemed it necessary, they introduced such significant relaxations of the rules that our rabbis of today would recoil if they were expected to introduce such measures. These were relaxations concerning not merely some milder interpretation of a passage in Scripture or the suspension of a Synodal decision, but indeed, in some instances, they discontinued the practice of certain precepts altogether.

It is only due to ignorance and the excessive anxiety of later days that our religion has taken on a mummy-like appearance, that indeed it has become isolated from real life by a deep chasm; that it consists of thousands of precepts which the people do not heed or do not even know. Most parents no longer know how to proceed in order to give their children a religious education which is to last them for life. The decrees of the various Synodal assemblies were of the character of laws which are binding for all times. Had the scribes issued laws for all times, one might well ask: Why were these laws not already introduced by Moses? However, a law, decree, which at its very inception was understood to be temporary, cannot become irrevocable through the fact that the authority which created it has ceased to exist. Its validity ceases by itself, with the fall of that power, and particularly so in the case before us, when it is a matter of obeying only the authorities of one's own time.

This, however, does not mean that all measures and decisions of the ancient scribes should be disregarded. To do so would rob us of all those useful means in the observance of the Pentateuch which we owe the Talmud, and would put us into the labyrinth in which the Karaites have found themselves for many centuries, without being able to achieve a satisfactory organization of their religious affairs. On the contrary, we wish to leave untouched many a custom which, through universal esteem, has attained even in our own time a high degree of venerableness. Take, for instance, the beautiful, scientifically accomplished calendar computation, of which it can be said, indeed, that it is an attestation of our wisdom and insight before the eyes of the other nations. It is only necessary that, in our awe for tradition, we do not exceed the boundaries which our ancient sages themselves would have set for us, had they foreseen our present-day conditions and had they not firmly believed that Israel's dispersion would not last half the time that it has lasted already. These boundaries can be described in a few words and can be narrowed down to these few maxims:

We recognize every interpretation of the scriptural passages, propounded by the regularly constituted synods, either as traditional or as derived by means of the well-known hermeneutic rules -- provided such interpretation was reached in unanimity. On the other hand, wherever there was a case of divided opinions, we follow the less strict version so long as it does not contradict our own conviction.

However, we shall maintain institutions and legal safeguards only if they still factually exist in most communities, and if they are of such character that the Israelite can continue existing with them; in other words, if he, as merchant, worker, farmer, and civil servant can practice his profession without grievous restraints. Within these boundaries lies, at the same time, the assertion of the degree of obligation that we concede to the statements of the Talmud; yet it is better that we also discuss this matter clearly. Let us proceed with all the candor and love of truth that befits an Israelite, and let us fear neither the accusation and heresy by the few Jews whose convictions we may offend, nor enmity on the part of certain Christians whom, in any case, we shall never be able to please.

We recognize the Talmud as being, at least for the present, a serviceable means for the interpretation of those ritual commandments which, according to the individual concepts of each man, are binding to this day; and we adhere to these interpretations in observing them within the already established boundaries.

We regard those portions of the Talmud which do not elucidate the Mosaic laws as merely humanly instituted decrees;

however, for the furtherance of good morality and pure piety, we gladly avail ourselves of anything that appeals to our reasoning.

We consider those passages in the Talmud which are not consistent with the principle of the universal love of man as outbursts of passionate hatred of which, unfortunately, quite often the best men cannot free themselves when they are oppressed in a disgraceful way, and when they see that all considerations to which the dignity of human nature gives them undeniable claims are being violated against themselves. Statements of that kind, regardless of where and into what book they might have gained entrance, are not only alien to the spirit of our religion, but indeed, contrary to its letter.

Question:

1. The Early Reform Movement:

   a) What was the attitude of the early Reform Movement toward the Talmud? Toward the Bible? Why was there a difference in attitude toward them?

   b) The Karaites rejected the whole notion of an Oral tradition and wanted to return to the "authentic" Judaism of the Written Law only. Why might we think of identifying Reform Judaism with Karaism? (Consider the Reform position on the Talmud, which is, after all, the Oral Law.) Why are both Schorr and Creizenach concerned to distinguish Reform Judaism from Karaism? (Consider the biblical injunction of "an eye for an eye, a tooth for a tooth." The Talmud interprets this in terms of pecuniary retribution, i.e., one who injures another gives him the <u>money</u> which his eye is worth. The Karaites interpreted the injunction literally, however; i.e., the one who injures must actually give the injured party his eye. Now do you know why the Reformers wanted to distinguish themselves from the Karaites? Think of other examples which would make them want to make such a distinction.)

   c) How free are we, according to the Reformers, to change the law in order to fit modern needs? Explain how their interpretation of what the rabbis of the Talmud did supports their view on what we can do with the Law today.

d) Recall briefly Hirsch's reaction to the Reform position which you described in a) and c).

(B) MODERN REFORM POSITIONS

Reading: Reform Responsa by Solomon Freehof, "Introduction"

<u>Reform Judaism is strong in ethical idealism but weak in legal discipline.</u> It calls to the personal conscience and points to social progress; but it deprecates old ceremonial habits and neglects the literature that treasures them. The central source of its inspiration is the Prophetic literature; the weakest influence upon its thought is the Halachic tradition, extending from the Talmud to the codes.

The Reform Movement was well served by this emphasized Prophetism, which also enabled it to exert a strong influence on the Jewish community. <u>In an era of fading tradition, where multitudes were abandoning their faith, Reform saved thousands of deserters by giving them an acceptable ideal and proclaiming it Jewish.</u> In a time of expansion and prosperity, it imposed decency upon wealth and helped build the organized charities in every great American city. And within itself, Reform felt that it was a purified, a noble, Judaism.

Yet this confidence has considerably faded. The Reform Movement is no longer certain that it has found in Prophetism a sure foundation for its Judaism. Basic debates now arise in almost every national meeting. The discussions reveal a search for a broader religious foundation, a quest for a revised relationship with the post-biblical legal literature. Although no one suggests a reacceptance of the old codes, some propose the development of some new codes or guides to give authority to the ceremonial practices. The Bible and its ethical ideals no longer seem sufficient. Reform is groping toward a new appreciation of the Jewish legal tradition.

Whatever adjustment will be made, it will never be a return to mere obedience. Reform hopes to find a new balance between discipline and liberty. If it succeeds, it will be stronger and more widely appealing than ever before in its century and a half of history.

The tens of thousands of Jews who, at the beginning of the modern era, fell into the habit of neglecting the ritual law, et cetera, and who had ceased to consider themselves religious Jews, came into very little contact with the rabbinate. But the Reformers, who were also neglectful of ritual, yet insisted that they <u>were</u> religious Jews, came necessarily into violent clash with the rabbinate. The general Orthodox rabbinical opinion on Reform is set forth in full detail in "Eleh Divre Habris," the responsa collection gathered in 1818 to denounce the Reformers in Hamburg. The general mood of these responsa is that it is utterly forbidden to make any changes in the traditional ritual. Thus, it immediately became evident that no adjustment in Jewish services or ceremonies could be made as long as the authority of the Orthodox rabbinate remained unchallenged. If there was to be Reform, there was no other way than to renounce the authority of the old rabbinate. The Reform Movement was therefore, from the beginning, anti-rabbinical, and hence, averse to the rabbinical literature, the Talmud, and the codes, which were the source of the rabbinical authority. The early Reform Movement became essentially Biblical. Its leaders held proudly to the inspiration of Scripture -- or, at least, of the Ten Commandments revealed on Sinai -- and of the inspired prophets.

At first it was easy to maintain this preference of Bible over Talmud. The Bible was the common source of religion in the Western world. It was idealistic and inspiring, while the rabbinical literature could be easily envisaged as merely legalistic pettifogging. Yet this rejection of the Talmud and the choice of the Bible as the sole foundation for Reform Judaism, appealing as it appeared to be, could not be long maintained.

The weakness of the position was primarily that the self-description of Reform as being solely Biblical was simply not true. <u>All of Reform Jewish life in all its observances was actually post-Biblical in origin</u>. None of the arrangements of worship, the hours of service, the text of the prayers, no matter how rewritten, was primarily Biblical.

The whole of Jewish liturgy is an achievement of post-Biblical times. The religious calendar, based indeed on Scriptures, was elaborated and defined in post-Biblical times. Marriage ceremonies and burial rites were all post-Biblical. The Bible, of course, was the source of ethical ideas, but the actual religious life could not avoid the historic rabbinic constructs that lived in the pageantry of the Jewish mode of life.

This was understood early by Isaac M. Wise, when, in the Cleveland Conference (1885), he agreed with the Conservative leader, Isaac Lesser, and his group, that the Bible must be interpreted through the Talmud. David Einhorn and the "radical" Reformers of the Eastern Seaboard denounced Wise as a compromiser, recreant to the ideals of Reform. But he said that any attempt to expound the Bible without the aid of tradition would lead to the sterile word-worship of the Karaites. That Rabbi Wise was right is clear to us. We see that, although the Bible is the sunlight, the source of the primary ideals, the Talmudic literature has created the spectrum of our daily life. Whatever percentage of the total traditional legislation Reform Jews observe, it is all mainly post-Biblical in origin. <u>Our life is inspired by the Bible, but organized by the Talmud</u>.

The practical fact that our actual religious practice springs from the Talmud made it impossible to maintain the first Reform insistence that the Bible alone was the source of religious inspiration. Moreover, the special status of the Bible as the preferred source of religious inspiration soon became weakened. Soon after the beginning of the Reform Movement, the Bible itself began to be subjected to the new criticism which taught that the Torah was a hodgepodge of fragments. How, then, could it now be the sole source of religious inspiration? That is why, for example, Rabbi Wise attacked the Higher Criticism and held firmly to the doctrine of Biblical revelation. But his position was difficult to maintain in the face of the expanding, new Biblical science, which, in its earlier days, held the field without a strong rival. If, then, neither the Talmud nor the Bible was divinely revealed, what could remain as the religious foundation of Reform?

It was becoming clear that Reform Judaism, with all the other liberal forms of religion, <u>must now grope toward a new definition of authority and revelation</u>; otherwise, its form of Judaism would degenerate into a mere convenient construct of willfully chosen observances, where the will of God is only metaphorically present and where there is really no such thing as a commandment.

A doctrine of divine revelation that can reach the heart of modern man is still to be developed. Yet it is sure that whatever descriptive definition may be arrived at, the human personality will no longer be described as an entirely passive recipient. He must also be an agent. In some way God reveals Himself, if not entirely, then surely in part, through the searching and striving of man. If man is an agent, then his total experience may become religiously significant. Biography and history are vehicles of revelation. If that is the case, there need be no sharp distinction in principle between Biblical and post-Biblical literature. God may well speak through both. The clearness of the divine Presence may be less in the Talmudic debates than in the prophetic orations, but, then, there are parts of the Bible which seem less inspired than parts of the Talmud. We cannot completely deny God's presence in the rabbinic literature.

We obey many rabbinic customs and neglect many more. As long as we are thus selective, we cannot believe that rabbinic law is God's mandate. It is, of course, possible that by some future date our part of the tradition will grow, first habitual, then legal, then authoritative. But it is not authoritative now, and cannot, and perhaps should not, be declared so to be. If, then, it is not a God-given authority, what does the law mean to us? Why do we so regularly consult it, and how do we react to the answers that we receive?

The law is to us a human product. That does not mean that God does not somehow reveal Himself in the "language of the children of men." Perhaps He does, but if He does, His self-revelation is not so perfect, nor so clear, nor so final, as to make the whole law His sure commandment. To us the law is human, but nobly human, developed by devoted minds who dedicated their best efforts to answering the question, "What doth the Lord require of thee?" Therefore, we respect it and seek its guidance. Some of its provisions have faded from our lives. We do not regret the fact. But as to those laws that we do follow, we wish them to be in harmony with tradition.

Even this guidance, confined to those observances that are still vital, we do not consider to be absolute. If, for example, a study of the law should reveal that a full marriage service can be conducted only in the presence of a minyan of ten (which, by the way, is open to some question), that decision would certainly influence us, but we would still occasionally conduct a marriage ceremony in the rabbi's study in the presence of only two witnesses. If a study of the law should reveal that only a pious mohel may perform circumcision (which is also open to question), that would influence us toward the use of mohelim, but would hardly prevent us from using the skills of a surgeon, especially a Jewish surgeon. In other words, the law is authoritative enough to influence us, but not so completely so as to control us. <u>The rabbinic law is our guidance but not our governance</u>.

Reform responsa are <u>not directive, but advisory</u>. They thus differ in basic doctrine from Orthodox responsa. They also differ in mood. The Orthodox mood is, at the present, extra strict because it is deemed dangerous in these non-observant days to make concessions. For example, a recent responsum discussed whether it is permissible to use the same oven for meat dishes and for milk dishes (not at the same time, of course). The Orthodox author admits that, according to the law, it is quite permissible to do so, but that nowadays, when there is so much laxity, it is better to prohibit such use (Hama-or, Shevat, 1954). The author is not concerned with whether such a decision is practical, whether it will be obeyed, or whether it will increase the number of people who will find it impossible to be observant. His concern is not the people, but the law. He is not helping the people; he is building a fence to protect the law.

Our concern is more with <u>the people than with the legal system</u>. Whenever possible, such interpretations are developed which are feasible and conforming to the needs of life. Sometimes, indeed, a request must be answered in the negative when there is no way in the law for a permissive answer to be given. Generally, the law is searched for such opinion as can conform with the realities of life. If no such answer can be found, it is so stated, and then the law must take its chance in the struggle with life.

Question:

2. The Modern Reform Movement (Freehof, Petuchowski): The Modern approach accepts the Talmud and selects from it rather than rejecting it outright.

   a) <u>The reason for this change</u>: Why, according to Freehof, do Modern Reformers find it necessary to reckon with both the Bible and the Talmud? Or, in other words, what is wrong with the early Reform attempt to base Judaism on the Bible only? (Hint: The answer involves a change in attitude toward both the Talmud and the Bible. Describe the change in attitude toward each separately.)

   b) <u>The nature of the change</u>: In what sense do Modern Reformers "accept" Tradition? (Hint: Consider Freehof's statement, "The rabbinic law is our guidance but not our governance.") What is the underlying assumption of the Reform approach to the Bible and Talmud as far as divine Revelation is concerned? (Be careful: Reform Judaism does <u>not</u> deny Revelation. It does bring man into the picture in a "new" way, however. What is it?)

Reading: <u>Ever Since Sinai</u> by Jakob Petuchowski (pp.108-114)

What, however, is this modern Jew supposed to <u>do</u> by way of practicing the provisions of the Torah? He could, of course, <u>voluntarily</u> subject himself in one "leap of action," to borrow a phrase of Abraham J. Heschel's, to the full regimen of Orthodox Jewish Law. That is to say, he could silence his own doubts, and terminate the anguish of his own personal search, by finding complete spiritual fulfillment in the traditional modes of Jewish living. He could do so even without becoming "Orthodox" in theory by regarding this step as purely his own personal solution, and by refraining from taking a censorious attitude towards those who are unwilling to take the identical step.

Yet it is unlikely that this step would appeal to the majority of modern Jews -- gratifying as it might well be in the case of individuals. Here we must revert to a point already made in chapter V: the distinction between "legislation" and "commandment." <u>"Legislation" is something that is "on the books." A "commandment," on the other hand, is addressed to me personally.</u> Now, it may well be that much of the legislation found in the Torah originated as "commandments" experienced by ancient Israel. But it is also true that, in the course of time, it did become "legislation," and as such, applicable only to the everyday life of a community governed by this legislation.

The modern Jew, as we have defined him, lacks the awareness of living in such a community, and therefore, also the prerequisite for re-translating the cold letter of legislation into the personally meaningful and significant sounds of commandments. This is not to say that the modern Jew rejects the idea of "community" as such. Even the non-religious Jew in America is often very community-minded. But it just is no longer the kind of community which would accept a 16th century, or even 3rd century, formulation of Jewish Law as its constitutional basis. The large American Jewish community, with its hospitals and its welfare funds, with its Jewish Centers and its "defense agencies," is, basically, a <u>secular</u> community. It may contain the seeds out of which a religious revival might one day sprout. But the religious revival itself has not yet taken place. This much, then, is clear: that the kind of "holy community" which enabled the Jew in the past to experience legislation as commandment is one no longer known to the modern Jew.

"Listening for the Commandment" --
By thus stating the diagnosis we have already hinted at the cure. In the first place, <u>the modern Jew must regain the frame of mind in which he is able to experience the "commandment" addressed to him.</u> It is a frame of mind which the Rabbis of old attempted to create, when they insisted that the Revelation at Sinai must be as topical to the Jew as if it had happened to him "today." It is also a frame of mind to which the modern Jew <u>can</u> attain, as has been demonstrated by Franz Rosenzweig, both in his thought and in his way of life.

How does one set about listening for the commandment? There could hardly be a hard-and-fast rule for this. But one of the prerequisites is undoubtedly the willingness and the readiness to shape one's whole life according to the pattern which God gives us to see. And we do not have to start from nothing! The accumulated heritage of the Jewish past is ours to select from, ours to experiment with, in our endeavor to find out what God wants _us_ to do.

Consider, for example, the case of the man who, after sober reflection, has come to the conclusion that one of the ways in which he can make God more real in his life is that of _self-discipline_. He cultivates the habit of saying "no" to himself occasionally. He is now looking for a regimen which would place this kind of self-discipline on a more permanent basis. He might hit upon the idea of abstaining from certain kinds of meat, such as beef or lamb.

Now, if this man were a Jew, a moderately informed kind of Jew, he would find such a system of self-discipline ready-made for him in the pages of the Torah. This he could adopt as a whole, or in part. The meat from which he abstains would, then, not be lamb, but pork. Moreover, in addition to cultivating self-discipline for his own spiritual welfare, he would, at the same time, strengthen his links with the Jewish past and the Torah tradition. Above all, he would furnish an example of how a cold letter of dietary legislation could become a living "commandment."

It is thus clear that the modern Jew in search of the "commandment" addressed to him must, as a starting point, engage in intensive Jewish study. A daily period set aside for this task is surely within reach of all. Yet, the moment a decision for Jewish study has been reached, an important "commandment" has already been accepted. Of all the things a man can do which, according to the Rabbis, would yield him enjoyment, both in this world and in the next, "the study of Torah" ranks as the greatest. For, with all the emphasis which is placed on "action" rather than on "study," the latter is far from being underestimated. The Rabbis recognized that "study leads to action." It will certainly do so in the case of the modern Jew who studies _in order_ to discover what to _do_.

And that is why study will have to go hand-in-hand with "experimentation." The modern Jew, fumblingly at first, and overcoming his initial shyness, will want to "try out" those practices and observances which _might_ contain God's commandment to _him_. Here, practice is the only way to find out. Only by actually _trying_ to observe it, will he be able to discover whether he is dealing with a "commandment" or just with another item of what is still only "legislation" to him.

Of course, all of this will be marked by a high degree of subjectivity. There is in it none of the certainty which Orthodoxy promises its adherents, none of the matter-of-factness of complying with the established legislation of a body politic. One individual's observance of the Sabbath, for example, is unlikely to be identical with that of another individual. The former might consider that to be forbidden "work" which, for the latter, is an indispensable ingredient of his Sabbath "delight." But this is the price which will have to be paid. For the majority of modern Jews, it will either be this or nothing at all.

It is a state of affairs well described by Franz Rosenzweig when he said that what we have in common nowadays is the landscape, and no longer the common road on which Jews walked in unity from the close of the Talmud to the dawn of Emancipation. The best we can do today is to work at our individual roads in the common landscape. Perhaps the future will again know of a common road, or, more likely, of a common _system of roads_.

"The Common Landscape" --

There is, however, a limit to too much subjectivity, just as there is the need to preserve the "common landscape." In the first place, it must not be forgotten that the modern Jewish individuals, with all their diversities, will, if they are interested in Torah at all, share a common ground and a common aspiration. What does it matter if there are variations in the minutiae of observance, as long as there is a willingness to "observe" at all?! It should be borne in mind that we are speaking of the modern Jew who is anxious to find his way back to the Torah, and not of him who is trying to run away from it.

The second consideration is that the very nature of Torah makes it impossible for the modern Jew to remain an isolated individual. Jewish living, in one form or another, is community living. The Jewish hermit is inconceivable. (The nearest approach we ever had to "Hermits," the sectarians who shunned Jerusalem and went to live near the Dead Sea, lived there in highly organized <u>communities</u>. The now famous Dead Sea Scrolls arose within a <u>community</u> framework.) And, if the old form of the community has broken down at the beginning of the modern Jew's devotion, a new form of the "holy community" is already in the making.

The Torah was given to the <u>People</u> of Israel. God's covenant is, as we have seen, with the "chosen <u>people</u>." But if the historical identity of Israel, in space and in time, is to remain intact, because, without the people there would be no covenant, it follows that, over and above the "commandments" which the modern Jewish individual accepts as his <u>personal</u> obligation, there will be others to which he submits as a member of the People of Israel.

An example will help to make this clear: A modern Jew has developed the habit of prayer. More than this, he regards daily prayer as a "commandment" which God wants <u>him</u> to perform. But this Jew does not know Hebrew. He prays in English. This, even from the point of view of the old rabbinic codes, is perfectly acceptable. But if, knowing that his English prayer is acceptable, this Jew were now to agitate for the abolition of Hebrew in synagogue and school, he would have to be told that he is acting contrary to his Jewish obligations. A pardonable ignorance is one thing. The imposition of this ignorance on generations yet unborn is quite another. For Hebrew happens to be a factor of supreme importance when it comes to the historic consciousness of the People of Israel, if not to its very survival.

The same might be said about the day of the week on which the Jewish Sabbath is observed, about celebrating the Festivals on their proper dates, and about many another "external" provision which is of no intrinsic merit in and by itself, but which gains its significance by maintaining the cohesion of Israel. In all such cases, an undue amount of subjectivism would be checked by the requirements of the "holy community." Yet, the "holy community" itself, in its modern form, will become possible only because of the personal commitments of Jewish <u>individuals</u>, who have learned to "observe" God's "commandments" to <u>them</u>. In this interplay of spiritual forces, of aspirations and of loyalties, there might well lie the hope of translating Torah from the realm of mere theory into that of "observing, doing, and performing."

<u>Question</u>:

3. It is important to note that most factions of Conservative Judaism accept Revelation in much the same way as Freehof describes it -- that is, through the process of "reinterpretation" by man. Consequently, the difference between Reform and Conservative Judaism lies largely in the differing <u>conclusions</u> which they draw from their <u>common</u> view of Revelation: the Conservative Movement holds that it is the <u>community</u> (as represented by its rabbinic scholars) which must reinterpret Judaism for modern times. On the other hand, Reform Judaism is marked by a staunch individualism: it is the <u>individual</u> who is to select what segments of Tradition he is to observe. a) What do you think is the motivation for the Reform individualistic approach to Tradition? (Hint: Consider Freehof's statement that "Our concern is more with the people than with the legal system.") b) Petuchowski describes a method by which the individual is to make his selections. Distinguish carefully between "legislation" and "commandment." Try to give an example of each in American Law. Now, then, according to Petuchowski, in order to decide what parts of Tradition he will observe, the individual must decide <u>for himself</u> what parts of Tradition are legislation and what parts are commandments. Why is study an important part of this process? What part does experimentation play? c) What is the danger in the Reform approach (called by Petuchowski "the price which will have to be paid")? Why is this a danger? (A very important question. Hint: How effective can one individual be in attaining the many social goals that are Judaism's? Or, in other words, why is there a need for concerted action? Moreover, even in terms of the many individual goals for which Judaism strives, why does one psychologically <u>need</u> to be part of a group to attain them? <u>Will</u> a person, in fact, persevere in striving for his own personal goals if he does not feel that others value his goals and support him in his efforts? d) What factor

does Petuchowski find it necessary to introduce in his "second consideration" in order to get around this danger? (Answer: He admits that there are obligations to the People of Israel.) Note that Conservative Judaism is going to expand the area of obligations that we have as members of the Jewish community and narrow the area of subjectively determined religious practice considerably.

Question:

4. If Reform Judaism makes observance of Jewish Law largely a personal matter, how does it differ from Christianity in regard to Law? (Hint: Consider the selections from Paul in chapter 10, and Petuchowski's statement that "the best we can do today is to work at our individual roads in the common landscape.")

(C) A CONCRETE CASE OF REFORM PRACTICE

Reading: Berhard Wechsler in The Rise of Reform Judaism, W. Gunther Plaut, ed.

Reform Judaism was essentially the response of a living people to the urgent demands of the time.

There were few areas in which practice and principle posed greater dilemmas than in the area of Sabbath and holiday observance. The whole question of the authority of tradition came here into sharpest focus. It need hardly be pointed out that many of the problems raised here still are matters at issue today, for, by definition, a dynamic Reform cannot give fixed permanent answers in matters of practices.

"What Work Is Permitted?"

At issue is the command not to work (on the Sabbath), the stoppage of all commercial activity. To what extent must an Israelite observe this? To the extent that he may not engage in any profession or activity which might at some future time force him to disregard the command? Does it extend so far that the observance of the Sabbath command supersedes all other obligations in case he has chosen such a profession or is subject to a collision of obligations under circumstances over which he has no control?

Does the Sabbath command yield to other obligations in such cases? What happens when someone is engaged in commercial activities which are incompatible with work stoppage on the Sabbath, because such activity must be carried on, even on that day, lest his entire temporal existence be threatened, and he be subject to the most severe losses and consequences? Is work stoppage commanded under such conditions, and is it an absolute obligation, or may an Israelite make some sort of arrangement of the carrying on of his business by eliminating at least his own personal direct participation in such activity? And, finally, the last question: What happens in some cases in which work stoppage would lead to the bitterest and harshest losses? Where the whole temporal happiness, either one's own or someone else's, is in question? May an Israelite make remedial arrangements? May he let non-Jews make such arrangements, if possible? And where not possible, may he himself make them?

Gentlemen, these are some of the questions and circumstances which we must consider and which we cannot avoid answering. These are no idle or casuistic questions. They are taken from present-day life. I need hardly tell you that our people expect from us definitive declarations and well-founded opinions on this point. These conflicts lurk everywhere and urge us on to make a decision. In my opinion, we should not, therefore, be frightened by the fact that, in making such a decision, we may have to make an independent judgment. For the traditional concept, even the Biblical point of view, gives us only sparse analogies and hints for the purpose of such a decision. We must be guided by our conscience and our conviction.

We turn first to the question of occupation. Here, above all, we must make a distinction. There is the occupation which we carry out as a consequence of our general obligations in life, one that we do not choose ourselves, but which comes to us because we are part of state, society, and community. The other is the kind of occupation which an Israelite chooses for himself, such as a teacher, lawyer, and so forth. In the case of the former, where it was our obligation to accept an occupation which is incompatible with work stoppage on the Sabbath (as a soldier, as a government official, etc.), it is not necessary to amplify the matter greatly. Everyone must carry out his obligations and must do what his office demands; even though the Bible and tradition are silent regarding such a collision of duties (they only speak clearly about pikuah nefesh, the saving of life), history, the development of man, and the ethical consciousness of the present speak of this the more loudly.

More difficult is the decision which concerns an occupation which is incompatible with the Sabbath, but is one that we have chosen ourselves, where we voluntarily took upon ourselves obligations which collide with the celebration of the Sabbath. Who forces anyone to become a doctor, lawyer, teacher, and so forth? But even here, I believe, we must overcome all scruples. Even here we must be satisfied with the answer: Life, conditions, our position in society in general, are forcing our hand. Should the Israelite today avoid all those higher professional activities which are not compatible with the observance of the ceremonial law, and especially the celebration of the Sabbath? Would his religion want this of him? Must he resolve to renounce all opportunities of education? Even if he would make such a resolution, it would not help, for times cannot be altered through resolution or authoritarian dicta. Incidentally, while we lack pronouncements on this subject, we do not lack analogies to dilute an all-pervasive observance of the Sabbath. Rabbis were doctors, government officials, and so forth, especially in the Moorish period, to cite just one example. However, we must draw a distinct line between the activity which is a consequence of obligations which have been assumed, and that which can be postponed without endangering the fulfillment of such obligations. Therefore, we must indeed ask of the doctor, even the soldier and official, that he should observe the Sabbath and stay away from occupational activity as far as his duties will allow. To be sure, we must leave it to his religious conscience to draw this line of distinction.

I shall now turn to the question of occupation. According to the Shulkhan Arukh, the Jewish customs collector may employ a non-Jew to take in taxes and customs, or to write receipts, or even to mint coins, with only the condition that he himself should not draw any gain from this activity, which does, however, not quite fit minting activities (Orah Hayim 244). The principle here is that the strictness of the Sabbath is meliorated because, without such concession, Israelites could not be tax or customs collectors. It is too bad that in the ancient days there were not other similar occupations, for, had there been, we would not have to search for meliorating excuses in today's occupational circumstances. Had this been the case, the manufacturer, the artisan, the merchant, would not be face to face with the sad alternative, either to leave his trade or act contrary to his religious duties. But why should we not be satisfied with these examples which make it possible to declare that the Israelite is obligated to withdraw on the Sabbath day from business and trade, and, wherever possible, to let these come to a complete standstill, but in all cases where such cessation completely interferes with his temporal existence, he would not be transgressing a religious obligation if he would make arrangements to have non-Jews carry out that which is necessary? From the rabbinic point of view, such an explanation falls under the category of <u>amira lenakhri shevut</u> (making arrangements through a non-Jew is a further safeguard of the command to rest). Therefore, it does not need any justification if we suspend such a <u>shevut</u> in the face of overriding needs in order to prevent further transgression. We do not find any command or prohibition in the Bible which could be applied to our circumstances, because the Bible does not know of any such collision of obligations. Therefore, we must turn to the spirit and the reasonable purpose of the Sabbath celebration. The day is meant to elevate, to strengthen, to encourage, to afford rest and recreation. How can this be when worry about one's livelihood lurks like a ghost and disturbs the equanimity of the celebration? When, on every Sabbath, the worry over one's livelihood battles with higher spiritual ideas?

But, it is said, there is greater danger when an Israelite allows a non-Jew to carry on business so that he himself would take part in such activities, that he would supervise them, pay attention to them, and thus be drawn away from the celebration of the Sabbath. Gentlemen, there is danger here as well as there. The question is: which is the least evil? The question is: how can we bring the present circumstances into possible accord with the needs of religion? To be sure, there is temptation, but that is not introduced through our declaration. It already exists, and it beckons already more than a little. It is our task to inquire what, in the spirit of our religion, is admissible, and what is not.

Who would doubt today that, in the spirit of our religion, it is permissible to violate the Sabbath when one's total possessions are in question, when the house is burning, when the elements are raging, and demand quick rescue of one's property? Who would doubt that it would be permitted to act in such cases, even on the Sabbath, rather than look on with outward calm and inner despair and disquiet, while misfortune crashes about us and perdition threatens our whole future? For here the principle applies: <u>Mutav sh'yehalel Shabbat ehad v'al yehalel Shabbatot harbe</u> (It is better to desecrate one Sabbath so that one should not be forced to desecrate many Sabbaths). What kind of resignation would be asked of us to observe the commandment in all its strictness? Must we not here remember the wise saying: The Torah was not given to the ministering angels? Who can help but publicly contradict rabbinic rigidity in such a case?

In conclusion, I would summarize my suggestions as follows, and would formulate the proposal of the committee in this manner:

The assembly should declare that the Israelite may follow the duties of his occupation in all cases where higher obligations (service of the State as a soldier, doctor, and so forth) come in collision with the celebration of the Sabbath and where they cannot be postponed. He is, however, obligated to observe the Sabbath as far as his professional obligations permit, and must let his business and profession come to complete rest.

The general duty to avert danger to life, be it one's own or someone else's, supersedes the duty to celebrate the Sabbath, and one is not only permitted, but even obligated, to do everything necessary in this regard and to withdraw from Sabbath celebration to this end.

The assembly should declare that, to be sure, it is the obligation of the Israelite not to seek a livelihood on the Sabbath, to abstain from any gain, and not to worry about his temporal existence, but, instead, to dedicate the day to God. There are occupations which do not admit of rest on the Sabbath because they must be carried on even on this day, and this is the case especially with artisans, manufacturers, and merchants, and some other types of business. Where this is the case, it is permitted to have non-Jews do what is necessary for the carrying on of the business, if personal direct participation by the Jew can thereby be avoided. Where it is a question of one's total material welfare, where one's total possessions or the means for one's future existence are in question and are threatened, a Jew would not transgress a religious duty if he takes remedial measures and, where others cannot assist him, attends to them himself.

Question:

5. The Concrete Example of Reform Practice:

Method: Probably the key portion in the whole article is the following: "For the traditional concept, even the biblical point of view, gives us only sparse analogies and hints for the purpose of such a decision. We must be guided by our conscience and our conviction."

a) "Conviction" to what?

b) Note that our Reform author does mention this conviction. Would Paul share this conviction? (Now perhaps you can answer question 4 better.)

c) The author implies that, had the tradition given more than "sparse analogies and hints," his present doubts as to the law would not have arisen. In other words, if the traditional law were specific, he would simply follow it. But is his problem really the obscurity of the law, or rather, how the law agrees with his "conscience"? Explain your answer.

d) Now let us examine his entire claim that the law is obscure. Do you really think that when the rabbis wrote the law they were totally unaware of the fact that, in some cases, "work stoppage would lead to the bitterest and harshest losses"? Why, then, did they nevertheless require work stoppage? (Hint: Consider the values of the Shabbat which they were trying to preserve; can they still be achieved if one works?) And what would _they_ say to an individual who claims that work stoppage brings him severe financial losses?

<u>Application</u>: What is Wechsler's decision? What does he consider to be the ideal practice in regard to working on the Sabbath? (Note here how the "conviction" of which he spoke earlier fits in.) Exactly where and for what reasons does Tradition disagree with Wechsler's decision?

Chapter 19

The Conservative Approach to Jewish Law

All readings in this chapter are from Tradition and Change, Mordecai Waxman, ed., The Burning Bush Press, New York, 1958.

I. Reading: "Introduction" by Mordecai Waxman

The Ideology of the Conservative Movement

The ideology of Conservative Judaism is more a matter of emphasis than of a radically new doctrine. The religious developments and the American Jewish character, described in the preceding section, did not, in the view of the founders and later leaders of Conservative Judaism, call for more than a shift in emphasis. Reform responded to the modern era by revolutionizing Judaism and Neo-Orthodoxy, in the persons of Samson Raphael Hirsch and other less articulate defenders, called for a resistance to the spirit of the times. The Conservative leaders, more traditional than the Reform and less obdurate than the Orthodox, were disposed to heed the admonition of the sages: "be as pliant as the reed and not as unyielding as the cedar." The pliancy led to new emphases. But it should be recognized that underlying them there were two firm principles.

1. The founders of Conservative Judaism had no intention of starting a new wing or denomination or party in Judaism. Their purpose and their philosophy were clearly expressed in the name they applied to themselves. They were conservative and their object was to conserve the Jewish traditions. Morais, Mendes, Kohut, and their successors in official leadership, Solomon Schechter, Louis Ginzberg, and Cyrus Adler, were all scrupulous in asserting that they represented a tendency and not a party. They conceived of their role as that of presenting an organized and meaningful alternative to the Reform movement and to Hebrew Union College.

When Morais suggested that the Seminary be called "The Orthodox Seminary," and when Mendes sought to organize the Orthodox forces and to rally them behind the Seminary, they were not playing politics. They believed that they represented traditional Judaism. And so did Schechter, who, in organizing the United Synagogue in 1913, asserted that he was providing a medium for all of traditional Judaism.

The Conservative movement has always clung to the position that it is not a denomination in the Jewish fold. It holds that it *is* Judaism. It is the Jewish tradition continuing along its path in time and space with its characteristic dynamism. It is true that there are other variants of Judaism -- Orthodoxy and Reform. But, then, there have always been movements to the left and right of normative Judaism. Mishnaic times resounded to the clash between the Pharisees, the Sadducees, the Essenes, and the early Christians. Eight centuries later Jewry was reft by the conflict between Rabbinites and Karaites. Ultimately, the Pharisees and their spiritual descendants, the Rabbinites, prevailed, and gave a specific tone to Judaism. Conservative Judaism sees itself as being in this tradition -- a sort of twentieth century Pharisee tradition. While it recognizes that Orthodoxy and Reform play a significant role in Jewish life, it feels that Reform is a revolutionary deviation from Jewish tradition, and that Orthodoxy, in stultifying the inner dynamism of Judaism, has taken itself on to a side path of Jewish life. To itself it assigns the role of being the staunch upholder of the Jewish tradition and of its inherent dynamism.

2. In making the conservation of the Jewish tradition their objective, the founders and leaders of Conservative Judaism were not blind to the pressures created by the American Jewish scene and by the modern world. They recognized that the survival of Judaism was imperilled by non-observance, by ignorance, and by intellectual confusion. But they were not prepared to make these factors the determinants of what Judaism is and should be. The Conservative movement has not really been a mass phenomenon, even though it has attracted the loyalty of a great number of Jews. It has sought to shape

the community rather than allow the community to shape it. Its thinking and goals have been derived from the Jewish tradition rather than from doctrinaire or sociological forces. It feels that the Jewish community is malleable, that it is reclaimable, and that it is, potentially at least, devoted to Judaism. The problem, as it sees it, is to state Judaism in meaningful terms, to focus attention on its essentials, and to communicate these things to the Jewish public.

Question:

1. "The Conservative movement has always clung to the position that it is not a denomination in the Jewish fold. It holds that it *is* Judaism." Frankly, that is a rather conceited statement to make. But the author, and the movement for which he speaks, are not just indulging in self-conceit when they make such statements. They offer objective facts to support their claims. To see this, consider the following:

   a) Who were the Pharisees? The Sadducees? The Essenes? The Rabbinites? The Karaites?

   b) Which of the groups mentioned in a) constitute "normative" Judaism? That is, if you were seeking to discover *the* Jewish view on any issue, to which of those groups would you turn for your answer?

   c) Why, according to Rabbi Waxman, does Reform Judaism fail to carry on the normative, Pharisaic-Rabbinite position?

   d) Why does Orthodox Judaism fail in this regard?

   e) How, then, does the general approach of the Conservative movement make it "a sort of twentieth century Pharisee tradition"?

Question:

2. How would a Reform thinker of our day answer the claim that Conservative Judaism is "the staunch upholder of the Jewish tradition and of its inherent dynamism"? How would an Orthodox thinker react to it? As we continue reading, we shall

note that these differences depend largely on the diverse ways in which the three groups interpret a) what went on in Jewish history; and b) what the present Jewish community now needs in order to preserve its Jewishness.

Question:

3. "The Conservative movement began as a liberalizing influence in reaction to the strict Orthodox way of doing things." True or false? How <u>did</u> it begin? That is, what was -- and is -- its purpose? How is this reflected in its method -- namely, "to state Judaism in meaningful terms, to focus attention on its essentials, and to communicate these things to the Jewish public"?

Reading:

Starting from these underlying principles -- that the Jewish tradition must be preserved and conserved, and that American Jewry must be moulded to that end, Conservative Judaism evolved not a doctrine, but a technique. The technique consisted of emphasizing the following aspects of the Jewish tradition:

A. <u>Catholic Israel</u>

The phrase "Catholic Israel" is, in its English form, a nimble paradox born in the fruitful mind of Solomon Schechter. But it derives from the solid and meaningful phrase, Klal Yisrael -- the totality of Israel. Jewish tradition has always maintained a sort of theological equation of its own whose best statement is found in the words of the medieval sage -- "God, Torah, and Israel are one." This formulation asserted the close relationship between faith in God and His primacy in life and history; the Torah as the means of coming close to God and His will by thought and action; and the Jewish people and its history through which the faith and the action are carried. To make the equation workable, it was always necessary to recognize not only the demands of God and Torah but the needs, the ability, and the situation of the Jewish people. Apparently this harmony was maintained rather successfully in Jewish history. In the modern era, however, it came to grief.

Reform Judaism in the early 20th century virtually eliminated the Torah as it had developed through the Jewish ages. It rejected many of the legal elements of the Five Books of Moses and it denied the relevance and validity of Talmudic law and thought and the codes which stemmed from it. Samuel Adler, one of the leaders of American Reform, put the matter quite clearly when, in a Passover sermon, he said: "We are like the Israelites at the Red Sea. Let us strike the sea of Talmudism with the staff of reason and, splitting it, pass through to the other side." Even as it rejected Talmudism, so did Reform spurn the Jewish people, the national element of the equation. It denied that a national sentiment existed, it extirpated the hope for a return to Zion from its prayer-book. It thus reduced the equation to one element -- God and an ethical religion.

Orthodoxy distorted the formula in its own way. God and the Torah remained primary in its equation. The Torah, indeed, was accepted in all its jots and tittles as it had been developed in interpretation through the years and as it was formulated in the 16th century code of Joseph Karo and in the 16th century commentary of Moses Isserles. The Jewish people, however, received shorter shrift. Some elements of Orthodoxy were bitterly opposed to Zionism and some minor groups still remain so, despite the existence of the State of Israel. The real distortion, however, appeared in the refusal to recognize the needs, the history, and the sociological condition of the Jewish people, as a factor to be reckoned with. Orthodoxy upheld the claims of the Torah, irrespective of the needs of "Catholic Israel."

The Conservative position has been that the balance in the equation must be restored. It eagerly accepts God and Torah as the fundamentals of Judaism. But it asserts that the national sentiment which is part of Judaism must be acknowledged, and so, Conservative Judaism has gone hand in hand with Zionism since its inception. It equally asserts that the needs and the state of the Jewish people must be taken into account, and so it has been concerned to face the current facts in Jewish life. English readings in the service, for example, is not a principle of Conservative Judaism, but rather, a realistic recognition that most Jews do not understand Hebrew and many do not read it. The retention of Hebrew in the service and the concentration upon it in the Conservative religious school, on the other hand, come out of the recognition that the Hebrew language is a cardinal binding force in Jewish life and a major element in Jewish history. Thus, the Jewish need is at once recognized and the national principle and historical outlook are maintained.

Question:

4. Distinguish "catholic" from "Catholic." What does the phrase, "catholic Israel," mean?

Question:

5. How did the early Reform movement distort the balance among God, Torah, and Israel? Give concrete illustrations. How did the later Reformers correct this, at least to some extent? How did the Orthodox movement distort this? Again, give concrete illustrations. What concrete policies of the Conservative movement indicate that it is attempting to restore the balance? Why is the balance important in the first place?

Reading:

B. Positive-Historical Judaism

The natural complement to concern with Catholic Israel is attention to the historical past of Israel. The Conservative movement has recognized the fact that every generation is "an omnibus in whom all...(its) ancestors ride." And so it has sought enlightenment for the perplexities of its day in the historical experience of Israel. Three attitudes have emerged from this emphasis.

A study of Jewish history has, first of all, made clear that each generation has builded on the past. No generation starts de novo. Judaism has been a historical growth which has sustained the Jewish people and has been sustained by it. It was because Reform Judaism was deficient in this sense of history, as applied to the Hebrew language, that Zacharias Frankel abandoned its Frankfort conference in 1845. In abandoning it, he proclaimed the doctrine of positive historical Judaism. Still later, it received elaboration at the hands of others, including Zunz, Graetz, and Schechter.

As a cardinal emphasis of Conservative Judaism it means respect for the Jewish past and a discernment of its guiding principles. Chief among them is that, as Saadyah long ago pointed out, "Israel is a nation only by virtue of the Torah." Respect for the historical character of Judaism, therefore, means respect for the religious-legal system which has been developed as the means of preserving and effectuating Judaism.

However, historical Judaism means something more. It involves a recognition of the fact that Judaism has changed through the ages, and with this it involves an understanding of why and how it has changed.

Conservative Judaism calls attention to the fact that Judaism through the ages has manifested an inner dynamism. It has proved able to adapt itself to changing conditions -- to move from a faith and a way of life based upon a physical fatherland to one which found its home in a "portable fatherland" (the Torah); to move from land to land, from age to age, and to remain contemporaneous. This is the fact of change. The reason is to be found in the internal dynamism of Judaism interacting with the external circumstances. The masters of Judaism did not, and could not, ignore the winds of circumstances and doctrines which swirled about them. When Judah the Patriarch found that his contemporaries were not observing the interdiction on the "oil of gentiles," he caused it to be revoked. When Maimonides found that philosophic doctrine constituted a threat to Judaism, he composed his "Guide for the Perplexed." The Jewish world reflected this propensity for change in accord with circumstances in other ways. While the essential forms remained the same, many customs of the Oriental Jews differed from those of the East European Jewry, and many of the prescriptions of the codes are accompanied by the statement, "In this we follow the custom prevailing in our land."

Conservative Judaism, being historically aware, thus confronts the need for combining reverence of the past with the fact that Judaism has changed. The third element that rises out of historical awareness is the manner in which change has been effected in Jewish life. And here it becomes quite obvious that the tradition has changed, not by revolution, but by evolution. It has itself provided the mechanism for legal change and interpretation and so has grown in the face of the exigencies of life, even as the common law or American Constitution has grown. A notable example of this is afforded by the Talmud, which is, as a whole, the cardinal example of the Jewish tradition being interpreted and expanded. The dispersion of the Jewish people inevitably led to the problem of what status to accord Jewish civil and criminal law when they were in conflict with the law of the land in which Jews resided. The problem is resolved in the Talmudic formula, "the law of the land is law." Thus, Talmudic law showed its capacity for modifying itself, even to the point of self-limitations, within the framework of the law.

These three elements, taken together, constitute the historical approach to Judaism which the Conservative movement has adopted. It holds that the religious legal tradition must be held in reverence, but that the need for changes and adjustments must be recognized when they become pressing, and it believes that the legal tradition of Judaism itself provides the remedy if we allow it to be implemented. An example of the application of these principles was recently afforded by the modified marriage contract (ketubah) adopted by the Rabbinical Assembly. The Assembly confronted the fact that it was often difficult for women who desired a Jewish divorce to secure one. The difficulty arose out of the refusal of the divorced or divorcing husband to grant the divorce as Jewish law requires. The Reform approach, which is to assert that there is no need for a Jewish divorce, is untraditional. The Orthodox stand that the matter should be left unresolved makes Judaism unlivable. The Conservative approach was to examine the alternatives available in Jewish law. The simplest remedy -- to empower a court to grant the divorce when the husband declined -- was held to be out of consonance with the structure of Jewish law. The alternative which was adopted was to make an addition to the marriage contract in which both bride and groom agreed to hold themselves bound, in the event of divorce, by the decisions of a court which was set up by the Assembly. This action was taken by the Rabbinical Assembly joined together with the faculty of the Seminary. Thus a felt need was recognized, the tradition was approached reverentially, and a solution in harmony with the spirit of the tradition was worked out.

Question:

6. Rabbi Waxman indicates the three elements of the Positive-Historical approach to Judaism which are of importance: a) reverence of the past; b) recognition of the fact that Judaism has changed; c) instituting new changes within the framework of the law. Where would Reform Judaism disagree? Can you generalize your answers somewhat and briefly describe how the three movements differ in their views of what happened in the history of Jewish law?

Question:

7. When a woman cannot obtain a Jewish writ of divorce (called a "Get"), she is called an "aguna," indicating that she cannot remarry until she gets one. This can be very serious, as, for example, when her husband is "missing in action," or becomes insane, in which cases she may have to remain a widow for life. Explain how each of the three movements treats the problem, showing how their treatment results from their respective positions as developed in question 6.

Reading:

C. Vertical Democracy

A third emphasis in Conservative Judaism and complementary to the ideas of Catholic Israel and Historical Judaism, is the idea of vertical democracy in Jewish life and thought. The underlying notion has not been formulated in this phrase, but it is implicit in the outlook of the movement. Horizontal democracy implies majority rule and looks for its majority to those who vote or are represented at any given time. It operates upon the principle that no system is enforceable or viable unless it receives the consent of at least the majority of the participants. To some extent, the Reform movement has been guided in its thinking by this concept. In point of fact, this is questionable doctrine, whether applied to a nation or a religion. Even democratic nations are not guided in their fundamental policies by the whims of the moment. Behind the democracy of Great Britain stand the English tradition and a mass of custom and the loose but powerful English constitution; American democracy must inevitably confront the constitution of the United States and answer the question of how would Lincoln or Washington have reacted to this proposal. Religious communities are even less susceptible to the majority rule of the moment.

They start with presuppositions which cannot be debated or rejected. The existence of God and His relation to man does not depend upon a majority vote. The festivals, the holy days, and much of the service, are beyond the reach of majority voting at any given time, since they represent the accumulation of the centuries.

The Conservative movement has tacitly recognized that even in an age which desires democracy in its institutions, the concept of democracy must be refined. Vertical democracy is a recognition that it is not only the present generation which has a voice in ongoing institutions. The past and the future must be allowed an equal vote. Thus, in evaluating Judaism in the present, we are constrained to let all the weight of past decisions play upon our own thinking, and we are impelled so to treat Judaism that it will live on for future generations.

This frame of mind, which would carefully balance the past and future with the present, has led the Conservative movement to be scrupulous in seeking to maintain the traditional patterns of Judaism, to be cautious in appraising the need for change, to be meticulous in making necessary changes, and to seek to create institutions and a frame of mind from which a stronger Judaism might grow. Thus, the Conservative synagogue initially offered the Sunday school pattern as an alternative to the several times a week Hebrew school. But, being aware that inadequate Jewish education was creating too great a gulf from the Jewish past and was incapable of developing a knowledgeable and traditionally rooted Judaism in the future, it has called for the discontinuation of the Sunday school and concentration upon the Hebrew school.

Question:

8. What does "Vertical Democracy" mean? Why is it important to give consideration to the past in making our present decisions? What about the future? <u>In practice</u>, does the concept of vertical democracy tend to make us institute changes more rapidly or more slowly? Why? Illustrate the effects of vertical democracy by citing the experience of the Conservative movement with Sunday schools. Would you now be prepared to go even further, claiming that only day schools would provide a sufficient Jewish education?

Reading:

D. Modern Thought

In according a voice to the past and in making its center of gravity the traditional pattern of Judaism, the Conservative movement is by no means prepared to ignore modern thinking. On the contrary, one of its principal emphases is that Judaism must be able to confront modern thought and research and assimilate it or harmonize it with itself, or disprove it. This has meant, in practice, that Biblical criticism, archeological and historical studies, the scientific emphasis of the modern age, the changing political and economic philosophies and the various philosophies of the twentieth century, ranging from pragmatism to existentialism and to neo-mysticism, have all found a receptive ear in the Conservative movement. It has, of course, not issued any formal statement which harmonizes these patterns of thought with Judaism. There is, rather, a general mood of awareness that the developments of modern thought must be taken into consideration. In many respects, this is achieved operationally by the individual rabbi. In some areas, individuals like Mordecai Kaplan and Abraham Heschel have presented their views in books which receive an attentive hearing, though not necessarily acceptance, in the Conservative movement.

In some fields, the Seminary, through its Institute of Social and Religious Studies and its publications, has brought Jewish and general thought to bear upon specific problems.

The emphasis is all-important in this area. In the Conservative movement it is felt that Judaism should be enriched but not dissipated by modern thought.

Question:

9. What philosophical problems do you think arise in Conservative Judaism as a result of its attention to modern thought? Does such thought have any bearing on problems of law? If so, how and where? If not, why not? (We shall discuss this more thoroughly when we get to the second article in this leaflet, the one by Rabbi Gordis.)

Reading:

E. Authority and Interpretation

The emphases described above are all meaningless unless they are accompanied by a further development, and that is a willingness to recognize that the principles of authority and interpretation which have secured to Judaism its inner dynamism apply to our own day. Reform has asserted the right of interpretation but it has rejected the authority of the legal tradition. Orthodoxy has clung fast to the principle of authority, but has, in our own and recent generations, rejected the right to any but minor interpretations. The Conservative view is that both are necessary for a living Judaism. Accordingly, Conservative Judaism holds itself bound by the Jewish legal tradition, but asserts the right of its rabbinical body, acting as a whole, to interpret and to apply Jewish law.

While this principle has, for most of the life of the Conservative movement, been honored more in theory than in practice, it remains a fundamental outlook, and, in the last few years, it has begun to be implemented. The most notable instance of it is the recently adopted modification in the marriage contract (ketubah). But many minor examples may be adduced from the decisions of the Law Committee of the Rabbinical Assembly.

Question:

10. In contrast to Reform Judaism, the Conservative movement asserts the authority of the legal tradition. Why is it important to do so? (Hint: Recall some of the problems with the Reform position which we mentioned in chapter 18.)

Question:

11. In contrast to Orthodox Judaism, the Conservative movement also asserts that at least some men of our century have the right to interpret the authoritative law. Why is this important? Why do you think that Orthodoxy virtually denies the right of interpretation to any modern? (Recall chapter 17.)

Question:

12. Who has the right and duty to interpret Jewish law, according to the Conservative position? Why specifically those people? Why is it important that only some people have the right and authority to interpret law? What does this mean in terms of the individual Jew's own practice if he decides to be a conscientious Conservative Jew (a member of "catholic Israel")? (An important question. Recall our discussions along similar lines when we considered the arguments in chapters 11 and 12. These issues will be more fully discussed in section G below, so return to this question after you have read that section.)

Reading:

F. Controlled Experimentation

The bent for interpretation of Jewish law and practice has also manifested itself in another way. Certain practices have grown up in Conservative congregations which are not the product of formal decisions, but rather, the outgrowth of practice. Thus, men and women are seated together at services, prayers in English are included in worship, the High Holiday ritual has been somewhat abridged, the priestly benediction by laymen has been eliminated. These are all products of the philosophy that, within tacitly recognized, but undefined limits, Conservative congregations may experiment in finding more effective forms for presenting Judaism. Some of these experiments have succeeded and have been generally adopted. Others have been attempted and abandoned. In this category, the Sunday school, as the alternative to the mid-week Hebrew school, deserves further notice. It was adopted as a response to the time pressures of American life. It was recognized as inadequate, and it has already been rejected by the movement as a whole and by the majority of its congregations.

Such experimentation could readily get out of hand. The element of control lies in the fact that there is an undefined but generally sensed set of standards in the Conservative movement and its congregations. The guarantee that these standards will be maintained is that discretion in these matters lies in the hands of the rabbi, and the rabbi, in turn, is a member of a limited group of some six to seven hundred, most of whom are graduates of one institution, and all of whom are members of the Rabbinical Assembly. In so small a group, which is organized to maintain its own standard of behavior and attitude, it is possible to create a general feeling of what is done and what is not done, and to enforce it.

Question:

13. "Certain practices have grown up in Conservative congregations which are not the product of formal decisions, but, rather, the outgrowth of practice." Give some examples. Note that the same thing has happened in Judaism as a whole: the yarmulke, the Bar Mitzvah celebration, as we know it, and Simhat Torah are all practices which became part of Judaism without any formal decisions to institute them as such. Can you think of any similar instances in regard to American secular life? (Hint: Consider how our style of clothes is set; and why do we have fireworks on the Fourth of July? Give other examples.)

Question:

14. What is the point of carrying on experimentation with certain Jewish practices? What is the danger involved? How is the danger alleviated, at least in part? (Note that the relatively small number of Conservative rabbis, together with the fact that, roughly, two-thirds are graduates of the Seminary, is crucial in understanding how the Conservative movement operates. For, as Rabbi Waxman notes, these two facts make "it possible to create a general feeling of what is done and what is not done," and thus there is a certain cohesiveness within Conservative ranks, even though its philosophy of law is much less straightforward than that of the other two movements, and much more difficult to apply.)

Reading:

G. The Theory of Leadership

The final question in any outlook or movement is, what is it supposed to achieve in practical terms, and how is it going to do so? All outlooks must have a theoretical foundation. This is equally true in the realms of science or religion. But the theory is of interest only to the professional or interested layman. It achieves meaning for the mass of people only when it is applied.

In the case of Conservative Judaism, this application involves its goal and the means that it takes to secure it. The means is the organizational structure which it has developed and which will be discussed in the next section. The goal is, very simply, to win the Jewish population to Judaism.

The goal is not as self-evident as it appears. In twentieth century America, two meaningful approaches to Judaism are possible. One is to make the attitudes and the behavior of the Jewish community the basis of thinking. The other is to start with the Jewish tradition, distinguish between its essential and peripheral elements, modify the peripheral, if necessary, and attempt to persuade the community to accept the result.

This, of course, presupposes an elite group which will select and communicate.

Conservative Judaism has adopted the second alternative. It has already been suggested that it is not a mass movement, despite its numbers. Its one million members have not made, or basically affected, the thinking or the emphases of the movement. They are, rather, a response to the ideas proposed and implemented by the rabbinic leaders of the movement over the last fifty years. The aims and the intellectual orientation of Conservative Judaism have been provided by a kind of elite which sought to mold the community without itself being molded.

This is not merely fortuitous. It is a basic policy which is much in consonance with the traditional theory of authority in Jewish life. It stems out of a belief that the form and character of Judaism are properly the concern of those who are both learned and interested. This has meant, in practice, in Conservative Judaism, that laymen have been discouraged and debarred from dealing with the ideology and basic policies. It has also involved a particularly high concentration of influence and policy determination in the Seminary and its scholars as against congregational rabbis. It has made it possible for the more traditional elements in the individual congregations to exercise a greater control over synagogue patterns than they would be entitled to by their numbers. It has made it possible to debate policies in a partial vacuum, ignoring the behavior and attitudes of the laity of the Conservative movement. This may seem an unrealistic pattern, but it is actually psychologically sound. In the area of religion, people do not expect to set beliefs and patterns; they rather expect to be guided in them. The Conservative movement has successfully operated on the assumption that if guidance were forthcoming, and if it were properly communicated in an idiom that people understand, it would be accepted.

(Go back and answer question 12 again.)

Reading:

II. "A Modern Approach to a Living Halachah" by Robert Gordis (in <u>Tradition and Change</u>)

Basically, the sanction of the Halachah lies for us in its Divine character. We regard the Law, both Written and Oral, as the revelation of God. What Moses, the prophets, sages, and rabbis taught, from Sinai to our day, is divinely inspired. That it has functioned so effectively, not merely for the preservation of Israel, but, what is much more significant, for the enhancement of human welfare and the elevation of human character, buttresses, but does not supplant, our faith that its source is God. Hence, we accept as fundamental to vital Jewish religion, the principle of <u>Torah min hashamayim</u>, "the Torah as a revelation of God."

Like our predecessors in rabbinic, medieval, and modern times, each of us is free to give the term a greater or lesser degree of definiteness and literalness of meaning. The common core in all such views, however, and the irreducible minimum, is the belief that the Torah, which encompasses the ethical and ritual tradition of Israel, inaugurated at Sinai and carried forward through Biblical, Talmudic, and post-Talmudic times to our own day, is an emanation of God, a revelation of Divine truth. This conception does not mean, for us, that the process of revelation consisted of the dictation of the Torah by God, and its passive acceptance by men. To be sure, this is implied in some, but by no means in all, rabbinic references to the subject, such as the explanation offered for the presence of the last twelve verses in Deuteronomy, which describe Moses' death: "Until this closing section, God spoke, Moses repeated and wrote it down. When this passage was reached, God spoke and Moses wrote in tears" (Baba Batra 15a).

Revelation depends not merely upon its infinite and Divine source, but upon its finite and limited human instrument. Just as traditional Judaism found no derogation of the creative power of God in describing man as "the partner of the Holy One in the work of creation," so Revelation is not impugned by viewing it as another aspect of this eternal partnership or cosmic symbiosis, where God depends on man, as truly as man depends on God.

That traditional Judaism recognized this variable human factor in Revelation is abundantly clear from our sources. The Bible itself distinguishes between the immediacy of relationship possessed by Moses and that of the other Prophets (Num. 12:6 ff.): "If there be a prophet among you, I the Lord do make Myself known unto him in a vision, I do speak with him in a dream. My servant Moses is not so; he is trusted in all My house; with him do I speak mouth to mouth, even manifestly, and not in dark speeches; and the similitude of the Lord doth he behold."

This distinction the rabbis amplify in their parable of Moses as a star-gazer with a clear telescope unlike the other prophets who had blurred instruments of vision (Yeb. 49b). The Talmudic comparison of Isaiah to a city-dweller looking upon the king and of Ezekiel to a rustic gazing in unfeigned astonishment at an unfamiliar spectacle (Hag. 13b), represents a distinction as well as an evaluation.

*****

Not only does Revelation differ in content and depth, varying with the individual, but it is not limited in time. In other words, it is not an event, but a process. After the period of the Patriarchs, Sinai marked the commencement, not the conclusion, of Revelation. The theophany on Sinai may be conceived of literally, mystically, or philosophically, but it represents a basic historical fact without which all the subsequent history of Judaism, and indeed of the Jewish people, is inexplicable. In increasing measure, contemporary Biblical scholarship is recognizing this truth and accepting the historicity of Moses and the Mosaic character of at least part of the Pentateuch. But scholarly analyses aside, for the Jewish religious consciousness, Revelation's first and greatest single hour was at Sinai. However, as Rabbinic literature abundantly recognized, there were revelations after Sinai. (Cf. Bernard Bamberger, "Revelations of Torah After Sinai," HUCA, 1941). The relationship between these stages and Sinai is expressed in an utterance of R. Johanan: "God showed Moses the derivations in the Torah and the words of the scholars, and whatever the scholars were to originate in the future" (Meg. 19b). The verb hadesh, "create anew," makes it clear that the rabbis recognized that their function was active, not passive; creative, not repetitive. The same view reaches classic expression in a passage which has been misinterpreted by some of its professed advocates, no less than by some of its strongest opponents: "Even that which an able pupil was destined to teach before his master was already said to Moses on Sinai" (Y. Hag. I, 76d). What this statement sets forth is the belief, which we share, that the entire development of Jewish law after Moses is implied in the giving of the Torah on Sinai, and that the organic unity binding it all together gives to it all the same Divine sanction.

This concept may be succinctly summarized in the words Torah missinai. Incidentally, this phrase, as far as we have been able to discover, unlike Torah min hashamayim, does not occur anywhere in Talmudic literature, except in the Mishna Abot I:1, where, however, it is not set forth as an article of faith. As a technical term, it is essentially late, being often used in modern Orthodox apologetics interchangeably, though incorrectly, as a synonym for Torah min hashamayim, and it is then taken to mean that the entire Torah, Written and Oral, was given to Moses on Sinai. Such a dogma means to pass judgment on a question which only historical and literary scholarship can legitimately decide, and which, contrary to widespread impression, is of little consequence for religious faith. At all events, for us both phrases summarize the belief that Jewish law, in its entire history and unfoldment, bears the same relationship to the Revelation at Sinai as a spreading oak to its original acorn, in which all its own attributes are contained.

That this concept does not commit us to a static concept of Halachah is clear from the Talmud itself. By the side of the passage just quoted, which emphasizes the unity of the Halachah throughout time, must be set the profound legend in Menahot 29b which describes its growing and changing character: "Moses found God adding decorative

crowns to the letters of the Torah. Upon asking the
reason, the Lawgiver was told, "In a future generation
a man named Akiba ben Joseph is destined to arise, who
will derive multitudes of laws from each of these
marks." Deeply interested, Moses asked to see him and
was admitted to the rear of the schoolhouse, where
Akiba was lecturing. To Moses' deep distress, however,
he found that he could not understand what the scholars
were saying, and his spirit grew faint within him.
Then he heard Akiba say, "The ordinance that we are
discussing is a law derived from Moses on Sinai," and
upon hearing this, his spirit revived. Hence the Sages
could say: "Things not revealed to Moses were revealed
to Rabbi Akiba and his colleagues" (Bamidbar Rabbah
19:6, Vilna edition). It is significant that the same
verb is here used of Moses as of the interpreters of
the law a millenium and a half later.

Revelation is therefore a never-ending process, suffering all the vicissitudes of human life, because human
beings, weak and imperfect, and varying widely in their
profundity and insight, are creative partners in the
process. Moreover, the process does not end with the
Mishna or the Gemara, Saadia, Maimonides, Jacob ben
Asher, or Joseph Karo, Rabbi Isaac Elhanan Spector, or
Rabbi Abraham Isaac Kook. It also follows that not
every stage is equally creative and fruitful. We venture to hope that the Rabbinical Assembly, dedicated to
the cause of a meaningful and vital Judaism, may prove
one of the instruments of divine revelation, and that
its contributions will ultimately enter the mainstream
of living Jewish tradition.

Question:

15. What is the principle of Torah min hashamayim? In being
    committed to that principle, is Conservative Judaism
    binding itself to a literal view of revelation? Is it
    precluding such a view? What is Conservative Judaism
    saying, then, when it asserts Torah min hashamayim? Why
    is that important?

Question:

16. Revelation, according to Rabbi Gordis, "is not an event, but a process." What implications for Jewish law does that evolving view of revelation have? Would Orthodox Judaism agree, either with the view of revelation herein presented, or with its legal implications? Why, or why not?

Reading:

The researches of Jewish scholars from the days of Frankel and Weiss to those of Chernowitz and Ginzberg reveal that the Halachah has a history. Hence, to decide what the law requires on any given issue means, not the discovery of a point, but the plotting of a line on a graph, where tradition is one coordinate, and contemporary life the other. To disregard either spells death to Judaism. In other words, it is important to know, not merely where the Halachah stands, but in what direction it is tending. This is possible only by exploring in each case the <u>ideals</u> which constitute its spirit and motivation and the <u>circumstances</u> under which it arose.

Having ascertained the position of the Halachah on any given issue and decided which <u>conditions</u> and <u>ideals</u> of contemporary life are to be reckoned with, it remains to determine the <u>method</u> of its <u>development</u>. In exceptional cases Rabbinic Judaism had recourse to legislation through <u>takhanot</u> and <u>gezerot</u>, positive and negative enactments, and this procedure is by no means to be summarily dismissed from consideration. However, many factors suggest that this device be used sparingly, if at all, today, and that only after the dominant method of interpretation has been proved inadequate. The <u>takhanot</u> and <u>gezerot</u> of earlier ages presupposed a far greater degree of homogeneity of outlook and practice in the Jewish community than exists today, and a correspondingly greater recognition of the authority of the rabbinate than any rabbinic group, particularly the Rabbinical Assembly, now enjoys. Moreover, during the past few centuries, the influence of historical conditions in Eastern Europe where the bulk of world Jewry was concentrated, impelled the <u>Aharonim</u>, who were their legal authorities, to adopt an ever more passive attitude toward the Halachah, avoiding any bold creative activity, and relying on the principle, "When in doubt the severer opinion is to prevail." As a result, the flexibility and the power of growth of Jewish law have been severely curtailed in modern times. Common sense would dictate that we walk before we run, and that interpretation be utilized to the utmost before recourse be had to legislation.

Historically, the growth of Jewish law through interpretation proceeded through two methods. The first, which many scholars regarded as the older, was the method of <u>Midrash</u>, "the searching of Scripture." It consisted of the analysis by scholars of the text of the Torah, both literally and through special canons of interpretation in order to deduce the laws from it. The <u>Tannaitic Midrashim</u> of the schools of Rabbi Ishmael and Rabbi Akiba, of which the <u>Mekilta</u>, <u>Sifra</u> and <u>Sifre</u> have reached us virtually intact, while others have survived only in part, are the literary monuments of this technique. The limits of this method, however, were reached early, and its results were relatively circumscribed, with the result that it was not generally utilized after the second century C.E.

Instead, the method of Halachah or Mishna proved far more fruitful. This approach derived its impetus, not from the text of Scripture, but from the context of life. By and large, the process would begin with a felt need among the people, of which the scholars became conscious. The spiritual leaders would then determine for themselves whether the particular need or aspiration was socially desirable and spiritually valuable. If not, they would oppose it, or seek to suppress and minimize it. Thus, Professor Ginzberg has suggested that the absence of angelology in the Mishna was due to the desire of the redactors to eliminate, or at least reduce, this element in Jewish folk-belief. That angels bulked large in the religious consciousness of the people is clear from the Apocrypha and the Pseudepigrapha, the Gemara, and the late Midrashim.

If the scholars concluded that the expressed need or ideal was worthwhile, they would seek to bring it into the mainstream of Jewish tradition by finding a basis for it in the text of Scripture as amplified by the seven norms of interpretation of Hillel, the thirteen principles of Rabbi Ishmael, and the elaborate thirty-two rules of Rabbi Eliezer,

Conservative Judaism views itself as a twentieth century version of Pharisaic Judaism.) How would Orthodoxy object to the Conservative program of expanding the law? What would the Reform movement say about the Conservative approach?

Reading:

Two more observations are in order with regard to the creative functioning of the Halachah. Common sense dictates a realistic approach to the contemporary problems of Jewish law, both with regard to the people for whom it is intended, and the areas of life where this process of interpretation is likely to prove most fruitful.

Attention has been called elsewhere to the need of recognizing the obvious fact that many modern Jews have all but completely surrendered the concept of Jewish law in practice, and, to only a slighter degree, in theory. To modify Jewish law in order to bring it into conformity with their way of life is tantamount to amending the Constitution of the United States so as to harmonize it with the viewpoint of an anarchist, however high-minded he may be. Such well-intentioned efforts can only succeed in undermining Jewish law for those sections of the Jewish people who still reverence it and seek to live by it, without winning over those who have strayed from the Jewish way of life. On the contrary, all experience teaches that the task of winning back the erring and the estranged, heartrendingly difficult as it is, is more often successfully achieved by traditional religion than by its non-traditional forms. This consideration aside, it is self-evident that only Jews who accept the concept of Jewish law and seek to observe it, can legitimately expect to mould the character of Jewish law and help determine its needs, direction, and aspiration. <u>Klal Yisrael</u>, or Catholic Israel, as a body competent to create in Jewish law, includes only such Jews as recognize the existence and authority of Jewish law. When the Talmud said, "Go see how the people conduct themselves" (Ber. 45a; Erub. 14a), it referred to a period when virtually all Jews qualified by this test. Had there been a large number of <u>Elisha ben Abuyas</u> or general Sabbath violators in their day, the Rabbis would not have consulted <u>them</u> as to how Sabbath observance should be conceived of.

Finally, after several centuries during which the entire field of Jewish law has lain fallow, it is obvious that all the broken fences cannot be mended at once. Hence, we should first take up the strand of development in those areas where our efforts are likely to have the most effect, and where the need is most acute. In the Diaspora, at least, the influence of the rabbinate is restricted largely to two areas -- family law and synagogue life. Without ruling out action elsewhere, it is both our duty and opportunity to deal courageously and reverently with such problems, fundamental problems, as the disability of women in Jewish law, which still exists in the synagogue service, marriage law, and religious life generally. Mixed pews which have become the norm without recourse to the Halachah, and the agunah proposal, which had recourse to the Halachah without becoming the norm, represent fields of productive thought and action which are open to us today. Other aspects of the same problem are the calling of women to the Torah, the Bat Mitzvah rite, and the counting of women in the Minyan.

The Sabbath Halachah, especially the problems of traveling and the use of electricity, are so fundamental to Jewish life and the future of Judaism in America, that we are justified in approaching them from the standpoint here presented -- the affirmation of the viability of the Halachah in meeting the problems of our age and its inherent value in ennobling human life and making man worthy to be God's partner in the universe.

Question:

18. Rabbi Waxman explained the concept of Catholic Israel before, but Rabbi Gordis now gives a justification for it. Why is it just, according to Rabbi Gordis, to ignore the practices of the vast majority of Conservative Jews and consider only those of observant Jews when we consider possible modifications of Jewish law? Do you agree? Why, or why not?

III. A Concrete Example of Conservative Legal Practice: "The Use of Electricity on the Sabbath" by Rabbi Arthur H. Neulander (in *Tradition and Change*)

Reading:

The great changes that have been effected by technological and scientific inventions and discoveries in our times force thoughtful Jews to re-examine the Sabbath Halachah, and reinterpret it to the needs of our day.

Electricity has become part of the warp and woof of our life. Our industrial system, our means of transportation and communication, the very conveniences of our home life depend upon electrification. In this paper, we limit ourselves to the legal adjustment required in dealing with the conveniences of home life. Lighting up our homes, telephoning, ringing our door-bells, using the elevator in our apartment houses, listening to the radio, watching television, refrigeration, washing and ironing, using electric razors, controlling our heating systems with thermostats, all involve the use of electricity. Many of these functions we normally direct consciously. Some are quite automatic, but all of these uses of electricity involve the application of Sabbath laws.

The earliest reaction to the problem of the use of electricity on the Sabbath was that of the mahmirim. This is a normal reaction. When studying history we frequently become aware of the fact that many forward steps in human civilization meet with resistance. New thoughts, new methods of procedure, new discoveries and inventions generally meet early disapproval by the conservative-minded, particularly in connection with religion which is traditionally conservative in bent; but later, these innovations are frequently accepted as the norm.

The use of electricity is something relatively new in human experience. The question of permitting its use for light on the Sabbath has been debated for the last two or three generations but has not been satisfactorily resolved. No individual opinion has won the approval of Klal Yisrael. The extensive literature on the subject, which continues receiving the attention of the scholars of our time, testifies to the fact that we are dealing with one of the living issues of the Halachah. Accordingly, we may address ourselves to it from our own point of view, and make decisions for the large group of Jews who look to us for spiritual guidance.

We do not pretend in this paper to make an exhaustive presentation of our views on the question of the use of electricity on the Sabbath. But the main line of argumentation is concisely sketched so that a conclusion may be reached and a decision made.

Those who disapprove the use of electricity on the Sabbath base themselves on the Biblical prohibition, "You shall kindle no fire throughout your settlements on the Sabbath day" (Ex. 35:3). They subsume electricity under the category of fire.

We find this identification between electricity and fire to be wrong, both on Halachic and on scientific grounds. In order to subsume electricity under the category of fire, it would be necessary to prove that electricity has the characteristics which the Halachah ascribes to fire.

According to the Halachah, fire is something that is <u>soref</u>, i.e., the substance afire is itself consumed in the process of burning and is turned to charcoal or ashes. This characteristic of fire is deduced from the following statement of Samuel (Shab. 42a): "We may extinguish a glowing metal coal in the public street so that people should not be injured by it, but not a wooden coal." Rashi, in commenting on the question of extinguishing coals on a festival (Shabbat 134a), points out that it is forbidden to extinguish a wooden coal because it becomes charcoal, i.e., is consumed; but that a metal coal may be extinguished because it is not consumed. Samuel's statement becomes the basis of the regulation, "A glowing coal, lying in a place where people may be injured by it, may be extinguished, whether it is of metal or wood. Maimonides, however, forbids the extinguishing of a wooden coal." (Shulkhan Arukh, Orah Hayyim, 334) The Magen Abraham explains this regulation on the grounds that "As regards a metal coal, there is no actual extinguishing, because it is not burned or consumed."

Thus kibuy (extinguishing) does not apply to anything that is not soref, undergoing the process of combustion or oxidation. Halachically, therefore, anything that is not soref is not esh (fire).

Another characteristic of fire, according to the Halachah, is that it must produce a flame. In a discussion in Pesahim 75a, it is said that if a man cut up the paschal lamb and placed it on a glowing coal, then Rabbi Judah regards it as though he had roasted it on fire. A glowing coal, in this context, is regarded as a wooden coal. A metal coal, though glowing, is not considered fire.

In an interesting Halachic discussion of the characteristics of fire, in an article on Lighting Electricity on the Sabbath published in the monthly Sinai, Vol. 12, No. 3, Rabbi S. Goronchick, chief chaplain of the Israeli Army, categorically states: "Any glowing thing which does not produce a flame when burning is not considered fire."

It therefore follows that, by both tests, electricity does not qualify as fire from the standpoint of the Halachah: (a) a filament of an electric light, when it becomes incandescent and gives off light, is undergoing no combustion, and (b) it gives off no flame.

The conclusion we have arrived at on Halachic grounds receives additional force because it is substantiated by science. On purely scientific grounds it is impossible for us to agree that electricity is a form of fire. On the contrary, the scientist considers fire one form of energy, and electricity another. It is not necessary for us to belabor this argument. Whoever has studied modern science will not question the conclusion that fire and electricity must be considered two distinct forms of energy.

Let us, furthermore, take into account the mechanical aspect of modern life and consider our dependence on automatic electrical devices, such as the thermostat that controls the heating system in many of our apartments and homes, or the thermostat that controls the cooling apparatus in our electric refrigerators. It becomes necessary even for the mahmirim, who hesitate to distinguish between fire and electricity, to modify their stand on the automatic use of electricity on the Sabbath on Halachic grounds. If they would ban such use of electricity on the Sabbath because of the principle that one may not do anything which will inevitably involve him in doing a prohibited act (pasik raishai n'lo yamut), then it would be necessary, strictly speaking, to ban the opening of a window to let in a bit of fresh air, or the opening of a door to enter or leave a house. The room temperature would inevitably be affected and the thermostat would automatically either hasten or delay the working of the heating mechanism. Are we expected, because of the application of the principle of pasik raishai, to sit in the cold and confine ourselves to our homes on the Sabbath, like Karaites? We may even go further. It is a scientific fact that every bodily movement sets in motion electro-magnetic waves. Some electrical home apparatus is thus inevitably affected by these waves that we ourselves radiate. Are we compelled to resuscitate the literal meaning of the Biblical verse, "Abide ye every man in his place, let no man go out of his place on the seventh day" (Ex. 16:29) which the Halachah reinterpreted centuries ago? Fortunately, loyalty to the Halachah as a living and growing influence does not require such a procedure. The principle of pasik raishai is Amoraic and quite unknown in the Mishna, which followed a more liberal attitude on a labor done unintentionally (melocho she'aino meetkaven).

We must follow the same line of reasoning in the use of electric refrigeration. In opening the door of a refrigerator to take out food, we necessarily raise the temperature within the refrigerator. Although, indirectly, we automatically hasten the turning on of the cooling apparatus, we must, in order to make life bearable, overlook Abbayae or Rava's principle of pasik raishai (being responsible for inevitable results) and follow the older Mishnaic concept of considering such acts as labor done unintentionally (and therefore permissible). Furthermore, we must utilize the principles that labor done unintentionally is permissible, and that labor which is not done for its own sake is similarly permissible when using such mechanisms as the telephone; for we are not interested in flashing a signal on the switchboard; we are concerned with talking to a friend.

In truth, scientists tell us that we cannot help setting electro-magnetic waves in motion at all times. Our very bodies are giving off this force, and every time we move a muscle these waves are increased. The insight and general responsiveness to life which characterized our sages of old leads us to assume that had they had our scientific knowledge they would not have applied the principle of pasik raishai where automatic use of electricity on the Sabbath is involved.

It is, therefore, clear that electricity is not to be regarded as a form of fire, either by Halachic definition or from the evidence of science. Its widespread automatic use in modern life underscores the inescapable necessity of reckoning with these facts practically in contemporary civilization.

It is noteworthy that recent authorities who, not having utilized the testimony of science, do not sharply distinguish between electricity and fire, nevertheless are led to various liberalizing decisions in detail.

In a Teshuvah by Rabbi Simcha Levy, issued through the Rabbinical Council of America, the use of electricity on the Sabbath and Yom Tov for a microphone is permitted in the Synagogue if the electricity has been turned on Erev Shabbos. In the same Teshuvah the statement is made that the use of electricity on the Sabbath for an elevator does not come under the category of fire, even though sparks are produced in the motor. This opinion is given in the name of Rabbi Eliyahu Henkin. We understand that our own Dr. Hyamson, of blessed memory, also permitted the use of an apartment house elevator on the Sabbath. Reference is also made to Rabbi Idelson, who states that turning on electric lights is not a type of work prohibited by the Torah. All this seems to indicate a tendency to be lenient about the use of electricity on the Sabbath when not used for work prohibited on the Sabbath.

A word is in order on the possible objection that using electricity on the Sabbath means producing something new (nolad) which is forbidden. Here the scientific facts clearly disprove the contention. Turning on an electric switch means using something which already exists, not creating anything new. The electricity has been produced through turbines or dynamos at the power stations and is stored in great condensers. It simply flows to us through cables and wires and is tapped by us in much the same way as water brought to us through mains and pipes from the great reservoirs is tapped by us by turning on a faucet.

In conclusion, Halachic consideration, coupled with scientific evidence, leads us to permit the use of electricity on the Sabbath. It is self-evident that this permission applies only to such uses as do not involve work prohibited on the Sabbath. Thus, we may permit turning on electric lights, telephoning, refrigeration, using a radio and television. But we cannot countenance the use of electricity for work prohibited on the Sabbath, such as cooking and baking, shaving with an electric razor, using the washing machine or an electric iron. The prohibition is here derived not from the use of electricity but from the nature of the work itself.

It must be clearly understood that whatever use of electric apparatus we permit on the Sabbath, we allow only on condition that use is in consonance with the spirit of the Sabbath. Thus, the telephone may be used for conversation to strengthen family ties, to foster friendship and neighborliness, to convey a message of cheer to the sick or for a similar debar mitzvah. But the telephone should not be used for shopping purposes, for making a business appointment, much less a business transaction. The first group is in keeping with the holiness of the Sabbath. The second group violates the menuhah shelemah of the Sabbath.

Similarly, in the use of radio or television, common sense should dictate that only such programs may be indulged in which are not vulgar and banal and do not desecrate the sanctity of the ideal Sabbath. Only programs of high esthetic taste, of high ethical content, instructive and of social value, are in keeping with our concept of a Shabbat Kodesh, and only such programs should be listened to and seen on the Sabbath day.

We humbly believe that this decision is in conformity with the spirit of the Halachah and not in opposition to its letter. This decision, taking into cognizance the needs of our day, we hope, will promote the goal of Jewish law which has always been to enhance life and add to man's joy in the riches of the world so that he may gratefully acknowledge the goodness of God's providence.

Question:

19. Refer back to the characteristics of the Conservative movement which Rabbis Waxman and Gordis enumerated, and explain how these characteristics are (or are not) reflected in the concrete decision on electricity. For example, in this decision, are the thinking and goals "derived from the Jewish tradition rather than from doctrinaire or sociological forces," as Rabbi Waxman says? Does the decision convey the notion that "the Jewish community is malleable," that "it is, potentially at least, devoted to Judaism," and that the problem, as the Conservative movement sees it, "is to state Judaism in meaningful terms, to focus attention on its essentials, and to communicate these things to the Jewish public"? Where does "Catholic Israel" play its part in this decision? What about "Positive-Historical Judaism"? "Vertical democracy"? Conservative notions of authority and leadership? And what method of legislation is being used here (legislation, Midrash, or Mishna)?

Question:

20. In sum, what are the strengths of the Conservative approach? What are its weaknesses?